THE FOX–NORTH COALITION

'Britannia Roused, or the Coalition Monsters Destroyed', Rowlandson.
From M. D. George, *Catalogue of Political and Personal Satires*,
Vol. **vi**, 1784–92.

THE FOX–NORTH COALITION

Crisis of the Constitution, 1782-4

BY

JOHN CANNON

Senior Lecturer in History
University of Bristol

CAMBRIDGE
AT THE UNIVERSITY PRESS
1969

Published by the Syndics of the Cambridge University Press
Bentley House, 200 Euston Road, London N.W.1
American Branch: 32 East 57th Street, New York, N.Y. 10022

© Cambridge University Press 1969

Library of Congress Catalogue Card Number: 70-85715
Standard Book Number: 521 07606 4

Printed in Great Britain
at the University Press, Aberdeen

CONTENTS

PREFACE

I should like first to express my gratitude to Lord Abergavenny, Lord Camden, Lord Kenyon, Lord Lansdowne, Lord Spencer and Mr Victor Montagu for permission to quote from family papers in their possession; to the Librarian of the University of Leeds for permission to consult the Brotherton Collection; and to the trustees of the late Sir Robert Dundas of Arniston, Bt.

I have much appreciated the kindness shown by my colleagues in the University of Bristol, particularly Patrick McGrath, James Sherborne and David Large, each of whom has shown great interest in the undertaking and listened with patience on many occasions. The staff of the University library have been invariably considerate, and I should especially like to thank Mr M. G. Edwards and Mr G. F. Richmond for the help they have given me over many years.

In the course of the volume I have in some places dissented from the views of my former colleagues in the History of Parliament Trust, the late Sir Lewis Namier and John Brooke. It therefore gives me particular pleasure to have an opportunity of acknowledging the many acts of kindness I received from them both, and my respect for the contribution they have made to our understanding of the eighteenth century.

Lastly, I must place on record my appreciation of the courteous treatment I have had from the staff of the Cambridge University Press. I hope that they too have enjoyed the gentle irony that a book which shows William Pitt in a less flattering light than usual should issue from the Pitt Building.

BRISTOL   J. A. C.
July 1969

ABBREVIATIONS

Buckingham The Duke of Buckingham and Chandos, *Memoirs of the Court and Cabinets of George the Third*, 1853

Debrett J. Debrett, *The Parliamentary Register*, 2nd series

Fitzmaurice Lord Fitzmaurice, *Life of William, Earl of Shelburne*, 1912

Fortescue *The Correspondence of King George III*, ed. Sir John Fortescue, 6 vols. 1927–8

Grafton *Autobiography and Political Correspondence of Augustus Henry, Third Duke of Grafton*, ed. W. R. Anson, 1898

Laprade *Parliamentary Papers of John Robinson 1774–84*, ed. W. T. Laprade, 1922

Leeds *The Political Memoranda of Francis, Fifth Duke of Leeds*, ed. O. Browning, 1884

Russell *Memorials and Correspondence of Charles James Fox*, ed. Lord John Russell, 1853

Stanhope Lord Stanhope, *Life of the Rt. Hon. William Pitt*, 1861

Wraxall N. W. Wraxall, *The Historical and Posthumous Memoirs*, ed. H. B. Wheatley, 1884

INTRODUCTION

The attempt by Charles Fox and Lord North in 1783 to establish their administration in defiance of the king's wishes marks the political and constitutional climax of the reign of George III. A party in command of a majority in the House of Commons was pitted against a monarch employing every weapon in the still formidable armoury of prerogative. The conflict was a struggle not merely for power, but between rival views of the constitution. From the beginning of his reign, George III had dedicated himself to the extirpation of party. In March 1783, reflecting on the previous twenty-three years, he wrote: 'When he mounted the throne . . . he had the pleasing hope that being born in this kingdom, he might have proved the happy instrument of conciliating all parties, and thus collecting to the service of the state, the most respectable and most able persons this nation produced. Of this object he has never lost sight.'[1] This was no personal whim on George's part, but a logical endeavour to check that development which was bound, in due course, to deprive the monarch of many of his powers, and in particular of the right to choose his own ministers. Any ruler, conscious of his own interest, would pursue a similar policy: it was hardly necessary to devise a melo-dramatic explanation in terms of Bute's indoctrination of high prerogative principles in order to account for George behaving as most monarchs had done. William III had struggled to resist party rule, and his successor had declared that party domination would render her a slave and mean her 'personal ruin'. Though the exigencies of the dynastic dispute with the Stuarts led the first two Georges to embrace party, with Frederick, Prince of Wales, the situation reverted to normal, and his programme included the determination to 'abolish for the future all distinctions of party'.[2]

[1] Fortescue, vi, no. 4259.
[2] *H.M.C. 9th Report, appendix*, 471–2; *Correspondence of John, fourth duke of Bedford* (1842–6), i, 320.

Opposition to the growth of party was, in fact, a standard monarchical attitude, and Gustav III of Sweden, George III's contemporary, assured his subjects at the time of his *coup d'état* that he was not establishing absolutism but rescuing them from 'the despotism of party rule': the parallel did not pass unnoticed during the acrimonious debates in Britain in 1784.[1] One hundred years later, in the midst of the controversy over parliamentary reform, Queen Victoria was still echoing the same sentiments: 'I do wish there was some patriotism, instead of Party, Party, in all this painful question.'[2]

But despite the disapproval of successive monarchs, political parties and combinations continued to flourish, and in the course of time acquired defenders. The old duke of Newcastle, whatever his practice, still professed devotion to the ideal of non-party government, and claimed to 'detest the thought of an *Opposition*'.[3] But a new generation of politicians openly declared party allegiance to be desirable. 'How men can proceed without any connection at all is to me utterly incomprehensible', wrote Burke in 1770, and in 1783 Fox proclaimed party as an article of his political faith: 'I have always acknowledged myself to be a party man ... a systematic opposition to a dangerous government is, in my opinion, a noble employment for the brightest faculties . . . Opposition is natural in such a political system as ours'.[4] This

---

[1] I. Andersson, *A history of Sweden* (1956), 279–80. Archibald Fraser referred to events in Sweden during the debate of 20 January 1784, and in caricature no. 6485, M. D. George, *Catalogue of political and personal satires*, vi, Pitt is shown exhorting the king to emulate Gustav III.

[2] Quoted in C. S. Emden, *The people and the constitution*, 2nd edition (1956), 115.

[3] Newcastle to Hardwicke, 17 August 1761, Add. MS. 32927, ff. 69–70. Historians have taken these protestations too seriously: the duke got over his dislike of a formed opposition. K. G. Feiling, *The second tory party, 1714–1832* (1938), 4, wrote: 'Nor, again, could there properly be, it was commonly thought, such a thing as "a formed Opposition". Till the Nineteenth century most retiring ministers followed the model of passive loyalty set by Walpole.' I do not see how this comment could survive an examination of the conduct of subsequent ministers. Bute retired from politics completely, and Shelburne for several years, but Newcastle, Devonshire, George Grenville, Grafton, North, Rockingham, Portland and Pitt all went into formed oppositions.

[4] *Thoughts on the cause of the present discontents*; Debrett, xii, 307–9.

George III would never concede. Opposition was to him inseparable from disloyalty. In November 1782, he wrote to North: 'I have no wish but for the prosperity of my dominions, therefore must look on all who will not heartily assist me as bad men as well as ungrateful subjects'.[1]

The confrontation between these conflicting views produced in 1783–4 the most acute political convulsion since the Revolution of 1688. Contemporaries talked of the possibility of civil war: Fox was likened to Oliver Cromwell, George to James II. For six weeks in the spring of 1783, while the country was still at war, government was in abeyance, with the king threatening abdication. For three months in 1784 the first minister was defeated in every major division in the House of Commons, yet would not resign. Every aspect of the royal prerogative was probed and discussed.

The tensions of the period 1779–80, at the time of Dunning's motion, have been described by Professor Butterfield as 'quasi-revolutionary to a degree which the world has since forgotten'.[2] His argument did not command complete acceptance,[3] and one may suggest that the description could more aptly be applied to the years 1783–4—by which time the ferments in Ireland had grown greater rather than less, the extra-parliamentary associations were still vigorous, the loss of the thirteen colonies was an undoubted fact, public credit was at a low ebb, there was serious disaffection in the army and navy, and Parliament and executive government were paralysed by constitutional deadlock. One may perhaps go further and see in the struggle between king and Parliament an English counterpart of the rivalry between monarchs and nobility that was so marked a feature of the European scene at this time. Though the people were no more than auxiliaries

---

[1] Fortescue, vi, no. 3973. This was an appeal to North's own position, as the 'ungrateful' jibe was intended to indicate.

[2] *George III, Lord North, and the people, 1779–80* (1949), p. vi.

[3] See, e.g., reviews by Richard Pares, *English Historical Review*, lxv, 526–9, and W. T. Laprade, *American Historical Review*, lvi, 340–1.

in the contest between the king and what Dundas termed 'an insolent aristocratical band', the unexpected by-product of the clash was an important extension of the role of public opinion in political life, as first the Rockinghams appealed to it in 1782 to coerce the king, and in 1784 the king, with even greater success, retorted it upon the Rockinghams. 'When the Crown and Nobility contend,' wrote Horace Walpole, 'both endeavour to conciliate the favour . . . of the people; and though the ultimate end of the contentions of the great is to oppress the people, many advantages are conferred on the latter to purchase their support'.[1]

No modern study of the central theme of these events—the formation of the coalition—has been undertaken. Indeed, the only full-scale treatment of the subject is in Nathaniel Wraxall's *Historical and posthumous memoirs*, published 150 years ago: though Wraxall's work is by no means as contemptible as its reviewers suggested, it is culled largely from the printed parliamentary debates, and is sometimes credulous and melodramatic. I have myself quoted from the debates of the time to an extent that some readers may find irksome, partly to do justice to the niceties of the constitutional arguments, and partly to convey something of the quality of a House of Commons that contained in North, Pitt, Fox, Burke, Sheridan and Dundas, six of the most effective debaters in parliamentary history.

In conclusion, it may be worth admitting at the outset that this is essentially a 'Whig' interpretation of the subject. I hope that this declaration will not lay me open to the charge of wilfully distorting the evidence, or of believing, as Horace Walpole did, that George III cherished a design to subvert the constitution and establish absolutist government. It means two things. First, that I have written unashamedly with an eye on the future, since I do not believe it possible for an historian to study the past 'for its own sake'. Secondly, I use the phrase in the sense employed by W. R. Fryer in his extremely useful attempt at synthesis, 'King

[1] *Journal of the reign of King George III*, ed. Doran (1859), ii, 626.

George III, His Political Character and Conduct, 1760–1784; a new Whig interpretation', *Renaissance and Modern Studies*, vi, 68–101, with whose argument I am in general agreement—*viz.* that George III is much more open to criticism than has sometimes been allowed, and that on occasions he strained his prerogatives and infringed established constitutional usage. Indeed, I believe that his intervention against Fox's India Bill was indefensible according to both the constitutional theory and practice of his own day. Finally, I think one can hardly too often stress the desirability, in the study of constitutional problems, to anchor one's investigations to the practice of politicians and not rest content with a survey of theory, which is often to be found lagging decades behind. Usages continue to be deplored while everyone knows that they are necessary and inescapable. In no field is this tendency more apparent than in relation to political opposition. Even though it is generally understood that opposition is at the heart of democratic government, people are sometimes uneasy, as though it were still faintly reprehensible. The practice is less ambiguous. When Mr Heath declared, immediately after the Labour victory of 1966, that 'if the government does pursue policies which we regard as being in the national interest, then we shall support them', few can have supposed that he would not lead his party into a formed Opposition.[1]

[1] *The Times*, 2 April 1966.

THE ROCKINGHAM ADMINISTRATION

On 27 February 1782 a motion in the House of Commons against the further prosecution of the war in America was carried by 234 votes to 215.[1] Lord North's ministry was doomed, and the Rockinghams, after a sixteen years sojourn in the political wilderness, could see the promised land. But the birth pangs of the new administration were arduous and protracted. The king did all he could to avoid a step which would certainly entail recognition of the independence of the American colonies. His first attempt was to try to shore up the existing ministry by bringing in Lord Gower and Lord Weymouth, remnants of the old Bedford party, with the help of the duke of Grafton, 'the most temperate of all the opposition'.[2] On 7 March they declared themselves unable to give any assistance, and North warned the king that it would prove 'very difficult to form a mixed system'.[3] The king next authorised Thurlow, the Lord Chancellor, to negotiate the formation of a ministry on a broad basis, not excluding the Rockinghams. These approaches also proved abortive as the king clearly hoped they would. Rockingham was not prepared to join forces with the existing ministry, and demanded specific assurances that the king would not obstruct the grant of independence to America, nor the introduction of

---

[1] Technically, the division was on a government motion for the adjournment.

[2] Fortescue, v, no. 3543. All three had at one time been colleagues of North in his administration. Grafton was Lord Privy Seal from 1771 to 1775; Gower was Lord President of the Council from 1767 to 1779; Weymouth was Secretary of State for the Southern Department from 1775 to 1779.

[3] Fortescue, v, no. 3545. I cannot agree with the suggestion by J. Norris, *Shelburne and reform*, 147, that there was a negotiation with Shelburne at this stage. The critical document is Fortescue, v, no. 3542, which appears to have been misdated by the editor. It is the reply to no. 3632, and was presumably written on 6 April.

economical reform. This the king treated as a personal affront, broke off the negotiations, and began talking of abdication.[1]

The next round of negotiations was triggered off by a further blow to the ministry. On Monday 18 March Lord North, who had survived a direct vote of no confidence the previous Friday by a mere 9 votes, learned that a sizeable group of country gentlemen was no longer prepared to support him. In a letter which was a model of tact and cogency, he advised the king to abandon his search for a 'broad-bottom' administration and come to terms with Shelburne and Rockingham. The king's reply was rude and peremptory:

After having yesterday in the most solemn manner assured you that my sentiments of honour will not permit me to send for any of the Leaders of the Opposition and personally treat with them, I could not but be hurt at your letter of last night. Every man must be the sole judge of his feelings, therefore whatever you or any man can say on that subject has no avail with me.[2]

But the prospect of being left with no ministry at all while the war still raged, and two more urgent representations from North, induced the king to change his mind and instruct Thurlow to reopen discussions. On Wednesday 20th, North announced his resignation rather than face another vote of no confidence. The following day the king saw Lord Shelburne and offered him the lead on the assumption that the Rockinghams would be prepared to follow. Shelburne was obliged to refuse. His own parliamentary following, though distinguished, was small, and there was no chance of the Rockinghams enlisting under his banner. After another unsuccessful approach to Lord Gower, the king reconciled himself to offering Rockingham the ministry, though Shelburne was to be built up as a counterpoise to the Rockinghams, and was to have complete charge of the negotiations. To his confidant

---

[1] Fortescue, v, nos. 3555, 3561, 3564 & 3563. The last of these letters seems to be misdated. Thurlow's 'little excursion' began on 17 March (see *H.M.C. Carlisle MSS.*, 597), so presumably the letter was written on 18 or 19 March. Rockingham's terms are given in no. 3564; Leeds, 62; and Albemarle, *Memoirs of the marquis of Rockingham and his contemporaries* (1852), ii, 451-3. [2] Fortescue, v, nos. 3566 & 3567.

Charles Jenkinson the king wrote on Sunday 24th: 'I have seen Lord Shelburne; his language is fair: he dreads the R(ockingham) party, and will I believe offer to take a secondary part if he can gain them. He knows I will not treat *personally* with Lord R(ockingham)'.[1]

Time was now running out. If a new administration were not formed by Monday 25th, the opposition threatened to bring forward a resolution expressing 'the anger of the House'. Not until the very last moment did the advice of Shelburne and Thurlow prevail; Dunning was empowered to inform the House of Commons that an administration was under construction.[2] The rest of the day Shelburne spent with Rockingham working out the arrangements, and reported to the king that he hoped he had been able 'to keep things within the bounds prescribed by Your Majesty'. The *rapprochement* between Shelburne and the king was developing fast, and George replied with some degree of cordiality: 'Lord Shelburne's Note I look upon as an instance of *personal* attention, and feel it as such; I trust from it he has stood firm, and will have remembered that the powers intrusted to him in the Ministerial line, according to his own sentiments, gives him strength with more vigour to resist all others'.[3] The first of the new ministers kissed hands on Wednesday 27 March.[4]

---

[1] *The letters of King George III*, ed. B. Dobrée, 151–2.

[2] Debrett, vi, 509. There is no evidence to support the assertion in Albemarle, ii, 464 that Rockingham had an audience with the king before kissing hands. Horace Walpole wrote to W. Mason, 1 April 1782, that Rockingham's friends had persuaded him to swallow the rebuff, and this is confirmed by the account given in Russell, i, 291.

[3] Fortescue, v, nos. 3581 & 3582.

[4] The cabinet numbered eleven. Thurlow stayed on as Lord Chancellor and watchdog of the royal interest. Shelburne, who took the seals of the Home Department, had his close ally Dunning (raised to the peerage as Lord Ashburton) with him as Chancellor of the Duchy of Lancaster, and might expect support from the ex-Chathamites, Grafton and Camden, serving as Lord Privy Seal and Lord President of the Council. Rockingham's staunch supporters Fox and Lord John Cavendish were Secretary of State for Foreign Affairs and Chancellor of the Exchequer, and he could normally expect support from Keppel at the Admiralty and Richmond at the Ordnance. General Conway, the Commander-in-Chief, stood somewhat aloof from the main groups, and his politics

In the king's handling of these negotiations may be seen the seeds from which the Fox-North coalition was ultimately to spring. His objective from the beginning was to drive a wedge into the opposition, and he was not unduly squeamish in his methods. In January 1780, when similar discussions had been in progress, a reminder from the opposition that they would expect all his confidence drew from him an indignant declaration: 'I think I know sufficiently the extent of my duty in this respect, and have never been wanting in the discharge of it'.[1] Yet this deference to constitutional propriety hardly squares with his refusal to see Rockingham, or his pretence that he knew nothing of the specific measures Rockingham was insisting upon. Rockingham complained repeatedly during the negotiations of royal evasiveness: 'I must confess that I do not think it an advisable measure, first to attempt to form a ministry by arrangement of office—afterwards to decide upon what principles or measures they are to act'.[2] Even after this clear indication that Rockingham was not to be side-tracked, Thurlow warned the king through North:

He had never owned to Lord Rockingham his having mentioned his Lordship's four propositions to Your Majesty, but had always treated them as inferior, and subsequent considerations to be settled after the formation of a ministry, and not as conditions of acceptance. He advises, therefore, that Your Majesty should not appear acquainted with that part of Lord Rockingham's conversation . . .[3]

Since there was no alternative to Rockingham, these prevarications were merely futile, and after North's resignation Rockingham had to be given the assurances he demanded.

It was equally unfortunate that Rockingham was not made aware of the extent of the king's commitments to Lord Shelburne. Although the king had talked of Shelburne taking a 'secondary

---

were unpredictable. The situation was, of course, fluid, and it is not possible to say precisely where each man stood. A rather different classification of the cabinet is given by A. S. Foord, *His Majesty's Opposition, 1714–1830* (1964), 373.
[1] Fortescue, v, no. 2916.
[2] Albemarle, ii, 459.   [3] Fortescue, v, no. 3566.

part', it is clear that he intended him to be joint first minister.[1] It is most improbable that Rockingham would have accepted this situation had it been explicitly stated at the outset. If the king's intention was to sow dissension, it could hardly have been done more adroitly, and Charles Fox was not alone in drawing the conclusion that the new administration 'was to consist of two parts—one belonging to the king, the other to the public'.[2]

To the king it no doubt seemed indecent that a subject should attempt to strike bargains with his sovereign: all good men should be willing to serve without question. But this desire to subordinate the discussion of great political questions to his personal honour was also sound tactics, and gave the king a last card to play when all else failed. Rockingham's trump against this was to bring the force of public opinion to bear, in precisely formulated demands, a proceeding sufficiently novel in the world of eighteenth-century politics to justify Macaulay and others finding it significant.[3]

The prospects for the new administration were far from auspicious. On almost every major issue the cabinet was at variance.

---

[1] It is instructive to compare the two drafts prepared by the king in answer to Rockingham's subsequent complaints. In the first, submitted to Thurlow for consideration, the king's promises to Shelburne before the negotiations commenced are very clearly stated: 'he was assured that he should not only be fully consulted on the Plan of the new administration, and that the changes proposed should be communicated to the King by him, but that after the Administration should be formed, all Ecclesiastical and Civil Preferments should be jointly recommended by the Marquis of Rockingham and him.' This seems to have been thought too candid, and in the version communicated to Rockingham on 7 April, no mention was made of these specific assurances. Instead, the king took refuge in the disarming observation that he would 'receive the advice of both separately with great attention, but certainly with the more if it meets with the concurrence of the other'. Fortescue, v, nos. 3632 & 3639.   [2] Russell, i, 292.

[3] Its comparative novelty can be gauged from the slightly bemused fashion in which Lord Stormont wrote to the king: 'their purpose is to draw advantage from insisting upon points which they have contrived to make popular for the moment.' Fortescue, v, no. 3587. Mr John Brooke, who distrusts the attempt to find 'uniqueness' in the Rockinghams and regards opposition policies merely as a cloak to cover political nakedness, nevertheless admits that 'on one occasion (in 1782) under the stress of a national disaster, the programme was actually put into effect when the Opposition achieved power'. See his stimulating essay entitled 'Party in the Eighteenth Century', in *Silver Renaissance*, ed. A. Natan (1961).

5

Whereas the Rockinghams had demanded independence for America, Shelburne was on record against it. In 1778 he had committed himself somewhat imprudently to the proposition that the moment independence was granted 'the sun of Great Britain is set', an opinion he reiterated as late as December 1781, declaring it would 'ever be a stumbling block' between himself and Rockingham.[1] To parliamentary reform, Shelburne, Fox and Richmond were sympathetic, Rockingham and Cavendish lukewarm, Thurlow stoutly opposed. On economical reform, while only the Chancellor dissented, the ministry suffered from the lack of candour at its inception, Rockingham presuming that the reform of the royal household would be by legislation, while the king assumed that he would be left to undertake it himself.[2] There were, in addition, other pressing problems, particularly in overseas affairs. The country had to be extricated from a war in which the Americans had been joined by the French, Spanish and Dutch. In Ireland the formidable force of the Volunteer Army demanded that Britain should renounce her claim to legislate for that kingdom. The Mahratta War in India was still unfinished, and the reports of the Secret and Select Committees on Indian affairs would soon compel the government to define its attitude towards Warren Hastings and towards the future of the East India Company itself. Horace Walpole doubted whether the ministry would survive to receive a quarter's salary.[3]

There was not even a honeymoon period for the new ministers: bickering broke out at once. Within less than a week of kissing hands and before the final arrangement of places was complete, the question of patronage was causing irritation. On 5 April the king wrote to Thurlow:

I stated to you shortly on Thursday that the Marquis of Rockingham had been with me that morning, wanting to get all Patronage into his hands, to the

---

[1] Fitzmaurice, ii, 14; Leeds, 48. [2] Fortescue, v, no. 3648.
[3] Walpole to Mason, 1 April 1782.

exclusion of Lord Shelburne; not satisfied with the lengths he had gone, he came after you left me, and begun the subject again. I said I would see how I could accommodate them both; when Lord Shelburne was with me he expressed an uneasiness lest I should yield to the importunities of Lord Rockingham, which would reduce him to a Secretary of State, acting under the former, instead of a colleague . . .[1]

On this occasion, Shelburne and the king concocted a soothing formula.[2] But when Lord Ashburnham, a fortnight later, resigned as Groom of the Stole, and the king offered the place through Shelburne to Lord Weymouth, Rockingham complained bitterly of 'want of confidence, and that everything must go through him'. Wrangling over appointments provided an obbligato to the ministry's activities during the remaining two months: 'besides the ill-will that this competition excites', wrote Hare, 'the time of the cabinet is as much taken up in settling the Vice-treasuryship as the kingdom of Ireland'.[3]

In the meantime Shelburne consolidated his standing with the king by a mixture of attentiveness to the royal interest and flattery. When Shelburne warned him that the cabinet was to discuss the Establishment bill, designed to effect economies in the royal household, the king urged him to 'concert' with the Chancellor in advance and 'do for the best'.[4] The result was a difficult cabinet meeting, described by Fox in a letter to Fitzpatrick, whose sister was married to Shelburne: 'There were more symptoms of what we had always apprehended than had ever hitherto appeared . . . Nothing was concluded, but in Lord Chancellor there was so marked an opposition, and in your brother-in-law so much inclination to help the Chancellor that we got into something very like a warm debate'.[5] When the matter was debated by the

---

[1] Fortescue, v, no. 3632. See also nos. 3627 & 3628.   [2] See p. 5, n. 1.

[3] Fortescue, v, no. 3699; Russell, i, 328. There was particular acrimony over the Governorship of Portsmouth. Shelburne had obtained a promise from the king on behalf of Lord Pembroke, but omitted to mention it to Rockingham, 'not intentionally, but owing to the difficulties which . . . attended all communications between Lord Rockingham and me'. Fortescue, vi, no. 3782.

[4] Fortescue, v, no. 3646.   [5] Russell, i, 314.

House of Lords, Shelburne stepped forth as the king's champion:
'I insisted that the proposed reduction of ministerial influence', he
told the king, 'must make the struggle within and without doors,
who should contribute most to Your Majesty's Dignity Comfort
and Splendour'. This was a novel interpretation of economical
reform, but it won royal approval: 'nothing could be more
proper than Lord Shelburne's language on Monday in the House
of Lords', replied the king.[1] By 18 April, Lord Temple suspected
that Shelburne meant to play Rockingham false, and that there
was 'some secret plan of removing Mr. Fox and of course Lord
Rockingham and his friends'.[2]

Shelburne worked assiduously to build up his political connections from the moment of taking office. Of these the most
valuable was with William Pitt, only twenty-two years of age,
but already marked as a man of the future. He had rejected offers
of junior appointments in March 1782 and maintained a certain
distance from the two ministerial groups, but by May was
identified in Fox's mind as 'the man that the old system, revived
in the person of Lord Shelburne, will attempt to bring forward
for its support'.[3] Of more immediate consequence, however,
were Shelburne's overtures to Henry Dundas, who had retained
his post as Lord Advocate: his electoral influence in Scotland and
his growing command of Indian affairs, demonstrated in a powerful two and a half hour speech on 9 April, made him a man worth
acquiring.[4] The intermediary was Thurlow who, early in April,
explained to Dundas that Shelburne, 'if a breach of administration
should ever happen so as to leave him in possession of government', would undoubtedly look to him to lead the House of
Commons. Dundas, perfectly aware of his own political importance, was not over-anxious to cement an alliance with Shelburne,

---

[1] Fortescue, v, nos. 3665 & 3666.   [2] Leeds, 66–7.
[3] Russell, i, 325. Shelburne wrote to the king, 20 May, that Pitt was 'certainly hostile' to
the Rockinghams. Fortescue, vi, no. 3765.
[4] See Burke to Rockingham, 27 April 1782; William Adam to W. Robertson, 10 April
1782, Robertson–Macdonald MSS. 3943, National Library of Scotland.

against whom, he confessed, he had 'imbibed prejudices'. The result was a subtle sparring match between Thurlow and Dundas, two master-craftsmen in political manoeuvre. Thurlow suggested that the Keepership of the Signet for life, on which Dundas had set his heart, was his for the asking: Dundas replied that he would be glad to have it, but not at the price of being under a 'substantial obligation' to Shelburne. It would be difficult to arrange other-wise, thought Thurlow, for Shelburne would rely so much on Dundas that he would certainly wish him to feel the obligation as 'flowing directly from himself'. After these cautious explorations, the matter was taken further in a meeting between Shelburne and Dundas on 7 April. 'There was on his part', Dundas wrote to his brother, 'a great deal of civility and courtship rather a little over-done upon so slight an acquaintance.' The king had a rooted dislike of life appointments, which he regarded as an open invitation to disloyalty, but by June Shelburne was urging him to 'send for the Advocate and agree upon the best terms we can'.[1] The understanding with Dundas helped to strengthen the connection with Pitt, whom Dundas later described as the *sine qua non* of any non-Rockingham ministry, and opened the channel to Richard Rigby, whose small group would make a useful addition to Shelburne's parliamentary following.[2]

Grafton and Camden were also the objects of Shelburne's attention. Early in May Grafton described several dinner parties at which Shelburne revealed 'nothing like cordiality' towards Rockingham's ministry:

I noticed . . . that every engine was set to work, to bring from Lord Camden a declaration that he would go on with Lord Shelburne in case of such a separation. No artifice could prevail on Lord Camden to acquiesce, though Lord Shelburne

---

[1] Fortescue, vi, no. 3798; Henry to Robert Dundas, 18 April 1782, Dundas of Arniston MSS., R.H. 4 15/5, Scottish Record Office.

[2] Dundas to Thomas Orde, 6 July 1782, Melville MSS., Scottish Record Office. In an analysis of the House of Commons made in March 1783 by John Robinson (Melville MSS.), Rigby is shown as the leader of a small squadron of seven members. He was, in addition, a useful speaker.

pressed him in a manner which appeared to me to be by much too warm. On my part, I gave his lordship no expectation that he could depend on my assistance on such a juncture.[1]

Such time and energy as ministers could spare from these pursuits were devoted to affairs of state. The programme of economical reform went through both Houses of Parliament without great difficulty.[2] The Northites were for some time in disarray, attendances were thin, and the debates desultory. The main opposition came from within the ministry itself, Thurlow speaking with particular vehemence against the bill to debar contractors from the House of Commons and against Burke's Civil List reform. A bill to reform the corrupt borough of Cricklade afforded another opportunity for the administration to parade its disunity. Richmond, goaded beyond endurance by legalistic obstruction, accused Thurlow of 'opposing indiscriminately every measure of regulation or improvement' which was laid before the House: his cabinet colleague, in injured tones, retorted that he was 'but a plain man, who studied nothing but to convey his sentiments clearly and intelligibly'. In the House of Commons, a motion by William Pitt for a committee to consider parliamentary reform proved a further embarrassment, Fox and Dundas clashing in the course of the debate. In addition, the proposal gave Lord North's following a chance to climb back into the political arena on an issue that united them most, and with their help the motion was defeated by 161 to 141 votes. It had been 'a strange day', wrote Burgoyne to Fitzpatrick, 'friend against friend among us; on the other side the late Ministry voted in phalanx'. The Northites' morale was further boosted by the news of Rodney's great victory over de Grasse in the West Indies. Unfortunately for the ministry orders had just been

---

[1] Grafton, 320.

[2] This legislation is discussed in detail by J. Norris, *Shelburne and reform* (1963), 155–64; B. Kemp, 'Crewe's Act, 1782', *English Historical Review*, vol. lxviii; I. R. Christie, 'Economical Reform and the "Influence of the Crown", 1780', *Cambridge Historical Journal*, xii.

despatched for his immediate recall, leaving Fox to argue a very awkward case in the House of Commons.[1]

On Indian affairs, the lead was shared by Burke, working through the Select Committee, and Dundas, chairman of the Secret Committee. Both had come to the conclusion that Warren Hastings, the Governor-General, should be recalled. But Shelburne was well disposed towards Hastings, and through Ashburton had contacts with Sir Elijah Impey, Chief Justice of the Supreme Court, and one of Hastings' closest associates. When Dundas opened the attack upon Hastings, declaring that he preferred 'frantic military exploits to the improvement of the trade and commerce of the country', he was warmly commended by Burke. On 29 April he followed this up with a bill to restrain Sir Thomas Rumbold, former Governor of Madras, from leaving the kingdom while his affairs were investigated. General Richard Smith, chairman of the Select Committee, next carried a motion for the recall of Impey, and at the end of May Dundas was able to gain a majority for a resolution asking the Directors of the East India Company to recall Hastings himself. But at this point the friends of Hastings began to rally. The General Court of Proprietors of the Company opposed his recall, and insisted that the Directors should ignore the Commons' resolution. The rift in the ministry showed itself, Fox and Burke demanding strong action, Shelburne refusing to support a showdown: the differences, wrote Major John Scott, 'had been carried to great lengths'.[2]

The ministry's handling of Irish problems was more coherent, perhaps because it was almost completely dictated by events. Government in that country was breaking down, leaving power in the hands of Grattan, Charlemont, and the Volunteer Movement. But though ministers approached Irish questions with

[1] Debrett, viii, 281; Russell, i, 321–2; Debrett, vii, 185–6, 189, 205–6; Burke to Portland, 25 May 1782.
[2] Debrett, vii, 32; *Commons journals*, xxxviii, 961, 978, 1032; L. S. Sutherland, *The East India Company in eighteenth-century politics* (1952), 385–6; Scott to Hastings, 11 July 1782, Add. MS. 29155, f. 69.

amiable intentions, they had no very clear idea of the issues involved. The demand of the Volunteer leaders was that Britain should renounce all legislative and judicial authority over Ireland, and a special meeting of the Irish parliament had been summoned for 16 April, when an address to that effect was to be moved. The ministers played for time. Fox turned aside in the House of Commons a proposal by William Eden that the declaratory act of 6 George I, c. 5 should be immediately repealed,[1] and the following day presented a message from the king recommending the House to give Irish affairs 'their most serious consideration'. In the Lords, Shelburne, presenting the same message, declared that 'the voice of a people, however conveyed, ought to be attended to'—sentiments distinctly at variance with his private opinions.[2]

In the meantime the duke of Portland, the new Lord-Lieutenant of Ireland, made his journey with the utmost speed, and begged Grattan and Charlemont to agree to a postponement of the meeting of Parliament. This they resolutely refused to do, and on the 16th Irish demands were formulated by Grattan in his most celebrated oration. Fitzpatrick, who had accompanied Portland as Chief Secretary, wrote to Fox the following day:

> You have sent us upon a hopeless errand; for it was too late even to prevail upon them to consider for a moment what they were doing, and the real truth is, that there is no existing government in this country . . . I hope you will be speedy in your resolutions . . . Long debates in your cabinet upon these matters will be very dangerous.[3]

The ministers hoped to obtain some reciprocal guarantees from the concessions they would clearly have to make: 'giving way in everything', wrote Fox, 'without any treaty or agreement . . .

---

[1] The act of 1720 confirmed Poyning's law of 1494.

[2] His speech was taken in Ireland as an indication that the ministers would yield to all the demands made. But privately Shelburne was urging Fitzpatrick to stand firm, and in his correspondence with the king he deplored any negotiations at all while Britain was in so weak a position. Debrett, vii, 2–27 and viii, 251–3; Fitzmaurice, ii, 95–6; Fortescue, v, nos. 3644 & 3686.   [3] Russell, i, 398.

can answer no end but that of obtaining quiet for a few months'. But when Portland was at length persuaded to assist the government with his opinion, he insisted that legislative independence be granted at once and without condition: 'there is still *an appearance* of Government; but if you delay, or refuse to be liberal, government cannot exist here in its present form, and the sooner you recall your Lieutenant and renounce all claim to this country the better'.[1] This was unpalatable to the king, who complained to Shelburne that the despatches from Ireland could hardly be 'less comfortable'. But though Shelburne was the minister responsible for Irish affairs and had been highly critical of Portland's suggestions, he confessed himself baffled:

Of all the subjects depending, Ireland gives me most pain. Such is the difficulty of it, that I feel myself deprived of the assistance which I have in every other part of Your Majesty's affairs. It is the only subject through which I do not see some sort of way. However Your Majesty may depend upon its being never off my mind.[2]

An answer to Grattan's address could not be long delayed, and on 15 May the cabinet resolved to recommend the repeal of 6 George I, c. 5, together with a pious declaration in favour of 'some solid and permanent connection' between the two kingdoms. Resolutions to this effect were carried through Parliament two days later. For the time being, Irish opinion was satisfied: on 27 May a motion that no constitutional differences remained between the two nations was passed by a large majority in the Irish House of Commons, followed by a vote of £100,000 towards seamen for the navy as a gesture of loyalty. Conway, in a letter to Sir Robert Keith, boasted, prematurely as it turned out, that the ministry had effected 'the pacification of Ireland'.[3]

By far the biggest task facing the ministers was the negotiation of a general peace settlement. Fox and Shelburne were directly

---

[1] Russell, i, 411, 417. [2] Fortescue, vi, nos. 3713 & 3743.
[3] 3 June 1782, Add. MS. 35525, f. 252.

concerned in this, the first as Foreign Secretary, the second as Secretary for the Colonies, who would be in charge of negotiations with America until independence had been recognised. The situation was delicate and could easily have led to friction between colleagues on cordial terms. In fact, Fox and Shelburne disliked each other intensely and differed on matters of considerable importance. Fox came to office convinced that Britain should cut her losses in America, endeavour to drive a wedge between the Americans and their French allies, and above all end her perilous isolation by reaching an understanding with Russia and Prussia. In his view it was essential to recognise American independence at once and without conditions, partly as a gesture of goodwill on which harmonious future relations might be based, and partly to demonstrate that any continuation of the war could only be to satisfy French territorial aspirations. Independence once recognised beyond doubt, the colonists would have little incentive to continue the struggle, and this, in turn, might force France to consider peace. Shelburne's assessment of the situation was quite different. He had only recently reconciled himself to the need to grant independence,[1] and he had to consider the views of the king, who still regarded independence as a valuable bargaining-counter which might be used to extort concessions: 'Common-sense tells me that if unconditional independence is granted, we cannot ever expect any understanding with America, for then we have given up the whole and have nothing to give for what we want from thence. Independence is certainly an unpleasant gift at best, but then it must be for such conditions of Peace as may justify it'.[2] Both sides seem to have overstated their case. Fox persisted in the Rockinghamite illusion that the Americans would eagerly grasp a hand stretched out in friendship to them; the

---

[1] Fitzmaurice, ii, 127; Leeds, 52. In fact it is not absolutely clear that he had reconciled himself to it, judging by a conversation he had with Lord Carmarthen as late as November 1782: 'he told me he knew we agreed about America, and declared that if he was forced to acknowledge her independent, it should not be for nothing, but upon condition of a Federal union between the two countries.' Leeds, 76.   [2] Fortescue, vi, no. 3841.

king, on his part, had an inflated idea of what the formal concession of independence was worth after the surrender at Yorktown. But though a legitimate difference of policy, it assumed the proportions it took only because of the jealousies already within the administration. Fox suspected that the king would seize an opportunity to resume the war in America, particularly after Rodney's victory over de Grasse had restored British naval supremacy; he was therefore determined that the declaration of independence should be unconditional and irrevocable. The king saw Fox's insistence on immediate independence merely as a political manoeuvre, designed to bring all negotiations into his own hands as Foreign Secretary.

The manner in which the negotiations were conducted did nothing to dissipate these mutual suspicions. There was difficulty in finding a suitable emissary to make the first tentative approaches. Fox hoped to use Thomas Walpole, member of parliament for King's Lynn, who was living on the continent in financial straits. Another possible negotiator was Henry Laurens, the American commissioner to Holland, who had been captured in 1780. But in the meantime Benjamin Franklin, the American commissioner in Paris, sent a letter of friendly greeting to Shelburne, who thought that something might be built upon an exchange of views. After consultation with the king, he despatched Richard Oswald, a Scottish merchant, to sound Franklin. It was an unfortunate choice. Oswald was seventy-seven years of age, had no diplomatic experience, had never been in France, and did not speak the language.[1] Worse still, he was gullible and indiscreet, while Franklin, with whom he had to deal, was an accomplished and unscrupulous negotiator.[2] At their first encounter he

[1] *The Whitefoord Papers*, ed. W. A. S. Hewins (1898), 193.
[2] While Oswald was appealing to Franklin's 'ancient affection and regard for old England', Franklin was observing that a little success would make 'that changeable nation' as insolent as ever, and disseminating fake atrocity propaganda. C. C. van Doren, *Benjamin Franklin* (1939), 674–6. For an account of Franklin extorting valuable information on Gibraltar from the unsuspecting Oswald, see S. Conn, *Gibraltar in British diplomacy in the eighteenth century* (1942), 201–2.

persuaded Oswald that it would be in Britain's interests to cede Canada and Nova Scotia to the Americans, and provided him with a paper to that effect to show Shelburne. Although Shelburne rejected the suggestion out of hand, he did not inform his cabinet colleagues that he had received the paper, and they agreed to send Oswald back to make arrangements for a general peace negotiation. At the same time the cabinet resolved to open direct discussions with France, and Thomas Grenville, a younger brother of Lord Temple, was appointed at Fox's recommendation. Each Secretary of State now had his representative in Paris. The king approved of Oswald being retained in service: '(it) cannot fail of being an useful check on that part of the negotiation that is in other hands'.[1] Consequently Oswald on his return to France had very little of a diplomatic character to perform, and after several desultory discussions Franklin wondered why he had come at all. But his approach to representing his country's interests had at least the merit of novelty. To Franklin he confessed that peace had become 'absolutely necessary' for Britain, and added: 'Our enemies may now do what they please with us; they have the ball at their feet . . . and we hope that they will show their moderation and their magnanimity'.[2] He agreed with Franklin that Britain had no just claim against America on behalf of the loyalists, and explained that he had done his best to convince the British ministers of the wisdom of ceding Canada. Franklin was charmed with such a negotiator: 'he seems to have nothing at heart but the good of mankind.' He wrote to Shelburne that Oswald would be a most suitable person to conduct the full negotiations with America, and Shelburne agreed, once more omitting to mention the matter to his colleagues.

This diplomatic activity proved more damaging to the British government than to its foreign adversaries. Grenville soon discovered the intention to appoint Oswald a commissioner, and

[1] Fortescue, v, no. 3693.
[2] B. Franklin, *Journal of the negotiation for peace with Great Britain*.

wrote to Fox that it made his own position impossible. In the course of his letter, in which he begged to be recalled, he also referred to the Canada paper, leaving Fox to infer that proposals of great importance had been withheld from the cabinet. 'We cannot suffer a system to go on', wrote Fox in reply, 'which is not only dishonourable to us, but evidently ruinous to the affairs of the country'.[1]

But at this point, in the middle of June, the quarrel about negotiators was swallowed up in a greater quarrel about policy itself. This stemmed from the different interpretations placed upon cabinet decisions by Fox and Shelburne. On 23 May the cabinet had resolved to instruct Grenville to 'propose the independency of America in the first instance, instead of making it a condition of a general treaty'.[2] This was in accordance with Fox's line of policy. There is no doubt that Shelburne understood it in that sense, for he wrote to the commanders in America announcing the decision and stating specifically that independence 'was not merely held out to her in the way of negotiation by the executive power, but a distinct unconditional offer'.[3] Unfortunately this was the direct opposite of the briefing he had given Oswald, and reported to the king: 'Mr. Oswald goes away fully impressed of the propriety of making *Peace* either general or separate the Price of Independence, and that Your Majesty will not be bound by the propositions if Peace is not the consequence.'[4] To which the king had replied: 'It is of the greatest importance

---

[1] Russell, i, 359-70. In Fitzmaurice, ii, 141 it is argued that Grenville was mistaken in believing that Franklin's knowledge of Oswald's proposed appointment had made him uncommunicative. But Franklin to Oswald, 27 June 1782, F.O. 97/157 (P.R.O.) makes it clear that Grenville's suspicions were justified.

[2] Russell, i, 357.

[3] Fitzmaurice, ii, 135-6.

[4] Fortescue, vi, nos. 3777 & 3778. I am not sure whether Shelburne misunderstood the matter under discussion, or whether he was pandering to the king's views by pretending to have briefed Oswald in these terms. For Oswald wrote to him on 12 July (F.O. 97/157): 'I have in my letters to Your Lordship, and in conversation with Dr. Franklin, always supposed that the grant was meant to be absolute and unconditional.' Not even Oswald could have believed that if he had been told what Shelburne claimed to have told him.

that Gentleman should be fully apprized what must be obtained at the dreadful price now offered to America.'

Fox was subsequently surprised and indignant to discover that an issue which he regarded as settled beyond doubt by the cabinet decision of 23 May was still regarded by some as unresolved.[1] He raised the matter at a cabinet held on 26 June in Grafton's house. Rockingham was away ill, and only Cavendish, Keppel and Richmond supported him: the others, feeling that independence need not yet be conceded, reversed the former decision. Fox began talking of resignation, complained that Shelburne was trimming to the king, and declared he could send no further instructions to Grenville until he had tested the opinions of his colleagues once more.[2] On 30 June a second cabinet denied that the offer of independence was unconditional and irrevocable, and Fox gave notice that he would resign.

By this time, Rockingham was on his death bed, and Shelburne was busily engaged in making arrangements for what he already called 'my government'. He reported to the king a 'satisfactory conversation' with William Pitt, and discussions about Charles Jenkinson; he wished to consult the king on 'the weight which Your Majesty would think it proper to give Mr. Fox in case of any new arrangement'. To this the king replied: 'It may not be necessary to remove him at once, but if Lord Shelburne accepts the Head of the Treasury, and is succeeded by Mr. Pitt as Secretary for the Home Department and British Settlements, that it will be seen how far he will submit to it.'[3] The following day Lord Rockingham died.

Lord Shelburne's conduct in the course of this unhappy administration has found its defenders. It was 'not especially

---

[1] Portland to Burgoyne, 8 December 1782, printed in E. B. de Fonblanque, *Political and military episodes in the latter half of the eighteenth century* (1876), 413–17. It can be dated by reference to Portland's letter of 9 January 1783 in the same work. See also Debrett, ix, 7–20.　　[2] Grafton, 321–3.
[3] Fortescue, vi, nos. 3824 & 3825. See also T. Orde to Dundas, 30 June, Melville MSS., Scottish Record Office.

improper' of him to take advantage of the king's favour, comments one able historian[1]: the office of Prime Minister was not clearly established, nor the doctrine of cabinet responsibility fully developed. This is no doubt true, though Shelburne's subsequent conduct as first minister suggests that he had a high concept of the office when occupied by himself. But it was hardly the point at issue. There is nothing in the constitution, then or now, to say that one must not fawn or flatter, that one must inform and consult one's colleagues, that one must not try to adapt one's language to serve all occasions. It is not difficult, however, to understand why, on both private and public grounds, Fox did not relish the prospect of serving under Lord Shelburne.

[1] J. Norris, *Shelburne and reform*, 152.

CHAPTER 2

LORD SHELBURNE'S MINISTRY

While Lord Rockingham lay dying, the king complained bitterly to Shelburne at the absence of information, and concluded that the Rockingham party was hatching plans. The reverse seems to have been the case. The Rockinghams were taken by surprise, while the preparations that Shelburne and the king had made were put smoothly into effect. The same afternoon that he received the news of Rockingham's death, the king wrote to Shelburne offering him the Treasury 'with the fullest political confidence'.[1]

The rival camp was in great disorder. Sir William Gordon reported to Lady Gower, some hours after Rockingham's death:

All is confusion at present, for as his friends from the declaration of his physicians did not think him in immediate danger the blow is the severer. Nobody at present can say who will be the successor . . . C. Fox's idea at five o'clock this afternoon was in case His Majesty would not put the Duke of Richmond at the head of the Treasury to put the Duke of Portland there and to persuade the Duke of Devonshire to go to Ireland. They will not hear at this present moment of Shelburne . . . for a compromise they talk of the Duke of Grafton, but he has not nerves for it.[2]

Charles Fox, though by far the ablest parliamentarian, was debarred by his own reputation and by the king's known detestation from being a contender for the Treasury. The duke of Richmond, Fox's uncle, considered himself to have strong claims, but his views on parliamentary reform were too advanced for the party, and he was not personally popular. Eventually the leaders decided to settle for the duke of Portland, who had deputised for Rockingham in the past, and came nearest to the departed

[1] Fortescue, vi, no. 3827.   [2] Granville MSS., P.R.O., box 3.

chieftain in his qualities, being safe, uninspired and inarticulate: 'the proper man to keep the party together', thought Sir Gilbert Elliot.[1]

There was, however, no chance that the king would change his mind and accept Richmond and Grafton's proposal that he should be guided by the ministers: 'in truth', commented Shelburne, 'it is taking the executive altogether out of the King's hands.'[2] Since Shelburne had determined to accept the offer, though with becoming reluctance,[3] the question was whether to serve under him. Richmond and Conway were in favour of continuing, Fox and Cavendish were anxious to go, while Keppel hovered uneasily. Burke, though agreeing with Fox on the 'utter impossibility of your acting for any length of time as a clerk in Lord Shelburne's administration', argued that there were tactical advantages in delaying a resignation:

Now my notion is that *still continuing to be ministers, you should put the whole to issue steadily and resolutely in the House of Commons* . . . My reasons for thinking it plausible are that it is always better to fight on strong ground—I mean by that, ground of power, or at least the appearance of place and power. Secondly it will preclude the disadvantage of putting people to the trial of giving up

[1] Elliot to Lady Elliot, 3 July 1782, Minto MSS.
[2] Shelburne to Marlborough, 8 July 1782, Add. MS. 34418, f. 484. Commentators have usually agreed with Shelburne. Sir William Anson found the Rockinghams' attitude 'difficult to understand' (Grafton, 361), and Richard Pares suggested that it represented 'yet another new constitutional claim' (*King George III and the politicians* (1953), 121). But the claim is a good deal modified by the circumstances. The situation arising from the death of the first minister, when the cabinet remains in existence, is different from that on his resignation or dismissal, when the administration would usually be dissolved. Whatever the constitutional position, it would be prudent for the king to show some regard for the opinions of the remaining ministers, especially if he wished them to continue. This is in fact what had been done on the previous occasion when a first minister had died in office. George II had asked the cabinet to suggest a successor to Henry Pelham, trusting that 'they would not think of recommending to him any person who has flown in his face'. P. C. Yorke, *Life and correspondence of Philip Yorke, earl of Hardwicke* (1913), ii, 206; B. Williams, *Carteret and Newcastle* (1943), 189.
[3] The episode affords another example of Shelburne's meaningless ambivalence. To his brother-in-law Lord Ossory he wrote of the offer: 'You know enough of me to be certain that it is not an event which suits me or mine. In the situation of public affairs I do not think myself at liberty to decline.' His conversation the same day with Lord Temple was 'that it was natural that the Treasury should be an object to him, that he knew no reason why he was always to forego'. Add. MS. 47579, f. 141; Buckingham, i, 51.

their places . . . Thirdly, your going out now must give the appearance of being beat . . .[1]

The other peace-makers laboured hard to find an acceptable formula: Richmond was reported to have 'talked his voice quite away, and sunk his spirits and health' in the process.[2] He was able to extract a half-promise from Fox that he would stay if Lord John Cavendish remained in the cabinet as Secretary of State for the Home Department. In the morning of 4 July, the issue was still undecided, and Fox wrote to Fitzpatrick:

The Duke of Richmond has been with me and says he thinks Lord Shelburne willing (as I thought he would be) to give up the point of America. He is now gone to persuade Lord John to be Secretary of State, in which, if he succeeds, I shall have a hard task to refuse, but am still of opinion that *even in that case I shall do it* . . . I did not think it had been in the power of politics to make me so miserable as this cursed anxiety and suspense does.[3]

But Lord John Cavendish had already received a strong hint from the king that his services were dispensable,[4] and his refusal to continue decided Fox. On the afternoon of the 4th, Fox attended the levée, confirmed with Shelburne that he intended to accept the Treasury, and resigned on the spot, leaving his seals of office with the king. Next day he took his place on the opposition benches in the House of Commons, while William Pitt moved over to the government side—situations they were to occupy for most of the rest of their lives.

'Mr. Fox's consequence in his retreat', Grafton advised Shelburne somewhat unnecessarily, 'depends on the numbers and weight of that party which he can be able to draw with him; to prevent which will be Your Lordship's effort.'[5] The key figure

---

[1] Add. MS. 47568, ff. 104 & 106. The handwriting is identified by the editor of *The correspondence of Edmund Burke*, vol. v, as that of Richard Burke, jr.

[2] Lady Sarah Napier to Lady Susan O'Brien, 6 July 1782, *The life and letters of Lady Sarah Lennox*, ed. Countess of Ilchester and Lord Stavordale (1902), ii, 18.

[3] Russell, i, 460-1.

[4] The king had told him in audience the previous day that he 'could not be expected to remain under a new first lord, but that it was wished to place him in an office that might suit him'. Fortescue, vi, no. 3830.   [5] 5 July 1782, Bowood MSS.

was Richmond, Fox's uncle and Conway's son-in-law, who persuaded most of the Rockinghams to suspend judgement until a party meeting could be held. When forty of them gathered at Lord Fitzwilliam's house on Saturday 6 July, the atmosphere was tense and heated, and the discussions acrimonious:

Every one in office argued in favour of a general resignation except the Duke of Richmond . . . Mr. Baker is said to have pressed him closely in consequence of his resolution so contrary to one he had joined in about four months ago which went to the secluding Lord Shelburne at all events from Minister, being a man with whom it was impracticable for his contemporaries to act on a fair footing. His Grace admitting this, said he was become of a different opinion, from the satisfaction he had had since in office of knowing his sentiments so fully respecting America. Here Mr. Fox interposed with a question to His Grace, which the latter answered in the affirmative, and I understand was to this purpose. If His Grace was not on a question concerning America proposed in the cabinet by Lord Shelburne or one of his friends in a minority? After this Your Lordship will not wonder that the Duke is among his old friends in a state of damnation . . .[1]

According to Carlisle, Richmond finished the meeting in tears, and Richmond himself admitted that he found Fox and his friends 'very warm indeed'.[2] Among the cabinet ministers, only Cavendish went out with Fox; Conway and Richmond decided to stay, and Keppel remained to see the naval campaign through.

The following week, while resignations began to trickle in and Shelburne worked to fill the vacancies, controversy broke out whether the motive for Fox's resignation was pique or policy. Neither side conducted a flawless campaign. Fox was handicapped in his explanations by the need to preserve some degree of cabinet secrecy, though in the debate of 9 July first Conway and then he revealed more and more of the dissensions in the ministry over America. Nor was he assisted by Burke who, in defiance of the

[1] Sir George Jackson to Lord Lisburne, 9 July 1782, Egerton MSS. 2136, f. 195.
[2] Carlisle to Gower, 8 July, *H.M.C. Carlisle MSS.*; Richmond to Lord George Lennox, 8 July, *H.M.C. Bathurst MSS.*; other accounts of this meeting are in Leeds, 72; Walpole to Mann, 7 July; Walpole to Mason, 8 July; Shelburne to the king, 9 July, Fortescue, vi, no. 3837; T. Pelham to Lord Pelham, 14 July, Add. MS. 33128, f. 83.

need to avoid personal rancour, launched a wild attack upon Shelburne, bombarding him with lurid invective. But when Pitt told Fox that he should have called a cabinet meeting before taking so hasty a step, Fox was able to retort that this was precisely what he had done.[1] Shelburne, on his part, tried to minimise the political differences that had taken place: 'he had no quarrel on public grounds that he knew of with Mr. Fox', he told Lord Carmarthen, and in letters to potential supporters he insisted that Fox's resignation was solely over the Treasury.[2] On 10 July he repeated the allegation in the House of Lords: 'though much had since been insinuated relative to the business of America, yet those ministers could all vouch that in the cabinet no reason of that nature or complexion had been assigned for the late resignations.' Fox wrote at once to demand a retraction, and on the following day Lord Derby denounced Shelburne in the Lords as guilty of 'a direct deviation from the truth'. Shelburne's reply was pitiful: 'he had made no such assertion; but he had certainly said that "in his opinion" that was the cause, and the exclusive cause; but he had not asserted it as a fact.' His discomfiture was completed by Richmond and Keppel rising in turn to admit that Fox had unquestionably declared that he would resign on matters of policy before Rockingham's death. The arrival of the king to prorogue Parliament saved Shelburne from further embarrassment, but his debut as first minister had not been auspicious, and the world understood a little better why his adversaries asserted that he was not to be trusted.[3]

When the dust had settled, honours seemed roughly even. The loss of Conway, Keppel and Richmond was a severe blow to Fox,

---

[1] Debrett, 286–319.

[2] Leeds, 72; Add. MS. 47579, f. 141; Shelburne to Marlborough, 8 July, Add. MS. 34418, f. 484; Shelburne to Edmund Pery, 9 July, *H.M.C. Buckinghamshire MSS.*; Pitt to Lady Chatham, 5 July, Chatham MSS.

[3] Debrett, viii, 366, 369–70. Fox's letter is not extant, but Shelburne's reply is printed in Fitzmaurice, ii, 164–5. He suggested that Fox's declaration was not seriously intended: 'Sunday was not the only cabinet council at which you talked of resignation.' The reply could hardly be more damaging to his own case.

but there was a good prospect that some of them would not stay long with Shelburne, and the total of resignations was in the end respectable. Portland and Fitzpatrick gave up their posts in Ireland; Sheridan and the Burkes went out; so did three of the remaining four Lords of the Treasury,[1] and two of the Lords of the Admiralty[2]; John Lee gave up his post as Solicitor-General and Lord Robert Spencer the Vice-Treasurership of Ireland. If Rigby's estimate that Fox had taken into opposition with him some fifty or sixty of the Rockinghams is correct, he had salvaged the greater part of the voting strength of the party.[3] But since Parliament was prorogued, this could only be matter for speculation: much would depend on the way the campaign was waged in the House of Commons in the autumn, and the arrangements that could be made before then.

In the cabinet, Fox's place was taken by Lord Grantham, an experienced diplomat, Cavendish's by William Pitt, and Shelburne's old post as Secretary for the Home Department by Thomas Townshend; Lord Temple replaced Portland as Lord-Lieutenant of Ireland, with William Grenville, one of his younger brothers, as Chief Secretary. The junior posts went mainly to followers of Shelburne, such as Samuel Estwick and John Aubrey, who had been disappointed in the spring.

Political opinion, which had almost universally condemned Fox's resignation as rash and precipitate, began to veer when the new appointments were announced. Even in the cabinet there were misgivings: Camden confessed himself 'not very sanguine', and Thurlow thought the new reinforcements 'not all of the most promising sort'.[4] Archibald Macdonald, Lord Gower's ambitious

---

[1] Lord John Cavendish, Lord Althorpe and Frederick Montagu.

[2] Lord Duncannon and John Townshend. Hugh Pigot had been sent to the West Indies to replace Rodney; he resigned on his return in December 1782.

[3] I. R. Christie, *The end of North's ministry* (1958), 218 puts the Rockinghams' strength a little earlier at between 70 and 80. Rigby's opinion is in a letter from Thurlow to Gower, printed in *H.M.C. 5th Report, appendix*, 211. It should be dated 11 July 1782.

[4] Camden to Stewart, 11 July, Camden MSS.; Thurlow to Gower *H.M.C. 5th Report, appendix*, 211.

son-in-law and no friend to Fox, reported that the 'general opinion' was 'against the duration of the new administration'.[1] Camden's considered view, as one who had watched the antagonisms from close quarters, was that the split had been inevitable:

He (his son-in-law) is mistaken if he thinks it was possible for Fox and Shelburne to have remained in power together a week after Lord Rockingham's death; one or the other must have submitted to be subordinate. The first was at the head of a powerful party, and the second was possessed of the closet, so that the different views, ends and measures of these two situations would have enacted a perpetual contest in the cabinet . . . The event would have been the same if Lord Rockingham had lived, and as they could not be united, their separation was the least evil of the two.[2]

These convulsions were watched from the sideline by Lord North and his supporters with the keenest interest. North had retained in his fall a powerful following, partly the result of twelve years command of patronage, and partly a tribute to his remarkable character and abilities. His stay in the vale of despondency had been brief. Without any exertion on his part, always an important consideration with North, circumstances had swept him back to the centre of politics. All intelligent observers appreciated that only some form of coalition could produce a stable and effective administration: Lord North had but to wait, and offers would arrive. The days when impeachment for the loss of America had seemed a distinct possibility were over, and politicians of varied hues began to remember his amiability and integrity.

Throughout the rest of July there was a steady buzz of political activity. Shelburne's first overtures were directed at North's colleagues with the aim of detaching them from the main group. Immediate steps were taken to secure Henry Dundas: the price was the Keepership of the Signet for life, and the Treasurership of the Navy.[3] Dundas delayed until he could receive North's

[1] Macdonald to Lady Gower, 9 July, Granville MSS., Box 4 (P.R.O.)
[2] Camden to Frances Stewart, 22 July, Camden MSS. [3] Fortescue, vi, no. 3841.

blessing, but by the end of the month had accepted: 'Lord Shelburne, I dare say, will have no objection to have it known that Lord North approves of the Advocate's taking part in the present arrangement', wrote Lord Sackville.[1] This success was followed up by approaches to Dundas's allies Rigby and William Adam, who agreed to give general support to the ministry, while opposing any parliamentary reform.[2] Meanwhile, Shelburne turned his attention to Charles Jenkinson, North's former Secretary-at-War, too unpopular to be given office at this stage, but with too many connections at court and in the city to be neglected. Jenkinson's initial response does not appear to have given Shelburne complete satisfaction, and the king was brought in to make a personal appeal: 'The mask is now certainly cast off; it is no less than a struggle whether I am to be dictated to by Mr. Fox, who avows that he must have the sole direction of this country; Lord Shelburne certainly must and shall have my fullest support; I therefore desire Mr. Jenkinson will give him every degree of assistance.'[3] Jenkinson's cooperation opened up the line in turn to his close friend, John Robinson, patronage secretary in North's government, and the recognised expert on political allegiancies and electoral matters. With Shelburne confessing to total ignorance about the House of Commons, the collaboration of Robinson was of critical importance. On 23 July Jenkinson advised Robinson that he should certainly see Shelburne, 'and converse with his Lordship on any subject he may mention to you', though Lord North should be kept informed. The outcome was that Robinson agreed to provide Shelburne with a state of the House of Commons showing the probable affiliation of members.[4]

Shelburne followed this up with an appeal to William Eden, Chief Secretary in Ireland under Lord Carlisle, and one of the

[1] Sackville to Knox, 29 July, H. V. Knox MSS., *H.M.C. Various collections*, vi, 187.
[2] Rigby to Dundas, 17 August; Adam to Dundas 17 August; Melville MSS., GD 51/1.
[3] Fortescue, vi, nos. 3832, 3846 & 3847.
[4] *H.M.C. Abergavenny MSS.*, 53–4.

most adroit political tacticians in North's group. 'He talked', wrote Eden, 'of the necessity of making friends . . . his personal partialities to connect himself with particular people . . . some broad but indefinite hints of some intentions in view respecting me'.[1]

Having drummed up a certain amount of support among North's lieutenants, Shelburne opened the attack on North himself. With great precautions for secrecy, the king wrote to him through Robinson on 7 August:

Lord North has so often whilst in office assured me that whenever I could consent to his retiring he would give the most cordial support to such an administration as I might approve of, that I should not think I either acted properly to my own affairs or placed the confidence in his declarations if I did not express my strongest wishes that he will give the most active support the next session of Parliament to the administration formed with my thorough approbation on the death of Lord Rockingham, and that during the recess he will call on the country gentlemen who certainly have great attention for him to come early and show their countenance by which I may be enabled to keep the constitution from being entirely annihilated, which must be the case if Mr. Fox and his associates are not withstood . . .[2]

This appeal was premature. North could hardly be expected to commit himself before he knew what the peace terms would be, and he was still resentful of the king's treatment of him over the election expenses incurred during his ministry.[3] He had no liking for Shelburne who, according to his own account, had moved in the cabinet to bring him to a public trial,[4] and he was being offered nothing in exchange for his services save the king's esteem. He therefore returned a guarded answer. It was true that he had, while in office, received the support of several independent

---

[1] Eden to Loughborough, 31 July, Add. MS. 34418, f. 523. [2] Fortescue, vi, no. 3872.
[3] The king had repudiated a debt of nearly £20,000, leaving North to pay it as best he could. Fortescue, v, nos. 3663, 3668 & 3669, 3674 & 3675, 3691; vi, nos. 3715 & 3753. On 8 September, North complained to Robinson that there was 'not the most distant hint of any intention to do me justice'. H.M.C. Abergavenny MSS., 54; Laprade, 60–2. The episode is investigated by I. R. Christie, 'George III and the Debt on Lord North's Election Account, 1780–84', English Historical Review, lxxviii, 715–24.
[4] Fitzmaurice, ii, 104.

country gentlemen, but he did not know whether he could venture to ask them to support the present ministry, and he was afraid that 'he may give them some offence if he were to attempt it'.[1] Robinson thought the reply 'cold and reserved', and the king complained that North's protestations of loyalty had soon evaporated.[2]

North was, in any case, already being wooed with assiduity by the other party. As early as 24 July he received messages from Fox that their differences were not irreconcilable and that they should unite. By the middle of August he was being offered 'a good office, but by no means in any superintending situations; this . . . was quite impossible'. North turned aside the suggestions 'in great derision'. Free at last from the strain of fifteen years in office, he was gradually recovering his old jauntiness, fortified by a holiday in the Peak District and a visit to Manchester, where he was received with great enthusiasm and entreated to resume the government.[3] Gibbon saw him in mid-September on his way to Dover looking 'not so fat and more cheerful than ever'.[4] To his father, Lord Guilford, North wrote of the political situation:

I really do not see any plan that will quite satisfy my mind, and that appears honest and honourable, but support to the general measures of government, and opposition to all innovations of the constitution. I believe I shall speak openly in a few days, but I wish first to converse with some friends, and learn what following I am likely to have; one would certainly wish to appear with as much dignity and importance as possible.[5]

The tug-of-war to influence North continued all through the autumn, Jenkinson and Robinson pulling him towards the ministry, Eden and Loughborough propelling him towards a reconciliation with Fox. The resultant forces, assisted by North's constitutional sluggishness, produced total inertia. 'When he leaves me

---

[1] Fortescue, vi, no. 3873.
[2] Jenkinson to Robinson, 16 & 22 September, *H.M.C. Abergavenny MSS*, 54–5.
[3] Eden to Loughborough, 24 July, Add. MS. 34418, f. 513; Robinson to Jenkinson, 24 July, Add. MS. 38567, f. 101; Eden to Loughborough, 22 August; Loughborough to Eden, 24 & 25 August, Add. MS. 34419, ff. 18, 20, 22.
[4] Add. MS. 34884, f. 272.   [5] 12 September, MSS. North d 26, f. 36, Bodleian.

he seems to acquiesce', wrote Robinson dejectedly in October, 'but afterwards somehow or other it is drawn back, and nothing gets done . . .'[1]

North was not the only politician experiencing difficulty in estimating what the line-up would be when Parliament re-assembled. William Eden's guess in October was that Shelburne would have 140 followers, North 120, Fox 90, and the rest uncertain. Selwyn, a little later, quoted very similar figures.[2] These computations, however tentative, revealed how doubtful the outcome was, both from the evenness of the three groups and from the large number of members who could not at that stage be classified—more than 200 according to Eden's estimate.

The least plausible of all the estimates was the one obligingly provided for the government by John Robinson, who must share some responsibility for Shelburne's misfortunes by lulling him into a state of absurd optimism. There seem to have been two editions of Robinson's list, in August and in October.[3] It grossly exaggerated the degree of cordiality towards the new administration, including under the category 'Hopeful' many members, like Lord North himself, whose final allegiance was still undetermined. The 'pros' and 'hopefuls' together totalled 439, against a mere 106 described as 'doubtful' or 'con'. These misjudgements were bad enough, but Shelburne seems totally to have disregarded Robinson's warning that the allocations were highly speculative. On 13 November he told Lord Carmarthen that he would have the support of 'almost all the property of the country, and that he did not believe his opponents in the House of Commons would exceed 60, a circumstance he added which he had reason to be

---

[1] Robinson to Jenkinson, 12 October, Add. MS. 38567, f. 117.

[2] Gibbon to Sheffield, 14 October, Add. MS. 34884, f. 275; Selwyn to Carlisle, *H.M.C. Carlisle MSS.*, 633–4. The editor had dated Selwyn's letter July, but from internal evidence it appears to have been written in mid-November.

[3] A memorandum from Robinson to Shelburne, dated 7 August, is printed in Laprade, 42, and is followed by the beginning of a detailed analysis. On 28 September Thomas Orde reported to Shelburne that Robinson had been ill, but had promised the 'immediate completion' of the list. Bowood MSS. This I take to be a revised version.

assured of tho' it appeared scarce credible'.[1] Three days before
Parliament assembled he remarked airily to Fitzpatrick that he
understood nothing of the House of Commons, 'but that they
show him a *very good list*'. He had always professed contempt for
parties and party organisation, and was to pay dearly for it.[2]

By inheriting Rockingham's office, Shelburne became heir to
the problems that had afflicted the previous ministry. The
implementation of economical reform proved to be tedious and
thorny: 'it is impossible to describe to you', he wrote to Grafton,
'how provokingly my time is taken up with the nonsense of Mr.
Burke's bill. It was both framed and carried through without the
least regard to *facts*.'[3] Parliamentary reform also proved to be full
of hazards. Its advocates greeted Shelburne's advent to power with
enthusiasm, since he was known to be much more sympathetic
than the previous first minister, and Christopher Wyvill, the
organiser of the Yorkshire Association, was delighted to receive
in August an assurance from Shelburne that he would 'act nobly'
by the Association. But Shelburne was in a most delicate situation. Dundas, Rigby and Adam had made it clear that they would
oppose reform, and their views were shared by Thurlow and
Jenkinson. Not only would such a measure raise difficulties with
them and with the king, but it would rule out any understanding
with the rest of the Northites, whose dislike of reform was
cardinal. As soon as Wyvill began to spread the glad tidings
among his colleagues, he was told that Shelburne's letter was
meant 'as a contribution to him personally', and not as a statement
of government intention.[4]

Rockingham's settlement of the Irish question proved to be
short-lived. Agitation flared once more upon reports that there were
reservations in the grant of legislative and judicial independence,

[1] Leeds, 76.　　　　　　　　　[2] Russell, ii, 10.
[3] Grafton, 338. Shelburne's policy is discussed fully by J. Norris, *Shelburne and reform*,
ch. x–xii.
[4] C. Wyvill, *Political papers* (1794–1802), iii, 333–62; J. Norris, *op. cit.*, 254–6.

and whatever goodwill there had been towards England was soon dissipated. Temple, the new Lord-Lieutenant, reported that the situation was critical, and the cabinet was ultimately obliged to bring in a Renunciation Bill to quieten Irish fears.[1]

But the fate of the ministry depended on the peace negotiations, which continued to be plagued by the confusion arising from Shelburne's ambiguous attitude towards American independence. The fierce recriminations that followed Fox's resignation aroused suspicions in the minds of the American commissioners that the minister was employing double language. On 12 July Franklin wrote directly to Shelburne for an explanation of rumours that he had opposed 'Mr. Fox's decided plan of unequivocally acknowledging American independence:' he could not believe this had ever been in dispute.[2] In reply Shelburne authorised Oswald to show Franklin his letter of 5 June to the commanders in America without mentioning that the cabinet had twice since refused to confirm that decision. For good measure Oswald was to assure Franklin that 'there never have been two opinions since you were sent to Paris upon the most unequivocal acknowledgment of American independence'. To Oswald's dismay, this show of candour failed to remove all doubts, and he was forced to report that unless the Americans received the most explicit and categorical assurances that independence would be 'absolutely and unconditionally granted', the negotiation was at an end. In the face of this ultimatum Shelburne could prevaricate no longer. Although the king protested that he did not see how 'the present ministry can consent to independency but as the price of a certain peace', the cabinet empowered Oswald to concede independence 'absolutely and irrevocably', if possible as the first clause of a treaty, but if necessary by previous parliamentary declaration. Thus the point for which Fox had contested in June was established, and Shelburne had at last succeeded in getting his two interpreta-

---

[1] A motion for leave to bring in the Irish Judicature bill was moved by Townshend on 22 January 1783.   [2] F.O. 97/157, P.R.O.

tions of policy into harmony. Grafton wrote to him to congratulate him on the 'manly manner' in which he had been prepared to sacrifice his own opinions.[1]

The sacrifice turned out not to be necessary. Their growing distrust of French and Spanish territorial ambitions, strengthened by knowledge of the financial difficulties faced by Congress, prompted the American commissioners to hasten on a separate settlement. They agreed to waive their claim to a previous recognition of independence provided that Oswald's commission was amended to refer to the 'United States' and not 'the colonies'. This the British cabinet conceded on 19 September. The main obstacle to a treaty was now the question of reparations to the loyalists. On this point the Americans proved adamant, taking refuge in the argument that Congress had no power to instruct the states to pay compensation, but would 'earnestly recommend' it. With this paper promise, Shelburne had to be content. Oswald's other efforts to obtain some modification of Franklin's original proposals obtained little more success, save for a slight rectification of the boundary of Canada and the deletion of a clause permitting the Americans to dry fish on Newfoundland. His conduct of the negotiations was much criticised, particularly by Richmond, who complained that 'every other member of the cabinet had long seen that he plead only the cause of America, not of Britain'.[2] But he had been given a poor hand to play, and was not helped by the common knowledge that Shelburne must have a peace settlement before Parliament reassembled.[3] On 5 November the

---

[1] Fitzmaurice, ii, 167–9; Oswald to Townshend, 17 August, F.O. 97/157; Fortescue, vi, nos. 3891-4 & 3907; Grafton, 339.

[2] Fortescue, vi, no. 4009. Even Shelburne thought Oswald too accommodating to the Americans, and warned him, 21 October, against 'going before the commissioners in every point of favour and confidence'. Fitzmaurice, ii, 193–4.

[3] Parliament was to have met on 26 November, but was prorogued until 5 December. On 23 November Townshend sent a public letter to the Lord Mayor of London stating that the negotiations would be brought to a 'decisive conclusion' before Parliament met. The English commissioners were then instructed to press for better terms for the loyalists. They were asked whether this constituted an ultimatum, and when they admitted that it was not, the Americans refused to make further concessions.

articles were sent back to England for final consideration. The king unburdened his bitterness to Shelburne:

> I cannot conclude without mentioning how sensibly I feel the dismemberment of America from this Empire, and that I should be miserable indeed if I did not feel that no blame on that account can be laid at my door, and did I not also know that knavery seems to be so much the striking feature of its inhabitants that it may not in the end be an evil that they become aliens to this kingdom.[1]

After a fruitless last-minute attempt to extract better terms for the loyalists, the preliminary articles were signed on 30 November.

The negotiations with the European powers were still in progress when Parliament met. The course of the discussions was much affected by the fact that the war was still being vigorously prosecuted: Spain launched her grand but abortive attack upon Gibraltar in September, and the French pinned great hopes on de Bussy's expedition to India. The object of both the French and Spanish was to reverse the decision of 1763; the Dutch, for whom the war had been a series of unmitigated disasters, demanded full restitution of their territories and a new maritime code.[2] When Thomas Grenville resigned with Fox in July 1782, negotiations were still at an exploratory stage. The precise demands of France and Spain were not officially formulated until 6 October, after long private discussions between Shelburne and Rayneval, the special envoy of Vergennes, the French Foreign Minister. France demanded the abrogation of the Utrecht clauses prohibiting the fortification of Dunkirk; exclusive fishing rights off the west coast of Newfoundland; Dominica and St Lucia in the West Indies; Senegal and Goree in Africa, and extensive commercial and territorial concessions in India to restore the situation to what it had been in 1754. The Spanish demanded participation in the Newfoundland fishery; both the Floridas; the Bahamas; the elimination of the British logwood settlement in

---

[1] Fortescue, vi, no. 3978.
[2] The maritime issue is discussed in I. de Madariaga, *Britain, Russia and the armed neutrality of 1780* (1962).

Honduras; Providence, Minorca and Gibraltar; in exchange for the last, they were prepared to offer Oran.

The most formidable part of the negotiation concerned the Spanish claim to Gibraltar, which, despite the total failure of their attack, they refused to abandon. The king was anxious to exchange it for West Indian possessions, particularly Porto Rico, on whose wealth he hoped an economic recovery might be based. The preliminary discussions were to find an acceptable equivalent. Shelburne at once rejected Oran as inadequate, and as a counter-proposal suggested that Spain should restore West Florida, the Bahamas and Minorca, and that in addition Britain should have either Porto Rico, or Guadeloupe and Dominica, or Martinique and St Lucia. In the event of either of the last two pairs, which belonged to France, being ceded, Spain would give France the other half of San Domingo as compensation. At this stage the French, alarmed at the progress made in the American negotiations, exerted pressure on the Spaniards to be less obdurate. Spain would not give up West Florida, or permit the continuation of the Honduras settlement, but offered to support the exchange of Guadeloupe and Dominica for Gibraltar. This the king and a majority of the cabinet would have been prepared to accept, but in the meantime public opinion had come out so strongly against any surrender of Gibraltar that Shelburne had to abandon the exchange proposals. He now offered to give up both the Floridas and Minorca provided the British kept Gibraltar, and this the Spaniards, under strong French pressure, accepted on 16 December. By the preliminary articles signed on 20 January 1783 France received the substance of her original demands,[1] except in India, where the absence of news about de Bussy's expedition forced her diplomats to be satisfied with more modest concessions. The negotiations with the Dutch, which had been particularly difficult, continued throughout most of 1783, after a truce had been arranged.

[1] She did not receive Dominica, but was given Tobago.

Professor V. T. Harlow, in a careful and informed study of the negotiations, expressed great admiration for Shelburne's conduct of affairs, which he called 'a diplomatic triumph . . . won almost single-handed'.[1] It is certainly true that Shelburne bore complete responsibility for the settlement, which he negotiated with scant reference to his colleagues. But it is doubtful whether the comparison which Professor Harlow made between the terms originally demanded by France and Spain and those ultimately accepted is a valid one. It is not unknown for negotiators to begin by asking for more than they expect to be granted.[2] By the same test the original British suggestion that the settlement should be based on the Treaty of Paris in 1763 emerged rather battered. Professor Harlow himself referred to the 'astonishing concessions' made to America; the greatest achievement against Spain, the retention of Gibraltar, had been forced upon Shelburne against his will; while the unexpectedly advantageous terms in India owed more to the failure of the French expedition than to any extraordinary diplomatic finesse.

Shelburne laboured under the conviction that he could make a peace settlement which would consolidate his ministry's position. But peacemakers are only blessed after successful wars—and not always then. Only a powerful ministry, resolute and united, could have hoped to survive the massive tide of disillusion that the end of such a war would bring. Shelburne's ministry was hardly that. At every stage he had ridden rough-shod over his colleagues: they now discovered the full significance of his remark on taking office that he 'could not bear the idea of a *round-robin* administration, where the whole cabinet must be consulted for the disposal of the most trifling appointments'.[3] In practice they were hardly consulted on anything. Lord Grantham, the Foreign Secretary, was little more than a clerk: Shelburne

---

[1] *The founding of the second British Empire 1763–93* (1952), i, 406. The negotiations are also examined in detail in R. B. Morris, *The peacemakers* (1965).
[2] I am forced to concede that Oswald is an exception.   [3] Leeds, 70.

thought of conducting the decisive negotiations with Rayneval without reference to him at all.[1] On 2 December, when these discussions reached their climax, he had the mortification to be informed of Rayneval's return by one of Fox's friends.[2] William Grenville, in London at the end of November to impress upon the government the gravity of the Irish situation, found the minister reluctant to summon a cabinet on the subject. 'If they were called upon the subject of Ireland', confided Townshend, 'nobody knows what other hare might be started there.' To his brother, Grenville commented: 'You will certainly think the mode of keeping a cabinet unanimous by never meeting them at all an excellent one.' A little later, exasperated at Shelburne's refusal to grant him more than a few minutes, he concluded that 'Lord Shelburne's evident intention is to make cyphers of his colleagues'.[3] Temple began to threaten resignation. Richmond and Keppel, already infuriated by Oswald's behaviour, would not hear of the proposal to abandon Gibraltar, and Grafton, Camden and Conway supported them.[4] Grafton, bearding Shelburne once more on the subject of Gibraltar, was told bluntly: 'As to Lord Keppel I should be happy to see him away from his board; the Duke of Richmond also must take the part he judges proper; I shall see it with indifference. But though it would be very unpleasant to me, and give me great concern to differ from you, yet I must bear it.'[5] This was Ercles's vein, but it was scarcely prudent to set forth on what was certain to be a stormy and decisive parliamentary session with half the cabinet in a state of mutiny.

---

[1] Harlow, *op. cit.*, 336.   [2] Fitzpatrick to Ossory, 2 December, Russell, ii, 9.
[3] Buckingham, i, 76, 84.
[4] The king commented on new proposals during December that they would enable Richmond, Grafton, Camden, Keppel and Conway 'to fight the whole peace over again, and to form fresh cabals'. Fortescue, vi, no. 4021.   [5] Grafton, 350.

CHAPTER 3

FORMATION OF THE COALITION

The intense political activity of the autumn of 1782 did little to clarify the parliamentary situation. Lord North maintained his detached position against increasing pressure from some supporters to declare himself before his following began to drift, and against more and more captivating offers.[1] On 4 November, in accordance with his promise to the king, he reported that the country gentlemen seemed 'in general, well inclined to concur in such measures as shall be necessary for the support of H.M.'s government'—a distinctly tepid assurance that drew from the king the reply that all who would not heartily assist him were 'bad men as well as ungrateful subjects'.[2] North did not take the hint, and in letters to his followers summoning them to Parliament, reserved his position:

I wished to explain to my friends how I stand with respect to the contending parties in the House of Commons; I am connected with neither, but as I can not consistently with my principles engage in faction, or consistently with my former professions refuse my assistance to carry on the war, I do intend to give my voice for the necessary supplies . . . But I am equally determined to resist all ideas of altering, or as it is called amending the representative body . . . With regard to any unforeseen measures, being in no connection, I am open to approve or disapprove of them as they arise.[3]

At a meeting on the eve of the session, North resisted attempts to

---

[1] Edmond Malone heard in November that Fox had 'even offered, I am told, to take a subordinate office under him'; a little later it was rumoured that Shelburne was prepared to serve as Secretary of State in a North ministry. Although it is most unlikely that either offer was made in these terms, discussions were obviously afoot. Sackville wrote on 26 November that 'Lord North is courted by all parties'. *H.M.C. Charlemont MSS.*, i. 422; Sir John Marriott to Lord Sandwich, 25 November, Sandwich MSS.; *H.M.C. Stopford-Sackville MSS.*, i, 143.

[2] Fortescue, vi, nos. 3972 & 3973.

[3] North to Lord Lisburne, 19 November, Egerton MSS. 2136, f. 213.

force a more positive attitude on the group. Sir Gilbert Elliot described the discussion after North had outlined the case for benevolent neutrality:

Lord Nugent said he supposed then they should all attend the cockpit at the reading of the King's speech the day before the meeting. Welbore Ellis said by no means for that would imply a personal approbation of the minister. Rigby was there but said nothing and it was conjectured that he had either connected himself with Lord Shelburne or that more probably he meant to follow Lord Advocate . . . It is added that Wallace and Mansfield talk the most determined opposition language and that Eden does the same.[1]

Most observers still believed that ultimately North would rally to the support of administration. Thurlow thought that 'he has it not in his power to go wrong'; Robinson that 'he will act right in the end though he will lose all the merit and grace of it'; and Pitt that 'in the end the part to be taken by North cannot be *hostile*'.[2] Shelburne appears never to have entertained the slightest doubt on the subject, assuring an incredulous William Grenville that the 'sure foundation' of the government was a 'moral certainty'.[3] Each of them overestimated not only North's loyalty to the king but the extent to which he was a free agent. He had a powerful following, but they would not follow him blindly. The treatment of the American loyalists in the peace settlement might well prove decisive, and on that subject North and several of his friends had already expressed the greatest uneasiness.

Charles Fox's position at the opening of Parliament was far from good. He was the leader of the smallest of the three parties, and his followers were not renowned as devoted attenders. His service as Foreign Secretary had done nothing to soften the king's enmity: on the contrary, the king wrote that his opinion had been 'if possible more rivited by three months experience of him in office, which has finally determined me never to employ him

---

[1] Elliot to Harris, 16 December, Minto MSS. M. 43.
[2] *H.M.C. 5th Report, appendix*, 211-12; *H.M.C. Abergavenny MSS.*, 55; Pitt to Lady Chatham, 2 November, Chatham MSS. [3] Buckingham, i, 89.

again'.[1] If North joined the ministry, Shelburne's position would be impregnable, and with Pitt as heir apparent the prospect for Fox's political future would be bleak. Against this Fox could oppose only his one asset, his extraordinary debating ability, and to this the ministry had no answer. Pitt was as yet too inexperienced to hold his own; Townshend was adequate but no more; Dundas, though formidable, was doubtfully committed to Shelburne, and Conway was more than half in sympathy with the opposition. The brilliant and sustained attack that Fox launched almost unaided upon the ministry in the winter of 1782–3 may be considered one of the greatest *tours de force* in parliamentary history.[2]

The king's speech opened the session with a long survey, announced that the provisional articles with America were agreed, and expressed the hope that a permanent union between the two peoples might still be constructed. The terms of the treaty were not yet published, and Fox, in an unusually full House, settled down to routine criticism. Aware that few members had heard from his own lips any account of the causes of his resignation in July, he repeated in full the story of his clash with Shelburne over American independence, and declared against the cession of Gibraltar, except for some 'valuable and adequate consideration'. North spoke, according to William Grenville, 'uncommonly well, holding off from both sides'[3]: he expressed his disagreement with Fox's attitude towards unconditional recognition, and defended his ministry's conduct of the war. He was surprised, he told the House, that anyone should attribute Rodney's victory, a mere fortnight after the Rockinghams had taken office, to the prowess of Lord Keppel's administration: 'he would say to the present naval Alexander, "True, you have

---

[1] Fortescue, vi, no. 3872.
[2] Burke was at this time almost an encumbrance as an ally, violent, maladroit and ponderous. He was repeatedly greeted with jeers and demonstrations when he rose to speak. In any case, his forte was the set-piece oration rather than the debating intervention.
[3] Buckingham, i, 79.

conquered, but you have conquered with Philip's troops!".' He concluded with a warning to the ministers not to abandon the loyalists. Pitt contented himself with a temperate reply, scored some neat points off Fox, and reminded members that in voting for an address of thanks they were not denying themselves the freedom to criticise the articles when they were made available. 'The day', admitted Portland candidly, 'was avowedly with Lord North, who seemed to feel the dignity and importance of his own situation much more than he ever did in administration.'[1] The address of thanks passed *nem. con.*[2]

But at this point the ministry suffered a severe setback that afforded its opponents excellent debating advantages and sowed more dissension in its own ranks. Lord Stormont, on the opening day, attacked the ministers for granting independence without condition. Shelburne at once denied it: 'the noble viscount was mistaken in his idea of unqualified, unconditional independence being given . . . this offer is not irrevocable; if France does not agree to peace, the offer ceases.' By this he presumably meant that the provisional agreement with the Americans would lapse if the negotiations with France were unsuccessful, though it is not easy to see how he could believe this after the ministerial recognition accorded by the change in Oswald's commission. But when, the following day, Fox asked for an explanation in the Commons, Pitt, Townshend and Conway gave the opposite interpretation and insisted that the provisional articles would remain valid until peace was ultimately concluded: 'nothing appeared to him more clear', stated Conway, 'than that the recognition was unconditional.'[3]

This divergence of opinion between the ministers was, admitted Shelburne to the king, 'awkward', and had created 'some uneasiness' in the House of Commons. The king, not informed of

[1] Portland to Burgoyne, 8 December, E. D. de Fonblanque, *Political and military episodes*, 414.
[2] Debrett, ix, 1–42.   [3] Debrett, xi, 14–15; x, 66.

the part taken by Townshend and Conway, put all the blame on Pitt's inexperience:

By Lord Shelburne's account, it very clearly appears that Mr. Pitt on Friday stated the article of independence as irrevocable, though the Treaty should prove abortive; this undoubtedly was a mistake, for the independence is alone to be granted for peace. I have always thought it best and wisest if a mistake is made openly to avow it, and therefore Mr. Pitt ought, if his words have been understood to bear so strong a meaning, to say; it is no wonder that so young a man should have made a slip; this would do him honour. I think at all events it is highly material that Lord Shelburne should not by any language in the House of Lords appear to change his conduct, let the blame fall where it may. I do not wish he should appear but in a dignified light, which his station in my service requires, and which can only be maintained by his conduct in the whole negotiation of peace having been *neat*, which would not be the case if Mr. Fox could prove that independence was granted otherwise than as the price of peace.[1]

Shelburne's balancing act between the king and the House of Commons was in evident danger. But worse was to follow. Pitt did not take kindly to the suggestion that he should make a public recantation, even to save his leader's dignity, and when the opposition probed the matter the following week he declared that his explanation had been given 'on mature consideration, and he persisted in it . . . recognition could not be revoked, even if the present treaty should go off'. In this interpretation he was fully supported by Conway.

The ministry was now wide open to attack, and John Courtenay, one of the wits of the House, enjoyed a field day at the expense of Shelburne, 'who was exceedingly well skilled and adroit in the dissemination of discordant opinions for the sake of unanimity'. Shelburne was in an impossible position. The king had forbidden him to recant, even if he had wanted to, and his colleagues in the House of Commons refused to. He fell back on the desperate remedy of all harassed ministers, and refused to

---

[1] Fortescue, vi, nos. 4014 & 4015.

answer questions on the subject. It was totally unprecedented, he argued, to ask a minister what his remarks meant:

There was no man less ready to fly to the forms and orders of that House for refuge against questions than himself, but nothing could be more unwise, and more unsafe, as well as more unparliamentary . . . He was bound, by his office, to keep the secrets of the King—he was bound by his duty to his King and his country to keep them inviolably, and he would do so with his life.

It was a pity that he had not remembered his duty when first questioned by Stormont, and that his friends in the House of Commons did not see theirs in the same light. Although to the king he passed off the matter nonchalantly, the damage was serious. He had alienated two of the remaining cabinet members who had until then given him steadfast support, and even the king could hardly fail to perceive that his minister's handling of the affair had been anything but '*neat*'.[1]

The rout would have been complete had Fox and his friends not overplayed their hand in the excitement of the chase. Determined to maintain the pressure, Fox moved on 18 December that the clause of the provisional agreement relating to independence be laid before the House. Thomas Pitt at once moved the order of the day, and the ministers were saved by North, who subjected them to sarcasm and ridicule, but led his cohorts to their rescue. 'He appeared', wrote Wraxall, 'throughout the whole debate not only pre-eminent in talents of every description, but as the arbiter of the scene.'[2] Fox rashly accepted a challenge from Conway to divide the House and was beaten by 219 votes to 46. Burke reflected gloomily on the debacle:

I was as clear as I ever was of anything in my life that it was proper to have a division. If it were in my Lord North's power to command our conduct whenever he thought proper to come, and that we could not move but at his pleasure, we could never consider ourselves as an independent party . . . Nothing could be so disgraceful to the gentlemen who act as ministers as the victory

---

[1] Debrett, ix, 71–94; xi, 21–7; Fortescue, vi, nos. 4025 & 4026.
[2] Wraxall, ii, 410–11.

obtained for them by Lord North. They looked, I assure you, more like captives led before the conqueror than parties in the triumph.[1]

The adjournment for the Christmas recess found both the ministerialists and the Rockinghams smarting from their wounds. Lord North, so often the despair of his friends from his irresolution and sloth, held all the cards. His situation, wrote Grattan, 'is singularly powerful'.[2]

Shelburne had a breathing-space of nearly two months in which to put his administration on a firmer foundation.[3] During the early part of January he appears to have made no move, though there were incessant rumours of negotiations, and a large number of private approaches being made; most of his attention was taken up by the peace settlement, which was not concluded by 20 January. He was also greatly embarrassed by the variety of views among his colleagues. He himself preferred an approach to North, and Dundas was arranging dinner parties with indefatigable zeal in the course of the month to effect a reconciliation with his old leader.[4] But Pitt, who had not enjoyed being the butt of North's pleasantries during the debate of 18 December, would not hear of negotiations in that direction, and he was supported by Keppel, Richmond, Camden and Grafton.[5]

[1] *The correspondence of Edmund Burke*, vol. v, ed. H. Furber (1965), 55–8.

[2] H.M.C. *14th Report, appendix IX*, Emly MSS., 175.

[3] Parliament was in recess until 22 January, and, apart from the Irish Judicature Bill, there were only desultory debates until the discussion of the peace preliminaries on 17 February.

[4] The personnel at these dinner parties was highly significant. Thomas Pelham attended one at Rigby's on 28 January, where Dundas, John Townshend, William Pitt, George North and Lord Lewisham were present. Loughborough reported a dinner at Dundas's for Shelburne, Rigby, Lewisham and George North, with another to follow 'next Saturday' for Lord North himself. This frenzy of entertainment was not purely convivial. Add. MS. 33128, f. 103; 34419, f. 89.

[5] Adam told Jenkinson, 3 January 1783, that North was anxious to know the impression his speech had made, and worried lest he 'might have gone too far'. As far as Pitt was concerned, he had. Jenkinson replied: 'Mr. Pitt is very much displeased with Lord North's last speech, and this disturbs Shelburne. I have done all I can to pacify him, and have made him disposed to send a message through me to North, but we agreed not to come to any resolution on this head till we have had another conversation.' Add. MS. 38218, f. 154; 38309, f. 77.

Although the first minister did not seem to realise it, it was a race against time. Unless he could bring in reinforcements quickly, there would be no garrison left to receive them. On 4 January, in audience with the king, Richmond and Keppel declared that they found their situation in the cabinet intolerable:

The former said it was impossible he could continue a member of the cabinet after at a meeting the Ultimatum had been settled, and that Lord Grantham had been authorised to offer Tobago in lieu of Dominica by a more intimate consultation; that he found Lord Keppel and General Conway equally ignorant of this transaction . . . [1] he could not be a member of council and consequently *answerable for measures of which he was ignorant* . . . Lord Keppel complained of having been constantly slighted, that duty to me made him silent till Peace was decided, but that he is convinced France will not conclude one . . .[2]

On 23 January Keppel formally tendered his resignation, telling Shelburne that he had long considered the peace terms 'such that I cannot bring myself to subscribe to'.[3] Richmond placed himself in a kind of political limbo by leaving the cabinet, but retaining his place at the Ordnance.[4] A few days later, Lord Carlisle wrote to announce his resignation as Lord High Steward. Though not a politician of the front rank, his connections through his father-in-law Lord Gower were important, and the reasons he gave for his decision showed where the difficulty in reaching an agreement with the Northites might lie:

[1] The Ultimatum was the final statement of terms agreed by the cabinet on 11 December. Richmond's complaint seems to have been well founded. The offer of Tobago, which was quite new to the negotiations, was made on 28 December after consultation, according to Grantham, 'with some of Your Majesty's principal servants'. Fortescue, vi, no. 4046. Nor is this the only example of Shelburne's cavalier attitude towards his colleagues. On 25 December William Grenville was at last able to get a reply to Temple's demand that renunciation should be explicitly granted. He wrote: 'Townshend has had this morning a long conversation with Lord Shelburne, the result of which is compliance with your wishes. But this will be done by an official despatch, and not by a cabinet minute, as they cannot venture to meet a cabinet upon it.' Buckingham, i, 104. Shelburne had a poor opinion of his cabinet colleagues, but since they were the only supporters he had, discretion might have suggested a little courtesy.

[2] Fortescue, vi, no. 4055.   [3] Bowood MSS.

[4] His letter to Shelburne, 22 January, is in the Bowood MSS. The fullest explanation of his attitude is in a letter of 27 January, printed by A. Olson, *The radical duke* (1961), 193–5.

That article of the depending treaty which seems calculated to prop and sustain the interests of all descriptions of men excepting those who have taken up arms against the United States in defence of Great Britain is I humbly conceive not to be maintained upon any ground of justice or humanity . . . I should esteem it to the last degree mean and contemptible to suppress that abhorrence of this treatment . . .[1]

In the meantime, the bargaining had at last commenced. Early in January Shelburne confided to Jenkinson that he would never coalesce with Fox, and would make overtures to North later. The withdrawal of Keppel and Richmond made it easier to originate these, though the opposition of Pitt made caution necessary, and it is doubtful whether he was kept informed.[2] Towards the end of the month, Shelburne authorised Dundas to tell North that he 'meant coalition with *the old government*', and would show every possible attention to him and to his son.[3] Both wings of North's following realised that a decision was imminent, and both were apprehensive that it would go against them. During the first week in February they redoubled their efforts to clinch the argument, and North was subjected to a bombardment of conflicting advice from his closest friends. On 3 February, John Robinson, after much heart-searching, wrote him a long and powerful appeal not to commit himself to an alliance with Fox: it could be neither permanent nor pleasant. On no account should he express disapprobation of the settlement:

A peace is made at the end of an expensive and in many parts unsuccessful war carried out under Your Lordship's administration, in which a most extensive dominion and valuable part of the Empire was dismembered and irretrievably lost in your opinion, before you had quitted His Majesty's service, and your uniform language has been that peace (although not an ignominious one) was

---

[1] Carlisle to Shelburne, 4 February, Granville MSS.

[2] On 6 February, Townshend assured William Grenville that he knew of no negotiations with North. Since Shelburne undoubtedly had been in negotiation, Grenville concluded that 'he keeps it from the knowledge both of Townshend and Pitt'. Buckingham, i. 143. Pitt's letter to Shelburne, 1 February, suggests that he had no idea that negotiations were in train. Bowood MSS.

[3] Robinson to North, 1 February, Abergavenny MSS. Robinson is reminding North of what he 'mentioned in the coach three days ago'.

necessary to this country, that we ought to make peace if possible ... does Your Lordship think that the objections to the articles of peace are such as would justify you to say that we should go on with the war? Will the country in general, although many exclaim against several articles of the peace, support this idea? ... will you not then be called upon to state why you did not endeavour to obtain a better?[1]

But Eden's counter-appeal was already on its way. As agitated and distressed as Robinson, he declared to North 'the purest and most affectionate regard for your Fame':

The whole tenor of my conduct towards you during eleven years has given me some right to be believed ... I have endeavoured for some days to divest my mind of all party prejudices and to think only of what is right to be done at present—and I cannot see any possible distinction under which you can admit the slightest approbation of the treaties without subjecting yourself and your late government to constructions that would hurt the feelings of your friends and beyond the power of words to express ...[2]

Dundas had little to offer in return for North's support. Pitt's uncompromising attitude ruled out any high office for North himself, and it was still impossible to say in what terms the resolution on the peace proposals would be worded. North seems to have suspected an intention to dupe him, to borrow his votes in exchange for vague promises of subsequent arrangements: a quarrel took place between him and Dundas, and the negotiation was broken off.[3]

Shelburne had no alternative but to seek an understanding with Fox on whatever terms he could get. On 1 February Pitt had warned him that in the state of the House of Commons, 'some decision soon is necessary'.[4] As soon as the negotiations

---

[1] Abergavenny MSS. The letter, a shortened version of which is printed in *H.M.C. Abergavenny MSS.*, 56–7, was dated 1 February but was extensively rewritten before being sent on 3 February to Jenkinson, with instructions to let North have it that night or early next morning.

[2] 4 February, Add. MS. 34419, f. 105. To Jenkinson, Robinson had written: 'it is by such perpetual teazing and writing that Eden gets his influence.' Add. MSS. 38567, f. 123–4.

[3] Jenkinson to Robinson, 7 February, *H.M.C. Abergavenny MSS.*, 57; Robinson to Jenkinson, 8 February, Add. MS. 38567, f. 127.   [4] Bowood MSS.

with North had broken down, Pitt was authorised to sound out Fox. The encounter was brief and to the point: 'Pitt told me today that it being thought necessary to make a junction with Fox, he had seen him today, when he asked one question, whether there were any terms on which he would come in. The answer was, None, while Lord Shelburne remained; and so it ended.'[1] Shelburne reported this 'absolute refusal' to the king, with the comment: 'I am confident this incident may be improved much to the advantage of Your Majesty's present and future government.' He had been handed his political death-warrant and could not decipher the message. Nor was the king much more in touch with reality:

I am not in the least surprised at Mr. Pitt's interview with Mr. Fox ended as abruptly as the hastiness and impoliteness of the latter naturally led me to expect. I shall certainly not object to any other quarter Lord Shelburne may with the advice of Mr. Pitt choose to sound; but I must insist that Lord Shelburne's remaining in his present situation be the basis of any plan . . . I can trust his own sentiments are too much exalted to think of supplicating any party; but that whoever he treats with must be expected to feel obliged for any offer that is made.[2]

It was too late in the day to think of Shelburne's dignity, nor was there any quarter to go to except back to North. The following day Shelburne hinted to Grafton that he believed North's friends would 'not be unreasonable', still cherishing the illusion that they would be prepared to take a purely subordinate part, providing the bulk of the government's voting strength, but making no claim to cabinet posts.[3] But events were now out of his hands, for the day after his interview with Pitt, Fox had sent a 'very civil message' to Lord North, acquainting him with what had taken place.[4]

[1] William Grenville to Temple, 11 February, Buckingham, i, 148–9. Grenville's letter is dated 11th, but the interview seems to have been on the 10th. It is dated by Fortescue, vi, nos. 4109 & 4110, and by Grafton, 355.
[2] Fortescue, vi, nos. 4109 & 4110.   [3] Grafton, 357.
[4] The remainder of this account of the manoeuvres before the coalition was formed is [based on the version given by William Adam, and printed in Russell, ii, 31–42. It is

A last minute intervention by Dundas, intended to coerce North into supporting the minister, had the opposite effect. He despatched Adam to tell North that it was his conjecture that Shelburne would resign, that Fox and Pitt would reunite, and that a subsequent dissolution of Parliament would liquidate North's following: only an explicit declaration from North that he would support the peace terms could save him. The technique was crude, but Dundas was in a desperate situation. North's resentment at Dundas's message was all that was needed to persuade him to send George North to arrange a meeting with Fox next day. Dundas and Rigby made one more despairing effort the following morning, but North refused to make any commitment before he had seen Fox.[1] In the afternoon, they met at George North's house. When, next day, Rigby called on Lord North with an invitation to discuss matters with Shelburne, he was told: 'I cannot meet Lord Shelburne *now*. It is too late.'[2]

At their first meeting Fox and North confined themselves to a general understanding and a discussion of the tactics for the forthcoming debate, leaving the question of the distribution of offices in any future administration to a later date. The most obvious stumbling block, reform, seems to have caused little difficulty. The greater part of the Rockinghams' programme for economical reform had been accomplished and it was agreed that no further measures should be introduced: parliamentary reform was to be an open question, Fox reserving the right to test the House once more. He has been accused on this point of abandoning his

---

clearly well-informed, and the letter from Dundas to Shelburne referred to is extant in the Bowood MSS. I am, however, sceptical of the account given by Dundas of his conversation with Shelburne, who does not appear to have inclined to resignation as early as that, and suspect that it may have been a picturesque embellishment, designed to point the threat to North's position.

[1] Dundas to Shelburne, 13 February, Bowood MSS.
[2] Russell, ii, 39.

principles,[1] but it is difficult to see what other stipulation he could have made: parliamentary reform, as the previous debate on the subject had amply demonstrated, was an open question inside the Rockingham party itself. North, on his part, concurred in Fox's demand that the king should not be allowed to rule by establishing a 'government by departments':

There should be one man, or a cabinet, to govern the whole and direct every measure. Government by departments was not brought in by me. I found it so, and had not vigour and resolution to put an end to it. The King ought to be treated with all sort of respect and attention, but the appearance of power is all that a king of this country can have.[2]

One of the most delicate issues was the treatment of the loyalists in the settlement. North and his friends considered this a base and deplorable betrayal, while the Rockinghams had for years disparaged the loyalists as the hirelings of royalism. They decided that a resolution condemning the provision made for them should be moved by North separately.[3]

The ministers had also concerted plans for the debate, agreeing that 'no triumphant words' could be carried in the address: instead, Parliament was to be invited to express 'satisfaction' at a settlement which promised 'perfect reconciliation and friend-

---

[1] E.g. in I. R. Christie, *Wilkes, Wyvill and reform*, 177–9.

[2] Russell, ii, 38. These sentiments from North are not as surprising as they may seem. He had never been a high prerogative man, and had always insisted that the American war was in defence of the authority of Parliament. In November 1778 he had argued the case for 'one directing minister, who should plan the whole of the operation of government, and control all the other departments of administration so far as to make them cooperate zealously and actively with his designs even though contrary to their own'. In March 1782, he had warned the king that 'in this country the Prince on the Throne cannot, with prudence, oppose the deliberate resolution of the House of Commons'. Fortescue, iv, no. 2446; v, no. 3566. For this account of North's discussions with Fox, I have also drawn on the document in the Waldeshare MSS., entitled 'What I said to the King from Lord North upon Lord Shelburne's going out'.

[3] The tactical understanding between North and Fox was reached the evening before the debate. A letter from Fox to Thomas William Coke on the subject is printed in A. M. W. Stirling, *Coke of Norfolk and his friends*, i, 169–70, where it is erroneously attributed to 1776. It is commented upon by A. Valentine, *Lord North* (1967), i, 419–20, who has been led astray by Stirling's misdating.

ship'.[1] But even at this late stage, the government was not spared one final convulsion. Keppel's place at the Admiralty and in the cabinet had been taken by Lord Howe: Carlisle's place as Lord Steward and Richmond's seat in the cabinet Shelburne gave to the young duke of Rutland. Grafton was outraged when he heard of Rutland's appointment from Townshend on the day of the debate, and, not in the least mollified by Shelburne's somewhat incoherent protestations that he had not had an opportunity of informing him, resigned on the spot.[2] The administration had lost four of its highest members in less than a month, and its own supporters were so unenthusiastic that even Pitt's urgent solicitation could not induce William Grenville to second the address of thanks.[3] Dundas made his own assessment of the situation in a letter to his brother just before the debate began: 'It is without exception the most singular day this country ever saw. The preliminaries of peace are to be taken into consideration and the Address to the King to be proposed is a very moderate one, but notwithstanding all that, and notwithstanding that administration are very sanguine, it is *entre nous* my opinion that we will be beat . . .'[4]

In the House of Lords no fewer than 145 peers are reported to have heard the debate, more than in any previous motion during the reign. Lord Carlisle moved that the settlement was 'inadequate to our just expectations and derogatory to the honour and dignity of Great Britain'. Since the ministers had not invited the House to do more than take note of the preliminaries with France and Spain, the main debate was on the American provisions, and

---

[1] Grafton, 357-8.
[2] Grafton, 359-61. Sir William Anson, Grafton's editor, criticised his views on the cabinet: 'Grafton seems to think that a Prime Minister might be dispensed with, but that the cabinet should be consulted before any addition was made to its numbers.' I think it was less a constitutional issue, than a simple question of man-management. Grafton was humiliated to be one of the last to learn of the appointment. William Grenville had informed Temple of it two days before.
[3] *H.M.C. Fortescue MSS.*, i, 193-4.
[4] Dundas of Arniston MSS., Scottish Record Office.

particularly the boundaries of Canada and the compensation for the loyalists. Keppel supported Carlisle, Grafton defended the administration, and Richmond and Gower declared they would not vote on the question. Lord Stormont, who had been Secretary of State under North, delivered one of the most powerful attacks, condemning Oswald, 'that very extraordinary geographer and politician', who had, he insisted, been 'overmatched' by the American commissioners. He expressed bewilderment at the term 'reciprocal advantages' which appeared in the preamble to the treaty: 'But at last he discovered that they meant only the advantage of America. For in return for the manifold concessions on our part, not one had been made on theirs. In truth, the American commissioners had enriched the English dictionary with several new terms and phrases; reciprocal advantages, for instance, meant the advantage of one of the parties.'

Shelburne's reply to the debate was uneasy, and full of theatrical flourishes—'Your Lordships must be told how many sleepless nights I have spent—how many weary hours of watching and distress. What have been my anxieties for New York! What have I suffered from an apprehension of an attack on that garrison.' He was able to demonstrate that he had consulted expert advice on the boundaries and trading opportunities, but in his general defence he tried to argue too many points at once. In reply to the charge that the trade of Canada was lost, he retorted that the trade was of negligible value, that it was not lost since the areas to the north were the more useful, and that, in any case, monopoly was a bad thing. Stormont had charged the ministry with abandoning their Indian allies: not so, retorted Shelburne, 'the Indian nations were not abandoned to their enemies; they were remitted to the care of neighbours'. Nor was it very prudent to proclaim, 'Gibraltar was saved!' when so many of his listeners knew the background story of the cabinet struggle on that subject. He finished by painting a gloomy picture of the total exhaustion of national resources, financial and military: 'were we not at the extremity of distress? Did not the boldest of us cry out for peace?'[1]

It was left to Thurlow to make the most effective defence of the ministry, striking some characteristically stout blows at the opposition:

When those persons apprehended that the difficult task of making peace would fall upon themselves, then our condition was painted in all, and perhaps more, than its real gloom; and their lordships were depressed and tortured with the accounts that were given of our navy and our resources. Then any peace, it was declared, would be a good one. A peace for a year even, nay, for a month, for a day was coveted . . . But when the grievous task was shifted to others, how did the language differ! The navy grew as it were by magic. The resources of the state became immense.

When the vote was taken at 3.30 in the morning, the ministry survived by the ominously narrow margin of 72 against 59— 'undoubtedly the smallest majority I ever remember in so full a House', remarked the king.[2]

Shelburne had to wait another four hours before he knew the fate of the preliminaries in the House of Commons. After Thomas Pitt and Wilberforce had moved the address, Lord John Cavendish proposed an amendment that the House would give the articles 'serious and full attention'. North, opening the attack, thought ministers would have been wiser to have copied Henry Pelham, who had introduced the peace of Aix-la-Chapelle without any attempt at commendation. He did not understand, in view of the many concessions made to France, how ministers could claim that the settlement was on the basis of *uti possidetis*. The generous treatment of the United States had not induced in exchange any guarantees for the loyalists, and he concluded by moving another amendment drawing attention to their plight. Dundas was amused at the cautious nature of Lord John Cavendish's amendment: 'could not the two noble lords, in the

[1] The fullest version of Shelburne's speech is that compiled from a variety of sources by Professor Harlow, and printed in *The founding of the second British Empire*, i, 434-43.
[2] Debrett, xi, 30-93; Fortescue, vi, no. 4122.

honeymoon of their loves, have begotten a more vigorous off-spring?' Fox denied that he had ever said that almost any peace would be good, but if he had, the minister's policy seemed designed to cause him every embarrassment: 'you call for peace, and I will give you a peace that shall make you repent the longest day you live that ever you breathed a wish for peace.' He did not believe that anyone could seriously maintain that the country's position was not greatly stronger than it had been in the spring. His union with North he defended in lofty terms:

If men of honour can meet on points of general national concern, I see no reason for calling such a meeting an unnatural junction. It is neither wise nor noble to keep up animosities for ever. It is not my nature to bear malice or to live in ill will. My friendships are perpetual, my enmities are not so. 'Amicitiae sempiternae, inimicitiae placabiles' . . . The American war and the American question is at an end . . . and it is therefore wise and candid to put an end also to the ill will, the animosity, the rancour and the feuds which it occasioned . . .

Pitt condemned the coalition with equal vigour: 'it stretched to a point of political apostacy, which not only astonished so young a man as he was, but apparently astonished and confounded the most veteran observers of the human heart.' But in his supercilious advice to Sheridan to reserve his talents for the theatre, Pitt laid himself open to one of the most crushing parliamentary retorts of all time. He would not comment, replied Sheridan, on the remark itself—'the propriety, the taste, the gentlemanly point of it must have been obvious to the House'—but should he ever take up his pen again, he would be tempted to improve on one of Ben Jonson's most celebrated characters—the Angry Boy in 'The Alchemist'. When the House divided, Lord John Cavendish's amendment was carried by 224 to 208: 'this is I think decisive', wrote Pitt to his mother.[1]

Perhaps the most remarkable feature of the voting was the extent to which the party lines stood firm: the revulsion from the coalition said to have been felt by many of Fox's and North's

[1] Debrett, ix, 224–89; 18 February, Chatham MSS. The *Whitehall Evening Post*, 15/18 February reported sixty members paired off.

supporters is not reflected in the division.[1] North's following had been estimated before Christmas at 120: he took with him into the division about 104 followers, or 117 if the 9 supporters of Sandwich and the 4 of Lord Hertford are included in his squadron. Fox's following had been put at 80 to 90: he brought up 72 votes. Shelburne's party, estimated at between 130 and 140, produced 126 votes. Very few regular supporters seem to have changed sides: North may have lost 3, and Fox 5, but in return they appear to have gained 3 from Shelburne.[2] The ministers attracted considerable support from among the independent country gentlemen, influenced perhaps by a forthright speech by Thomas Powys, knight of the shire for Northampton: of the 58 members for English counties who voted, 37 supported Shelburne and 21 the coalition.[3] But an ominous feature for Shelburne was the defection of a number of the Scots members, who could usually be relied upon to provide overwhelming support for administration: on this occasion they divided 18–18, an indication both of the growth of party feeling and their opinion of the government's prospects.[4] It was noticeable too that some courtiers appeared to have reservations: of the four Grooms of the Bedchamber and Gentlemen of the Privy Chamber in the House of Commons, 2 voted with the coalition and 2 abstained.[5] The

[1] This analysis is based upon the division list printed by the *Morning Post*, 27 February correlated against the estimates of allegiance made by Robinson on 10 March in a list in the Melville MSS. It can hardly be over-emphasised how tentative these assessments must be in the absence of precise corroborative evidence. J. Norris, *Shelburne and reform*, appendix ii, prints another analysis of this division: inevitably, our allocations do not always coincide.

[2] J. Vaughan, M. Brickdale and G. Daubeny, usually considered Northites, voted with the ministry: the first was disgruntled over patronage, while the other two may have been influenced by feeling in their constituency, Bristol. Fox appears to have lost Sir William Codrington, J. Hanbury, T. Scott, T. Lucas and Beilby Thompson. Shelburne's losses included John Curtis, S. Salt and, perhaps, Christopher D'Oyley.

[3] This is a crude definition of 'independent country gentleman', but any more sophisticated one, such as that attempted by Professor Norris, seems to me to founder on agonising niceties of judgement.

[4] *The House of Commons 1754–90*, ed. L. B. Namier and J. Brooke (1964), i, 171.

[5] Sir George Osborne and Sir Frederick Rogers voted; Henry St. John and J. C. Jervoise abstained.

absence of persons like George Selwyn, who made a show of his loyalty to the king on every possible occasion, was certain to be remarked.

There followed a week of great confusion. Although Shelburne's ministry had been dealt a blow, no one could be sure that it would prove mortal: the majority was small enough to afford a rearguard action, resolutely conducted, some chance of success. Dunning's motion in April 1780 had been carried against Lord North by a greater majority, yet his ministry had contrived to continue.

But Shelburne's government was in no shape to sustain an heroic defence: the crisis revealed how small was the fund of good will upon which he could draw. Camden, consulted on the morning of the 19th told him bluntly to resign, 'as unfortunately it plainly appeared that the personal dislike was too strong for him to attempt to stem', and the following day Grafton heard that Pitt had been asked by 'many of the most independent and respectable members of the House of Commons' to convey a similar message.[1] Meanwhile the opposition promised a further attack for the 21st. Shelburne was uncertain what to do: Carmarthen, who dined with him on the 20th, thought his conduct 'totally devoid of spirit'.[2] His resolution seems to have been sapped by the suspicion that the king was playing him false. Of this there is not the slightest evidence: the general distrust of Shelburne, dismay at the peace terms and North's influence is quite sufficient to account for his defeat in the Commons. Nevertheless his friends were soon reported to be saying that he had been betrayed, and when Carmarthen hinted to him that 'a certain person might not be acting a fair part towards him', he 'appeared struck at my suggestion'.[3] The day before the second debate he received a letter from Thomas Orde, recounting a

---

[1] Grafton, 364–6.   [2] Leeds, 82.
[3] *Life and letters of Lady Sarah Lennox*, ii, 29; Leeds, 82.

conversation with Hatsell, the clerk to the House of Commons, that put the argument explicitly:

The question of stability or downfall to your administration depends solely (as Your Lordship has always said) upon the *Highest*. It is not the difference of the peace. It is his will. Lord Guilford is notoriously liable to his influence in a complete degree—and Lord North is not less so to Lord Guilford's. That it would therefore be only necessary to represent to the King that the matter solely depended upon him; that if he was solicitous to continue the government in the present hands, he should speak to Lord Guilford and to such others as will be moved by the certainty of his interference, such as Sir George Osborne, etc.[1]

Shelburne could hardly fail to remember what a dusty answer the king's entreaties had received from Lord North the previous autumn, but he may have preferred to attribute his misfortunes to treachery rather than his own unpopularity. He decided to await the outcome of the second debate, fortified perhaps by rumours that Fox and North were already quarrelling over the distribution of places. 'No man at this hour pretends to say how the question will be decided', wrote General Cunynghame to Temple: 'one may get a bet of hundreds at either side.'[2]

The debate itself was something of an anti-climax, ranging over much the same ground as the first. The opposition's main resolution, moved once again by Lord John Cavendish, declared that the concessions to Britain's adversaries were 'greater than they were entitled to'. Pitt's reply was the first of his great ministerial orations: 'even his enemies or rather opponents unanimously acknowledged it to be the finest speech that ever was made in Parliament', wrote Thomas Pelham.[3] He pointed out that the opposition's attitude the previous Monday had been to reserve judgement: they had not reserved it long. 'In the short space of two days we are ready to pass a vote of censure on what we declare we have not had leisure to discuss.' The defects of the

---

[1] Fitzmaurice, ii, 247–8.   [2] Buckingham, i, 160.
[3] Add. MS. 33128, f. 254. For once the testimony was almost universal. See Fortescue, vi, no. 4124; Kenyon Diary, 21 February; H. Walpole, *Last journals*, ii, 588.

settlement he attributed to North's incompetent handling of the war, and the resolution he denounced as pure faction:

> I repeat then, Sir, it is not this treaty, it is the Earl of Shelburne alone whom the movers of this question are desirous to wound ... this is the aim of the unnatural coalition to which I have alluded. If, however, the baneful alliance is not already formed, if this ill-omened marriage is not already solemnised, I know a just and lawful impediment, and, in the name of the public safety, I here forbid the banns.

But though Pitt's oratorical triumph was undisputed, there was little comfort in the debate for Shelburne: indeed, the absence of enthusiasm for him even among supporters of the ministry was most conspicuous. Sir Cecil Wray admitted that 'various reasons concur to make me wish him out of power', and Thomas Powys remarked that the previous vote had been 'a pretty broad hint to that lord that he was not altogether so popular as he had imagined'. Pitt himself, though declaring that posterity would do justice to Shelburne, was 'far from wishing him retained in power against the public approbation', and delivered the obituary with unseemly haste.[1] Four members were reported to have rallied to the ministers since the first debate, but they were again defeated, by 207 votes to 190.[2] Next day Pitt and Townshend warned Shelburne that government could no longer be carried on.[3] On the 23rd, the duke of Rutland had the curious, if not unique, experience of attending his first cabinet meeting only to find it agreed that the ministry he had joined was at an end, and on the 24th, Lord Shelburne offered his resignation.[4]

---

[1] Debrett, ix, 297–369; *Parlt. Hist.*, xxiii, 499–571.

[2] Lord Hyde, Sir Cecil Wray, John Elwes and Archibald Macdonald were said to have changed sides on perceiving that the attack was not on the peace but on the man. Jervoise Clarke Jervoise, on the other hand, was reported to have paired off for Shelburne on the first vote, but to have divided against him on the second. 27 & 28 February, *Morning Post*. [3] Fortescue, vi, no. 4130.

[4] There is considerable confusion on this point. Fitzmaurice, ii, 252 states categorically that Shelburne resigned on 24 February, probably basing this opinion on an entry in H. Walpole, *Last journals*, iii, 588. This is repeated in the *Dictionary of National Biography*. But it seems that his resignation was not finally accepted until more than a month later, on Wednesday 26 March. Although Walpole noted this (609), he did not correct the

The formation of the coalition lay in the logic of the political situation. It had been envisaged by Loughborough a fortnight after Rockingham's death in a letter to Eden:

I have taken a notion that a strong and durable administration is not impossible . . . part of the old administration with the remnant of the Rockingham party could form a stable government. Their opposite faults would correct each other, and amongst them they would possess more character and more of the public confidence than any other assemblage of men. The first thing is to reconcile Lord North and Fox. The first, you know, is irreconcilable to no man; the second will feel his ancient resentment totally absorbed in his more recent hostility, which I think he has no other probable means of gratifying.[1]

The person most responsible for producing the situation in which some form of coalition was inevitable was the king, the success of whose plan to break the Rockingham ministry ensured that the political nation should be divided into three parts. The main responsibility for the coalition that ultimately emerged rests with Fox and Pitt, the first because of his proscription of Shelburne, the second because of his proscription of North. Fox's attitude towards Shelburne has already been discussed. It is not possible to gauge the proportion of personal and public motives in his refusal to work with him, nor, perhaps, are the two things ever separable: it may, however, be observed that no politician who held office with Shelburne wished to do so again. William Knox recorded the opinion that 'those who served with him in office abhorred him as a principal', and George Rose, secretary to the Treasury in his administration, parted from

---

former entry. The later date is confirmed in Buckingham, i, 208 and Leeds, 85. Shelburne told Carmarthen that he had waited 'to give the King time if possible to form an administration, and to see if the debate in the House of Commons would produce any new lights on that subject'. This I take to have been the important debate of Monday 24 March. Although he did not take part in business during the intervening month (see Fortescue, vi, no. 4216), the point is of some importance: his continuation in office may have encouraged the coalition's suspicion that the king never intended to deal honestly with them.

[1] 14 July 1783, *The journal and correspondence of William Eden, Lord Auckland*, ed. G. Hogge (1860-2), i, 9. This work is referred to hereafter as Auckland.

him in the determination 'never to be in a room with him again while in existence':

The alternate violence and flattery of Lord Shelburne . . . made my situation so thoroughly unpleasant to me that I felt the certain removal from office as a relief. There were other qualities in his Lordship that were uncomfortable to me; a suspicion of almost everyone he had intercourse with; a want of sincerity and a habit of listening to every tale-bearer . . .[1]

William Pitt, whose career was built on the ruins of Shelburne's, was careful never to make him an offer of employment during the remaining twenty-one years of his life. When Shelburne's allies found him insupportable, it is hardly surprising that Fox could not accept him.

Pitt's prohibition of North was the decisive factor in forcing him into an alliance with Fox, and the celebrated Pitt–Fox interview was the immediate cause of the coalition. Pitt's contempt for North sprang from the belief that the American War had 'originated in his pernicious and oppressive policy'.[2] In fact, North had always adopted a conciliatory attitude towards the colonists, often at considerable risk to his own political position: the protagonists of a strong line were men like Thurlow, Dundas, Jenkinson and Rigby, with whom Pitt was perfectly prepared to work. North was the first to admit his own incapacity as a war minister: Pitt himself was to learn, in the course of time, that the conduct of revolutionary wars is far from simple. His accusation that North's ministry was based upon 'influence and intrigue' was merely opposition rhetoric: North's responsibility was open and avowed, and his administration supported by a majority in Parliament: the only 'secret influence' at work had been that of Jenkinson and Robinson, who were soon embraced by Pitt as allies.[3]

---

[1] H.M.C. *Various Collections*, vi, 284; *The diaries and correspondence of the Rt. Hon. George Rose*, ed. L. V. Harcourt (1860), i, 25–8.

[2] Debrett, ix, 351.

[3] See *sub* Jenkinson in *The House of Commons 1754–90*, ii, 674–8.

One of Lord North's biographers has suggested that his motive in forming the coalition was self-preservation: 'he was seriously and fearfully alarmed at the prospect of impeachment and the block.'[1] There is no evidence to suggest that North ever considered himself in real danger, but certainly by 1783 impeachment was out of the question. The truth was simpler and less melodramatic. Despite his frequent protestations of incapacity and his recurrent bouts of sloth and indecision, North was deeply ambitious: during the last weeks of his life, we are told, he 'expressed considerable anxiety on the subject of his character and fame—that he would have wished to know how he stood and would stand with the world'.[2] In February 1783, at the very moment when everyone recognised his political importance, his future was placed in jeopardy by the arbitrary, and to North's mind vindictive, veto of a young man of twenty-three. Lord North's own account, as related to the king by his father Lord Guilford, leaves the matter beyond doubt:

He had no predilection for Mr. Fox, or any conversation with him till he was driven to it by that message brought by Mr. Pitt to Mr. Fox, which was calculated entirely to exclude him and his friends from being of any consequence and that Mr. Pitt had made a positive declaration that he would never serve in any administration in which Lord North had the least consequence. Mr. Fox sent to him on account of that message and desired to be upon good terms with him. He could not in that situation refuse to have any commerce with him, when he knew Mr. Pitt's declaration . . . that if he never had had any commerce with Mr. Fox it would have become necessary now.[3]

A good deal of the abuse flung at the coalition was synthetic and theatrical, designed to appeal to the political innocents. All informed politicians had understood for months that the situation could be resolved only by means of a coalition, and had known

[1] R. J. Lucas, *Lord North, second earl of Guildford* (1913), ii, 209.
[2] *The diaries of Sylvester Douglas, Lord Glenbervie*, ed. F. Bickley (1928), i, 61.
[3] "What I said to the King from Lord North upon Lord Shelburne's going out', Waldeshare MSS.

of the many negotiations in progress. Whichever grouping emerged, the isolated party would certainly complain of a dereliction of principles: it is unwise to take too solemnly the indignation of Henry Dundas, who had called loudly for a coalition in the spring of 1782 and had spent much time since then trying to reconcile Pitt and North. It was certainly easier to condemn the coalition as unnatural and unprincipled than to suggest any alternative, and the very men who had denounced Fox in the summer of 1782 for resigning office now denounced him with equal assurance for seeking it.

It is true that Fox had condemned North in the most vehement terms, and these were now dredged up and used against him, particularly in the newspapers, with great effect. Less than a year earlier he had assured the House of Commons that the moment he formed an alliance with North or his colleagues 'he would rest satisfied to be called the most infamous of men; he could not for an instant think of a coalition with men, who in every public and private transaction, as ministers, had shewn themselves void of every principle of honour and honesty; in the hands of such men he would not trust his honour, even for a minute'.[1] Not surprisingly, some of his associates found his 'inimicitiae placabiles' difficult to digest.[2] But it was the violence of the language that was reprehensible rather than the coalition itself, and even there extenuating factors may be found. Debates of the period were conducted in flamboyant terms, with withering denunciations and soaring encomiums. Fox, as an impetuous and passionate speaker, was peculiarly likely to give offence, but he was equally

---

[1] Debrett, vi, 367. The context of the debate helps to explain this immoderate declaration. Fox had just offered his services as a negotiator to end the war: he was anxious to assure his followers that he was not fishing for office, and seems to have been provoked by 'a learned gentleman' whom he saw smiling at the proposal.

[2] Sir George Savile wrote to David Hartley, 15 March: 'to unite as allies generally with men one ought to impeach . . . can be justified one way (if it can at all), viz. Lord Shelburne is worse . . . You must know I took great offence at Charles Fox's expression of 'amicitiae sempiternae, inimicitiae breves'. R. Warner, *Literary recollections* (1830), ii, 242–6.

ready to apologise. Immediately after the declaration quoted above he assured North that he had not meant to impugn his private character, nor 'such part of his public character as related to money matters, in which he was ready to admit that he stood clear from every imputation'.[1] He followed this up a few days later with another disclaimer of malice at a time when he could have no motive for wishing to appease North.[2] Moreover, though they were freely charged with insincerity in their declarations of mutual respect, Fox and North did succeed in working together harmoniously in the coalition, in defeat as well as in victory. It is hard to believe that either of them would have worked as amicably with Lord Shelburne.

There were, of course, circumstances in the politics of the period that made such a coalition easier to fashion and maintain than it might have been later. In a one-class system, the role of government was defined in narrow terms—the maintenance of law and order, protection of property, supervision of foreign relations, and the handling of such problems and emergencies as might occasionally arise. Public issues therefore tended to be ephemeral, and not necessarily closely related to one another: it was easier to wipe clean the past than in a contemporary political system. But in any case, it is hardly in the nature of politics to permit a straight and undeviating course, except to those on the fringe of events, never called upon to commit themselves categorically. 'The vicissitudes of politics', declared Disraeli, 'are inexhaustible', and the careers of most great politicians—Chatham, Pitt, Peel, Disraeli, Gladstone, Joseph Chamberlain, Lloyd George, Churchill—are marked by startling leaps and somersaults. It does not follow that politicians are more unprincipled than the

[1] Debrett, vi, 368–9.
[2] Debrett, vi, 432. 'He did assure the noble lord that in what he had said then, and in what he had said formerly, he meant not to press upon him in an unhandsome way, he meant not to goad him, or run him down, or say anything that should hurt his mind, or make him uneasy . . . He asked pardon of the noble lord if he had offended him, for he meant it not; but he must continue to urge him to retire, and the sooner he did so, the doing it would have the more dignity.'

rest of mankind, but that they face choices which other people can avoid.

Lord Shelburne passed out of office never comprehending what had happened to him. Prone to melodramatic explanations, he assumed that he had been betrayed by the king, of whom he spoke later in the most bitter terms as a man 'who obtained your confidence, procured from you your opinion of different public characters, and then availed himself of this knowledge to sow dissension'.[1] Historians have often speculated why he should have been so detested, but he is a sphinx without a secret. His fall was in part due to his inability to understand the growing place of party in the politics of his time, but more fundamentally to his total incapacity for working frankly, cordially and honestly with his fellow men. Trusting no one, he tried to do everything himself: harassed and overworked, he lost his way in his own circumlocutions and evasions. In his anxiety to be all things to all men, he finished up as nothing to any man; and within a month of his resignation, he was neglected and forgotten.

[1] J. Nicholls, *Recollections and reflections, personal and political* (1820–2), i, 389, quoted in Fitzmaurice, ii, 248.

CHAPTER 4

INTER-MINISTERIUM

'The *coup de pied* is given to Lord Shelburne', wrote Fitzpatrick on 18 February: 'who will succeed him is a matter for speculation.'[1] It remained in that state for the next five weeks—one of the most protracted cabinet crises in British history. The only certainty in the situation was that the king, lamenting his lot 'to reign in the most profligate age', would yield to the coalition with the greatest reluctance.[2]

The suggestion that William Pitt should be offered the lead was made rather casually by Shelburne to Dundas on the 23rd. Astonishing as the proposal would have seemed a few weeks earlier, it had much to commend it: Pitt's prestige had risen dramatically since his speech of the 21st, and it was not impossible that, freed from the incubus of Shelburne's unpopularity, the administration might survive. On the 24th, Dundas wrote to Shelburne that the proposal should be taken up in earnest:

To you who know him so well I need not deliniate his many qualities, they are indeed great and splendid, and in place of being an objection his youth appears to me a very material ingredient in the scale of advantages which recommend him. There is scarce another political character of consideration in the country to whom many people from habits, from connexions, from former professions, from rivalships and from antipathies will not have objections. But he is perfectly new ground against whom no opposition can arise except what may be expected of that lately allied faction, which I am satisfied will likewise gradually decline till at last it will consist of only that insolent aristocratic band who assumed to themselves the prerogative of appointing the rulers of the kingdom . . . I would scarcely have presumed to intimate it if by accident I had not sat upon the sofa at your house last night with Lord Weymouth, who lamenting

---

[1] Russell, ii, 16–17.
[2] Fortescue, vi, nos. 4125 & 4131.

the present state of the country, mentioned the very idea which had dropt from Your Lordship in the morning . . .[1]

The king acted at once on the suggestion and saw Pitt that afternoon, who 'received it with a spirit and inclination that makes me think he will not decline'.[2] The rest of the evening Pitt spent in consultation with Dundas: the following morning they were joined by Rigby, and went through a state of the House of Commons. 'I have little doubt', wrote Dundas, 'that he will announce himself Minister tomorrow'.[3] Pitt himself was less ebullient: 'I feel all the difficulties of the undertaking, and am by no means in love with the object', he informed his mother: 'the great article to decide by seems that of numbers.'[4] Though by the evening of the 25th, rumours that he had accepted were current, he remained full of misgivings, remembering perhaps the *very good list* they had shown Lord Shelburne, and fearful of being deceived by the court. On the 26th, Dundas, Rigby, Ashburton and Kenyon all tried to persuade him to accept, but 'he seemed averse, thinking he will not be supported in the House of Commons'.[5] Thurlow, inclined to be intrepid at other people's expense, could not understand such hesitation 'when to my notion the ball seems to be absolutely at his feet'.[6] Pitt agreed to go on holding office for the moment, but on the evening of the 26th told the king that only the 'moral certainty' of a majority in the House of Commons would allow him to accept the Treasury: 'I am clear I could not add any more', the king told Shelburne.[7] Next morning Dundas made a last attempt to demonstrate that a majority could be obtained for a ministry with Pitt at the Treasury and Gower as Lord President of the Council, and parted with him 'perfectly resolved to accept'.[8] Within three hours Pitt had changed his mind completely:

[1] Bowood MSS.   [2] The king to Thurlow, 6.30 p.m., Fortescue, vi, no. 4133.
[3] Henry to Robert Dundas, 25 February, Dundas of Arniston MSS.
[4] 25 February, Chatham MSS.   [5] Kenyon Diary, Kenyon MSS.
[6] Thurlow to Dundas, 26 February, Dundas of Arniston MSS.   [7] Bowood MSS.
[8] Henry to Robert Dundas, 27 February, 5 p.m., Dundas of Arniston MSS.

What you stated to me this morning seemed to remove all doubts of my finding a majority in Parliament . . . I have since most deliberately reconsidered the ground, and after weighing it as fully as is possible for me to do, my final decision is directly contrary to the impression then made on me. I see that the main and almost only ground of reliance would be this—*that Lord North and his friends would not continue in a combination to oppose.* In point of prudence, after all that has passed, and considering all that is to come, such a reliance is too precarious to act on. But above all, in point of honour to my own feelings, I cannot form an administration trusting to the hope that it will be supported, or even will not be opposed by Lord North, whatever the influence may be that determines his conduct. This resolution will, I am afraid, both surprise and disappoint you.[1]

Pitt's concluding observation was certainly right: 'I don't think I shall give myself any more trouble in the matter', remarked Dundas dourly.[2] Pitt was particularly anxious not to be involved in a fiasco at the outset of his career: 'it would be dishonourable not to succeed if attempted', he told the king.[3] His natural caution was reinforced by the advice he received from his father's old friend, Lord Camden, who warned him that 'the ground on which he was to tread was rotten . . . and that the court on which he was to depend for support could withdraw it at a nod'.[4]

When the House of Commons reassembled after a short adjournment, expecting to hear details of the new administration, nothing had been settled. 'Our internal regulations, our loan, our commerce, our army, everything is at a stand,' wrote William Grenville, 'while the candidates for office are arranging their pretensions; in the meantime we have no money, and our troops and seamen are in mutiny'.[5] On 1 March the king, confessing that Pitt's decision had put him into a 'great dilemma' consulted Charles Jenkinson, who was said to have 'thought much on the

---

[1] Pitt to Dundas, 27 February, 2 p.m., Dundas of Arniston MSS.
[2] Henry to Robert Dundas, 27 February, 5 p.m.
[3] The king to Shelburne, 27 February, 7.30 a.m., Bowood MSS.
[4] Grafton, 370.   [5] Buckingham, i, 170.

subject of possible arrangements'. But the outcome of his deliberations was depressingly unoriginal—to send once again for Lord Gower, who, as the *Morning Chronicle* subsequently remarked, 'is never brought forward by the court except when they despair of every other support'. Though Gower's sentiments were as handsome as ever, the project was a non-starter in the absence of anyone prepared to lead in the Commons against the coalition's array of talent.[1]

The king's next move was fairly predictable—an attempt to split his adversaries by sending for Lord North. North had gone into the coalition with misgivings, torn between his desire to sustain an important role and his dread of responsibility: 'I am perfectly miserable', he wrote to his father the day after his great victory on the peace preliminaries, 'and tremble at the vexations and troubles that are hanging over me'.[2] Four days later William Eden, observing his uneasiness of mind, devoted a long letter to assuring him that he had no cause to reproach himself.[3] Reports of his dejection convinced Jenkinson that he would be glad of an excuse to break off the alliance, and pointed him out as the obvious person for the court to approach.[4] On 2 March the king despatched Lord Guilford with an offer to restore him to his place at the Treasury, or, failing that, to include him in the cabinet of an

---

[1] The king to Shelburne, 28 February, Bowood MSS.; Jenkinson to Gower, undated, Granville MSS.; Atkinson to Robinson, 28 February, Abergavenny MSS.; Fortescue, vi, nos. 4140-3; *Morning Chronicle*, 7 March; B. Connell, *Portrait of a Whig peer* (1957), 134; Robinson to Jenkinson, 7 March, Add. MS. 38567, f. 128.

[2] Waldeshare MSS. The letter is undated, but was clearly written on 18 February 1783.

[3] Add. MS. 34419, f. 113. 'The play of parties . . . threw you into a junction of conduct with Mr. Fox and his friends; we had no cause either to plume ourselves at this or to disclaim it; we had no choice about it . . . We are now to see the government placed in the hands of Mr. Pitt. It is fair to say of Mr. Pitt that he is one of those ministers whose treaties we have recently censured as inadequate, that he is a mere boy in years and experience, that he is manly in nothing so much as a steady (tho' ill-founded) declaration of political enmity towards you . . . On the other hand, Lord John Cavendish, Mr. Fox, The Duke of Portland and their friends have publicly shown every disposition to atone for past differences, and every private proof of personal respect.'

[4] Jenkinson to Gower, undated, Granville MSS. Internal evidence suggests that the letter was written on 27 or 28 February 1783. Fortescue, vi, no. 4268 also refers to these transactions.

administration to be presided over by 'a peer not connected with any of the strong parties that distract this kingdom'.[1]

North's reply, delivered by Guilford, justified the coalition, declared that he had neither the ambition nor the spirit to undertake the Treasury or any post of administrative responsibility, but that he would serve in a coalition cabinet, provided that he could nominate the Lord President, Lord Privy Seal and the two Secretaries of State. Alternatively, if Pitt could be persuaded to continue, he would waive any claim to cabinet rank and support from the sidelines, with some of his friends in office, as an indication of his approval. On the main issue of the leadership,

> he thought by Mr. Fox's conversation he seemed set upon having the Duke of Portland first Lord of the Treasury, but that nothing was agreed . . . That Lord North would like extremely the idea of having a neutral person not connected with any party for First Lord of the Treasury, if Mr. Fox's party will agree to it, but he fears they will not, knowing their consequence and that it is impossible to form any ministry that will have the appearance of stability without them.

This answer the king found sufficiently encouraging to warrant further discussions, and on the evening of 3 March, in an audience with North, offered 'great, honourable and efficient' offices for Fox and his friends, provided that they would accept an 'independent peer' at the head. Fox's immediate reply was that they would only serve under Portland, and, at a second audience on the 4th, the negotiation was broken off.[2]

The point at issue was of considerable constitutional importance. The king's claim to choose his own ministers, and in particular his first minister, was the most effective of the remaining

---

[1] Fortescue, vi, no. 4150. I do not know of any evidence who the peer was to be, but a reasonable guess would be the inevitable Gower. Thurlow reported to the king that Gower had 'no personal objection to Lord North' (no. 4175). The editor has suggested the date of 10 March for this letter, but 1 March appears more likely, with no. 4143 as the king's reply.

[2] 'What I said to the King from Lord North upon Lord Shelburne's going out', Waldeshare MSS.; Fortescue, vi, nos. 4153, 4156-8, 4161; Fitzmaurice, ii, 254-5; *The correspondence of George, Prince of Wales, 1770–1812*, ed. A. Aspinall (1963), i, 103-4; Thomas Pelham to Lord Pelham, 4 March, Add. MS. 33128, f. 106; Buckingham, i, 173-4.

prerogatives of the crown. The right to veto legislation was in abeyance, and was, in any case, purely defensive; the power to create peers was a dubious method of enlisting support, and if used too lavishly could be self-defeating; the power of dissolution depended for its effect upon too many electoral arrangements to be a convenient weapon for the king. But the right to choose ministers was central, flexible and easily defended on the ground that the king ought not to be forced to do business with men who were personally offensive to him. In practice the distinction between personal and political offensiveness was hard to maintain: the king tended to find personally offensive politicians who held views other than his own. It is difficult to believe that his objection to Rockingham and Portland was basically a personal one, and in moments of candour he was even prepared to admit that Fox's manner was perfectly proper.

Against the royal prerogative, Fox and his friends opposed their own right to refuse to serve except under a man in whom they had confidence: there was nothing else they could do if they wished to avoid a repetition of the Shelburne affair, with the 'independent peer' in the leading role. The clash of views almost destroyed the delicate balance of the eighteenth-century constitution. It had long been recognised that the first minister should command the confidence of the king and the House of Commons: what was to be done if such a minister could not be found had been left unanswered. The operation of the balance depended upon the tacit agreement of both sides not to push their rights to extreme lengths, and on the assumption that the existence of several acceptable candidates for the position would render compromise possible. This assumption was increasingly challenged by the growth of party loyalty.

Fox went out of his way in a debate of 5 March to state his own position:

It had been argued again and again that the King had a right to choose his own ministers. In that particular, he rested upon the spirit of the constitution, and not on the letter of it . . . He ever would maintain that His Majesty in his choice of ministers ought not to be influenced by his personal favour alone, but by the public voice, by the sense of his parliament, and the sense of his people.[1]

It would be hard for the most bigoted royalists to deny this, but it was not completely candid. In practice, Fox asserted that the personal views of the monarch should not count at all, a view that the king could hardly be expected to embrace. Ironically, however, it was the triumph of Fox's principle that enabled the monarchy to survive at all, the price paid being its gradual elimination from power. George's concept of his rights must ultimately have led to a direct clash between the crown and the public, in which the existence of the monarchy itself must have been at stake.

The king's next move, almost out of habit, was to send for Lord Gower, who suggested that Thomas Pitt, cousin of William, might be prepared to lead the House of Commons: 'Mr. Thomas Pitt or Mr. Thomas anybody', was the king's distracted answer. But the interview between Gower and Thomas Pitt proved another disappointment. Pitt expressed the most gratifying detestation of the coalition, but declared himself 'totally unequal to public business, but most certainly unequal to a task like this'. His advice was to admit the coalition to office while withholding any mark of royal favour, leaving disappointments over patronage, the need for heavy taxation, and the difficulties arising from the reform programme to render it speedily unpopular. He concluded with a sombre warning:

That after all if His Majesty still persisted in his resolution to stand his ground against them, he should well weigh his decision, perhaps the most important of his reign; that every symptom of a distempered state seemed to prognosticate the danger of some convulsions if the temper of the times was not managed with prudence.[2]

---

[1] Debrett, ix, 422.

[2] 'Lord Ashburton's Narrative', Bowood MSS. This is printed in Fitzmaurice, ii, 253–61, but parts of it seem to have been misdated; Fortescue, vi, nos. 4165–9. Fortescue, vi, no. 4261 is Thomas Pitt's own account, and has been misdated by the editor.

The king, now 'in the utmost distress', was still unwilling to give way, though Pitt's advice was reinforced by Thurlow, who thought any administration better than none.[1] To Lord Ashburton, whom he now called in for advice, the king confided that, rather than surrender, he would throw himself upon the House of Lords and 'deliver a speech which, without assistance or communication anywhere, I have composed', hinting that he would abdicate if he did not receive assistance.[2] Ashburton dissuaded him from such a course, and the next few days were spent in an attempt to float a Gower administration, with Jenkinson as Chancellor of the Exchequer and Henry Dundas to lead the House of Commons.[3] Unfortunately the organisers were more enthusiastic than the participants. John Robinson did his best by providing Dundas with a detailed, meticulous and totally misleading analysis of the House of Commons, which he claimed demonstrated that such a ministry was practicable: of the 558 members, 316 were classified as potential supporters, 173 as opponents, with 69 doubtful. But the assumptions behind the allocations were highly questionable,[4] and Dundas declared himself 'perfectly resolute' not to embark. Jenkinson professed willingness to act as directed, but had little confidence in the arrangement, Gower would not move without Pitt, and the attempt collapsed.[5]

With the crisis in its third week and public business at a standstill, the king had no alternative but to yield. But yielding

---

[1] Jenkinson to Robinson, 8 March, Abergavenny MSS.; Fortescue, vi, no. 4172.

[2] This speech is presumably the one printed as Fortescue, vi, no. 4259, though that version is an appeal to the House of Commons.

[3] 'Lord Ashburton's Narrative', Fitzmaurice, ii, 257–9. It is printed as taking place on 26 March, but should, I believe, be 10 March: it should be compared with Fortescue, vi, nos. 4170, 4172, 4173.

[4] Robinson's state is in the Melville MSS., National Library of Scotland. He assumes the support of half of North's following, 11 of Sandwich's connection (though Sandwich had written of Shelburne's overthrow that there never was 'any political measure in which I more pointedly took the lead') and 5 of Lord Hertford's connection. If these members did not change sides, the potential majority would be 7, with 69 doubtful.

[5] Henry to Robert Dundas, 10 March, Dundas of Arniston MSS.; Atkinson to Jenkinson, H.M.C. Abergavenny MSS., no. 505. The events referred to date the letter as 16 March.

proved as difficult as resisting. On 12 March he sent for North, agreed that Portland should be First Lord of the Treasury, and asked for a plan of the administration as soon as possible. It was now the coalition's turn to run into difficulties. Portland's original assumption had been that the Rockinghams would have a monopoly of the 'responsible, efficient offices': this position he tried to maintain with Fox as Foreign Secretary, Lord John Cavendish as Chancellor of the Exchequer, Keppel at the Admiralty, and the second Secretaryship going to Carlisle who, though a nominee of North, was acceptable to the Rockinghams; North was to be a member of the cabinet without office, and Dartmouth and Stormont were to be Lord Privy Seal and Lord President of the Council respectively. But Stormont refused the proposed office, and the Rockinghams would not hear of his replacing Carlisle as Secretary. On this issue the negotiations ground to a halt. For good measure, the Rockinghams would not contemplate allowing Thurlow to continue as Lord Chancellor, remembering his equivocal conduct during their former ministry. On the 14th, North reported these disagreements to the king, who encouraged him to stand firm: this Portland interpreted as a royal ultimatum on behalf of Stormont and Thurlow, and returned at once an 'immediate and absolute negative'. A well-attended meeting of the Rockinghams called at Lord Fitzwilliam's for the 16th to hear details of the administration was told instead of the hiatus:

The Duke of Portland said very little at the meeting but Mr. Fox who spoke afterwards gave his opinion of the transaction. He thought Lord Stormont from his abilities entitled to some employment, but said there was a great difference between his being placed in a particular employment by those who were desired to form an arrangement, and being placed there by the King. In the former case, he was part of their connection; in the latter he stood upon different ground and was quite independent of them.[1]

In the meantime, however, the king, anxious to avoid the responsibility for a breakdown in the negotiations, decided upon

[1] Philip Yorke to Lord Hardwicke, 17 March, Add. MS. 35381, f. 62.

retreat, summoned North, and explained that his remarks on Stormont and Thurlow were merely his 'private and hasty thoughts': he would not give his mature opinion until the whole arrangement had been laid before him.[1]

Portland re-embarked on the negotiation with the utmost caution. He suspected the king of trying to play him off against North, an opinion shared by William Grenville, no friend of the coalition, to whom the king unburdened his thoughts in an audience on the 16th.[2] It was also apparent that, with the junction of two powerful parties, there would be disappointments in the distribution of offices: Portland feared that the king would lead him on to betray his full hand, break off the negotiation on some pretext, and recruit the deserters and malcontents into a new administration.[3] He therefore insisted that he should be granted an audience and receive the royal commands directly:

If it is His Majesty's pleasure to place me at the head of the Treasury, it is impossible to suppose that he means to withhold from me any part of his confidence, but it is very necessary that the public should be convinced of that circumstance . . . I feel an insurmountable difficulty in taking any steps which may uselessly commit any other person as well as myself . . .[4]

The coalition also decided that the time had come to put parliamentary pressure on the king. There were reports that they had considered refusing to renew the Mutiny Act when it expired on 25 March, or granting only a month's extension. Such an expedient would have been drastic at a time when there was considerable unrest in the armed forces, and Robinson was

---

[1] Fortescue, vi, nos. 4268 & 4203.   [2] Buckingham, i, 187–94.

[3] Fitzpatrick to Ossory, 16 March, Russell, ii, 60–1.

[4] Fortescue, vi, no. 4209 and enclosure. It is difficult to see how any potential first minister could accept the treatment the king intended for Rockingham and Portland. Chatham, who shared the king's detestation of parties, had made demands similar to Portland's when asked to form a ministry in 1778. North then reported: 'he wishes to speak to His Majesty in order that his plans may not be misrepresented; that he expects to be a confidential minister, that he must have the appearance of forming the ministry, that the most important offices being filled with efficient men, Lord Chatham's desire would be in everything to attend to the wishes of His Majesty.' The king's retort was that Chatham aimed to be Dictator. Fortescue, iv, nos. 2223 & 2224.

convinced that it would not be supported were Fox to attempt it.[1] Their procedure in the end was more orthodox. On 18 March, Thomas William Coke, the member for Norfolk, gave notice that, if an administration had not been formed within three days, he would move an address to the king.[2] On the 21st, negotiations having been resumed, it was agreed to postpone the address until the 24th.

In the meantime the king had withdrawn his objection to treating personally with Portland and granted him an audience on the 19th. But the disagreement about Stormont was still unresolved. North offered to take the Home Department himself, going to the House of Lords, a proposal that Fox welcomed[3]; but Stormont continued to refuse the Presidency of the Council unless it carried cabinet rank, and to this Portland could not agree. Consequently Portland was obliged to explain to the king on the 20th, that the coalition could not form a ministry. The king bore his disappointment manfully, brushed aside Portland's offer to try to construct a purely Rockingham administration, and summoned Pitt urgently the same night.[4] The following morning Dundas was invited to breakfast with Pitt, who was still in cautious mood:

I went and met the Duke of Rutland there. The result was that if they could not *agree* and the country by that means kept in anarchy, he (Pitt) would accept of the government . . . But he insisted to have the secret kept because he was determined to have it distinctly ascertained before going again to the King that North and Fox after making a profligate conjunction had quarrelled among themselves about the division of the spoils.[5]

It was now the turn of Portland to retreat. Immediately after his return from court, he wrote to Burke:

---

[1] Robinson to Jenkinson, 12 March, Add. MS. 38567, f. 132.
[2] Debrett, ix, 502.
[3] Russell, ii, 62. I take this letter to have been written on 19 or 20 March 1783.
[4] Grafton, 375; B. Connell, *Portrait of a Whig peer*, 135; H. Walpole, *Last journals*, ii, 604; Buckingham, i, 202-3; *The correspondence of Edmund Burke*, v, 77-9; the king to William Pitt, 20 March, 10.22 p.m., Chatham MSS.; Fortescue, vi, no. 4268.
[5] Henry to Robert Dundas, 21 March, Dundas of Arniston MSS.

The alarm among our *most principal* friends became so general after *we* parted, and their opinion so strong for acquiescing in Lord Stormont's appointment that I have submitted, on condition of Lord John (Cavendish) and Keppel's assent. I am going to both, from thence to Lord North's, and so to Coke's. It is a bitter draught after what has passed, but the situation of the country I believe makes it necessary.[1]

But the removal of one difficulty made way for an even greater. When Portland arrived on the 21st with the list of the seven members of the cabinet, the king refused to look at it, insisting that he had already made it clear that he would give no opinion until he had seen the whole arrangement. This the duke declared showed a want of confidence in him, and 'began to grow warm'.[2] Richard Atkinson, an ardent advocate of a Pitt administration, summed up the position laconically: 'if the parties quarrel *clearly* between themselves, the thing will do. If the King quarrels with them, it will not do'.[3]

Portland assumed that the king would be obliged to give way before the 24th, when the debate in the House of Commons was to take place. Although he and North worked on the composition of the new ministry, he made no attempt to communicate with the king, and on the 23rd he was summoned to bring the plan of arrangement at once. At the audience Portland maintained his former attitude that the king should first give his approval to the cabinet proposals: the most he was able to achieve was to importune the king into glancing at the list of names and handing them back without comment. Surely, he asked, the seven cabinet members might be trusted to make no improper nominations: 'this I replied', wrote the king, 'was asking more than any man above forty could engage to do'.[4]

The king's unexpected resistance stemmed from the fact that

---

[1] *The correspondence of Edmund Burke*, v, 77. The next letter, from Burke to John Lee, gives more details.
[2] Fortescue, vi, no. 4268; B. Connell, *op. cit.*, 135.
[3] Atkinson to Robinson, 21 March, Add. MS. 37835, f. 202.
[4] Fortescue, vi, nos. 4228, 4230–9, 4268; Fitzmaurice, ii, 259.

he was once more in close touch with William Pitt and convinced that he would at last come to the rescue. Early on the 24th, he wrote to Thurlow:

After every sort of chicanery from the coalition, to which I have opposed the only weapon an honest man can employ, straight dealing, I have brought it to the repeated refusal of laying a plan of arrangements before me for my consideration, upon which, with the consent of Mr. Pitt, I broke off all further negotiation last night. He has said every thing but that he will engage to remain at the head of the Treasury which his delicacy made him wish to defer saying till this morning when I am to expect him.[1]

But though Pitt had summoned Dundas out of bed at two in the morning for urgent consultations, he retained his habitual self-possession, and deferred the audience until the debate that afternoon had given him a chance to gauge the temper of the House.[2]

When Coke rose to ask whether any administration had yet been formed, there were more than 400 members present: it was generally assumed that Pitt would declare himself minister. The king, who always found it difficult to credit that any honest man could differ from himself, believed that a manly pronouncement by Pitt would produce 'an applause which cannot fail to give him every encouragement'.[3] But the debate proved to be a disaster for the court party whose tactics were totally uncoordinated. Jenkinson arrived at the House determined to oppose any address as a violation of the royal prerogative, only to find that Pitt intended to offer no objection. Archibald Macdonald, Lord Gower's son-in-law and a recent convert to Pitt's cause, then opposed it on his own initiative, could find no seconder, and ran into a hail of banter and sarcasm from Fox, Sir Charles Turner and North. Worst of all, the wave of indignation against the coalition failed to materialise: 'both the Advocate and Mr. Rigby', reported Atkinson, 'admit that these expressions were short of

[1] Fortescue, vi, no. 4242.
[2] Henry to Robert Dundas, 24 March, Dundas of Arniston MSS.; Fortescue, vi, no. 4243.
[3] Fortescue, vi, no. 4244. The language is Thurlow's but the king shared his sentiments.

their expectations'. Pitt was not at his best.[1] He made one telling thrust—'gentlemen talked of forgiving animosities and altering their political opinions with as much ease as they could change their gloves'—but for the most part the trumpet gave an uncertain note. At the outset, in reply to Coke, he declared that he knew of no arrangement for a new administration: later on he admitted that he had 'some reason to imagine' that an administration might be formed in two or three days. 'The whole of Mr. Pitt's conduct was inexplicable', thought Jenkinson. Coke's address, begging the king to appoint a ministry entitled to the confidence of the people, passed *nem. con.*[2] Pitt explained later to Lord Carmarthen:

He had in the debate on Monday in the House of Commons purposely endeavoured to collect the real wishes of the independent part of the House, but not finding any reason to expect a substantial support from thence, he should think it inconsistent with his duty to the King or to the public service, as well as highly detrimental to his own character as well as his future views, to undertake under the present aspect of affairs so weighty a charge as the government of the country.[3]

His report to the king described the debate as 'desultory', and added that it had done nothing to relieve him of 'the embarrassments' he had previously felt. 'I am clear Mr. Pitt means to play false', summed up the king.[4]

Pitt's conduct had put the king into an impossible position. In the expectation of his support the door had been slammed on the coalition so emphatically that there was now no alternative to surrender. Dundas declared that he would not listen to another word on the subject, and Atkinson wrote: 'all that can remain will be to give such support as one can to the government they form, for by Heaven I am convinced there are not materials in the country

---

[1] This must be a matter of opinion, and it is only fair to add that William Grenville thought his speech 'inimitable' (Buckingham, i, 207). Robinson implied that Pitt was disconcerted by Powys's failure to move an amendment he had expected. (Add. MS. 38567, ff. 143–4.)

[2] Jenkinson to Robinson, 24 March, Atkinson to Robinson, 25 March, Abergavenny MSS.; Debrett, ix, 512–39; Fortescue, vi, nos. 4245 & 4247.

[3] Leeds, 85–6. [4] Fortescue, vi, nos. 4245–7.

to form another.'[1] For another week the king held out, hopelessly re-shuffling the discard pile—Lord Gower, Lord Temple, Thomas Pitt. More and more his mind turned to abdication. 'I am the more pressing to attempt to catch at everything', he confided to Thurlow on 28 March, 'as I feel if someone will not assist me, I must within a couple of days take the step I have so often hinted to you'. His abdication speech, based on the appeal he had previously contemplated making, was ready.[2] In it he repeated his belief that an administration 'of the most efficient men of all parties' had been needed to negotiate the definitive treaties:

> But this patriotic attempt has proved unsuccessful by the obstinacy of a powerful party that has long publicly manifested a resolution not to aid in the service of the Empire unless the whole executive management of affairs is thrown entirely into its hands, from which it has not on this occasion departed; at the same time want of zeal prevents others from standing forth at this critical conjuncture. My obedience to the oath I took at my coronation prevents my exceeding the powers vested in me, or submitting to be a cypher in the trammels of a self-created band.

After announcing that the rest of his life would be spent in Hanover—a strange change of heart for one who, in his first public utterance had 'gloried in the name of Briton'—he called for a restoration of 'that sense of religious and moral duties in this kingdom to the want of which every evil that has arisen owes its source'. His conclusion, with echoes of Elizabeth's Golden Speech, was ungrammatical, dignified and moving: 'May I to the latest hour of my Life, though now resolved for ever to quit this island, have the comfort of hearing that the endeavours of my son, though they cannot be more sincere than mine have been ... may be crowned with better success'. The speech was never made, nor the letter to his son delivered.[3] The advice of Thomas Pitt,

---

[1] Atkinson to Robinson, 25 March, Abergavenny MSS.

[2] Fortescue, vi, nos. 4256 & 4260. The abdication draft is not dated, but I take it to have been composed during the last week of March.

[3] A draft of the letter to his son is printed in *The correspondence of George, Prince of Wales*, ed. Aspinall, i, 104.

augmented perhaps by that of Thurlow, convinced him that the game was not yet lost.[1]

On the 31st, the parliamentary attack was resumed. After Pitt had announced his resignation as Chancellor of the Exchequer, Lord Surrey moved a long address cataloguing the matters demanding urgent government attention and begging for an administration. Fox and North, anxious not to alienate moderate opinion, begged him not to press the matter to a division, and after Pitt had admitted that he 'naturally supposed' a ministry would be formed in a few days, Surrey agreed to postpone the address until the 3rd. Pitt's report to the king carried the clear warning that the postponement had not been agreed to 'without its being understood on all sides that an address to this purpose would not be objected to if that hope should fail'.[2]

The following day the king gave way, sending for North in the evening. He was the victim, he told Lord Temple, of 'the most unprincipled coalition the annals of this or any nation can equal':

I have withstood it till not a single man is willing to come to my assistance and till the House of Commons has taken every step but insisting on this faction by name being elected Ministers. To end a conflict which stops every wheel of government and which would affect the public credit if it continued much longer I intend this night to acquaint that *grateful* man Lord North that the seven cabinet counsellors the coalition has named shall kiss hands tomorrow and then form their arrangements as (in) the former negotiation they did not condescend to open to me any of their intentions.

A ministry which I have avowedly attempted to avoid by calling on every other description of men, cannot be supposed to have either my favour or confidence and as such I shall most certainly refuse any honours that may be asked by them; I trust the eyes of the nation will soon be opened as my sorrow may prove fatal to my health if I remain long in this thraldom; I trust you will be steady in your attachment to me and ready to join other honest men in watching the conduct of this unnatural combination, and I hope many months

---

[1] The king was much impressed by Thomas Pitt's argument, and his subsequent conduct followed closely on the lines suggested. Wraxall, iii, 36 records some plain speaking by Thurlow but gives no source.

[2] Debrett, ix, 547–82; Fortescue, vi, no. 4269.

will not elapse before the Grenvilles, the Pitts and other men of abilities and character will relieve me . . .[1]

In this state of uneasy truce, the leaders of the coalition arrived at St James's on Wednesday 2 April to kiss hands.

[1] Fortescue, vi, no. 4272. This letter seems to me to cast doubt on an observation in J. S. Watson, *The reign of George III, 1760–1815* (1960), 266, that 'there is no evidence to support the view . . . that George III schemed to destroy the coalition from its formation'.

CHAPTER 5

THE COALITION IN OFFICE

The king's determination not to show any favour to the new
ministers, and in particular not to grant any peerages or advance-
ments on their recommendation, brought into discussion yet
another aspect of the prerogative. The king's attitude was a
serious embarrassment to the coalition: Pitt, later in the summer,
thought it the point 'on which . . . almost everything depends'.[1]
It advertised in the most public way that the ministers did not
enjoy the king's confidence and that their tenure of office was
precarious: it could deprive them of the support of persons like
Sir James Lowther, Edward Eliot and Lord Paget whose primary
aim was honours and distinction, and it created difficulties in the
construction of the ministry. The original intention had been that
North should go to the House of Lords, possibly to strengthen the
government's debating resources there, that Lord Hertford
should be given a dukedom, and that peerages or advancement
should go to Lord Fitzwilliam, Lord Clive, Welbore Ellis, Robert
Vyner, and Sir Thomas Egerton.[2] The frustration of these plans
necessitated some delicate adjustments: Lord Hertford had to go
back to his old post of Lord Chamberlain, which had been originally intended for Lord Hillsborough, who was dropped completely. The coalition leaders must have been sorely tempted to try
to force the king on this point as well while they had the power,
but were deterred partly perhaps by the desire to avoid another
protracted dispute and partly by doubts about the attitude of the
independents in a matter so close to the personal wishes of the
monarch. The king certainly thought he would be fighting on

[1] Pitt to William Grenville, 10 September, *H.M.C. Fortescue MSS.*, i, 219.
[2] Portland to North, 22 March 1783, Waldeshare MSS. deals with the construction of the
ministry; Fortescue, vi, nos. 4185 & 4271.

strong ground, writing to Ashburton that he did 'not mean to grant a single peerage or other mark of favour . . . if they fly out at that I think, torpid as all collectively have seemed, I cannot fail to meet with support'.[1]

Apart from the sharp difference of opinion over Lord Stormont, the formation of the administration was carried through harmoniously, Fox and Burke both paying tribute to Lord North's conciliatory attitude. By far the greatest difficulty was an acute shortage of places. The union of two substantial parties flung great pressure on to resources that had just been curtailed by the economical reform legislation: the eight Lords Commissionership at the Board of Trade (worth £1000 p.a.), the three places in the Board of Works, and the six Clerkships and Clerk Comptrollerships at the Board of Green Cloth (worth £1,018 p.a.), all swept away by Burke's Civil List reform, would have been invaluable for stopping hungry mouths. In the end a system of rationing was adopted, and most of the great political families had to be content with one place.

In the cabinet, the Rockinghams were supreme, with four places against North's three: in the rest of the administration, the balance was slightly in favour of the Northites.[2] Burke resumed his post as Paymaster, Fitzpatrick became Secretary at War, and Sheridan joined Richard Burke as secretaries to the Treasury. The leading advocates of the coalition were well rewarded: Eden became Joint Vice-Treasurer of Ireland, George North became Under-Secretary at the Home Department, and Lord John Townshend went to the Board of Admiralty. A certain

---

[1] 2 April 1783, *H.M.C. 9th Report*, part I, *MSS. of Alfred Morrison*.

[2] Of the twenty-nine places referred to in Portland's letter to North on 22 March, seventeen went to Northites and twelve to Foxites. But Keppel, as First Lord of the Admiralty, nominated to two places at that board, which, in effect, brought the Foxite total to fourteen. The Northites had considerable success in capturing the snug places: Lord Weymouth resumed as Groom of the Stole at £2,000 p.a., Charles Townshend became Treasurer of the Navy at the same salary, Lord Dartmouth, as Lord Steward, received £1,460 p.a., and the needy Charles Greville collected £1,200 p.a. as Treasurer of the Household. The Postmastership was shared by a Northite and a Foxite at £2,000 p.a. each.

amount of discontent was to be expected. Conway, despite the king's efforts to stir up resentment, took his removal from the cabinet with equanimity and continued as Commander-in-Chief, but Richmond resigned the Ordnance and went into avowed opposition. Loughborough, whose ambition was the Lord Chancellorship, had to content himself with the lead in the commission set up to hold the Great Seal.[1] Lord Sandwich protested that the Mastership of the Buckhounds for his son, Lord Hinchingbrooke, was an inadequate recognition of his family's importance, bombarded North with menacing letters, and eventually had to be quietened with the Rangership of St James and Hyde Park.[2] The choice of a successor to Lord Temple in Ireland presented such difficulties that it was three weeks before an announcement could be made: after refusals by the duke of Devonshire, Lord Fitzwilliam, Lord Derby and Lord Althorpe, it was accepted by the 2nd earl of Northington, an amiable and intelligent man, but in poor health and without any previous experience of public affairs.[3]

The new ministry could boast considerable debating and administrative ability. Grafton, who condemned the coalition itself as disgraceful, admitted that 'no person questioned the talents of most of those who filled the principal offices of government'.[4] But the ministers were well aware that without some reconciliation with the king their prospects were poor. Such a reconciliation did not appear out of the question. The king's

---

[1] Lord Campbell, *The lives of the Lord Chancellors* (1847), vi, 169 explains that the king would not agree to Loughborough's appointment to the Woolsack, but it may also have been that it would have given him entrance to the cabinet and upset the Rockinghams' supremacy there. William Grenville wrote to Temple, 11 April: 'the news of the day is that they are quarrelling about having Lord Loughborough of the cabinet.' Buckingham, i, 235.

[2] Sandwich to North, 4 April, Sandwich MSS.; Sandwich to Robinson, 21 April, Abergavenny MSS.

[3] Buckingham, i, 232, 237; H. Walpole, *Last journals*, ii, 617; H.M.C. *14th Report*, appendix, part ix, *Emly MSS.*, 176; Fortescue, vi, nos. 4302 & 4317. Assessments of Northington are in H.M.C. *Charlemont MSS.*, i, 100–2; Wraxall, iii, 59.

[4] Grafton, 380.

prejudices were strong, even violent, but not immutable. Lord Chatham, Pitt's father, had run the whole gamut of royal opinion, beginning in 1760 as 'the blackest of hearts' and 'a true snake in the grass', transmogrified by 1765 into 'My Friend, for so the part you have acted deserves from me', only to finish up in 1778 as 'that perfidious man'.[1] Lord Shelburne, described in 1778 as a man 'who personally perhaps I dislike as much as Alderman Wilkes', had become a royal favourite four years later.[2] The duke of Portland, though the king had complained of 'personal incivility' during the negotiations, had some success in his attempts to close the breach: his condolences on the death of Prince Octavius in early May extorted an assurance that 'the Duke of Portland's very feeling expressions for my welfare and that of my family are not thrown away upon me'.[3] But all of Fox's overtures were received with stony contempt. At his first audience, according to Horace Walpole, he tried to exonerate himself from the charge of leading the Prince of Wales astray: 'he had never said a word to the Prince which he should not have been glad to have His Majesty hear'. There was no response.[4] On 16 April, he tried once more:

Mr. Fox hopes that Your Majesty will not think him presumptuous or improperly intruding upon Your Majesty with professions, if he begs leave most humbly to implore Your Majesty to believe that both the Duke of Portland and he have nothing so much at heart as to conduct Your Majesty's affairs, both with respect to measures and to persons, in the manner that may give Your Majesty the most satisfaction, and that, whenever Your Majesty will be graciously pleased to condescend even to hint your inclinations upon any subject, that it will be the study of Your Majesty's Ministers to show how truly sensible they are of Your Majesty's goodness.[5]

The effort was wasted: on the back of the letter the king wrote, simply, 'No answer.' Far from condescending to hint at his wishes, he retired into the defensive shell that his tutor, Lord Waldegrave,

---

[1] *Letters from George III to Lord Bute, 1756–66*, ed. R. Sedgwick (1939), nos. 57 & 60; Fortescue, i, no. 94; iv, no. 2224.
[2] Fortescue, iv, no. 2221.   [3] Fortescue, vi, nos. 4335, 4336, 4340, 4341.
[4] *Last journals*, ii, 613–14.   [5] Fortescue, vi, no. 4308.

had noted as his characteristic refuge when a boy. On the 18th Fox forwarded details of the definitive treaties, adding that if the king 'should wish for any verbal explanation upon this very great business', he was at His Majesty's command. 'I do not mean to call on Mr. Fox for further explanations on this subject', replied the king: 'unnecessary discussions are not my taste'.[1] Nevertheless, coalition supporters continued to hope that his rancour would soften, and throughout the summer reports of the royal mood were accorded the attention reserved today for public opinion polls.

The most urgent of the many problems demanding the attention of the new ministers were the state of the finances and the negotiation of a final peace settlement. The financial situation had been a main factor in forcing the king to surrender: according to Portland there was only £400,000 left in the Exchequer at the beginning of April against immediate claims of more than £3,000,000.[2] The shortage of money had had a serious effect upon the discipline of the armed forces, since it delayed the discharge of many servicemen whose arrears of pay could not be met. In January the 77th Regiment at Portsmouth had mutinied, and were soon joined by the 68th. The following month the disaffection spread to the seamen, and in March the 104th Regiment in Guernsey mutinied and was subdued only after a pitched battle. During April there were disturbances among the troops in Dublin, Wakefield and Rotherham, while angry seamen surrounded the Navy Pay Office threatening to pull it down.[3] Under these circumstances the negotiation of a loan of £12,000,000 was Lord John Cavendish's first task on taking office.

He found himself in the unfortunate position of having to negotiate at short notice and at a moment singularly unfavourable

---

[1] Fortescue, vi, nos. 4315 & 4316.
[2] Fortescue, vi, no. 4271; Debrett, xi, 175–6.
[3] *Gentleman's magazine*, 1783, part i, pp. 89–90, 171, 263, 266–7, 345–6, 356–8; Fortescue, vi, nos. 4089–92, 4098, 4126, 4132, 4137, 4147, 4252–3, 4313–14.

to government.[1] In his exposition to the House of Commons he was disarming, confessing that 'the bargain was more advantageous to the money lenders than he could have wished, but considering the danger of delaying the loan till after the holidays, he thought it better for the public to conclude the bargain then'. Pitt criticised the terms of the loan, and expressed concern that the reservation of a share to be allocated by ministers would leave room for jobbery. Fox at once retorted that Pitt, by retaining office for six weeks without attempting to negotiate a loan, was himself responsible for the poor terms.[2]

The debate in the House of Lords was more interesting, and took a curious turn. Lord Shelburne obviously intended to demonstrate that he was still in the political arena: his speech was carefully prepared and he had concerted plans with Pitt.[3] He opened with a protest that the House of Lords had, in the course of the century, allowed the Commons to appropriate to themselves all power over money bills: if unchecked, this could destroy the balance of the constitution. The loan itself he dismissed as improvident and reprehensible, and, partly to demonstrate the House of Lords' right to intervene in financial matters, he moved two resolutions—that any future loan should assist the reduction of the national debt, and that no reserve should be kept for the ministers' disposal. The set-piece went off without mishap, but the total effect was marred by a series of subsequent disasters. First Stormont showed that he was out of order, and his resolutions were saved for discussion only by Thurlow's ingenuity. Next, Loughborough, a vigorous and formidable speaker, fell upon the first resolution, ridiculing the suggestion that a loan could decrease debt. When Shelburne intervened to deny that he had been responsible for the delay in forming an administration, he put his case somewhat maladroitly: 'With regard to the

---

[1] D. M. Joslin, 'London bankers in wartime 1739–84', in *Studies in the Industrial Revolution*, ed. L. S. Pressnell, 172.
[2] Debrett, ix, 618–38.   [3] Fitzmaurice, ii, 264.

argument that he had lost the confidence of the House of Commons, he did not believe he had lost it. But, said the noble lord, let the House of Commons beware, or they will lose my confidence.' Finally, the debate degenerated into an extraordinary quarrel between Shelburne and his former colleague, Keppel, who accused him of having 'interfered with his office, through clerks, unknown to him, and in an underhand manner'. Shelburne then remarked that Keppel 'seemed determined to make a most direct attack upon him', to which Keppel replied, 'With all my heart.' The come-back ended miserably. The resolutions, to whose fate Shelburne professed himself 'perfectly indifferent', were rejected, the House of Lords declined his invitation to pick a constitutional quarrel with the House of Commons, and the Commons themselves bore with equanimity the loss of Lord Shelburne's confidence.[1]

The chief feature of Cavendish's budget, introduced on 26 May, was a tax on receipts, designed to bring in £250,000 p.a.; stamps to the value of 2d were required on receipts for payments of between £2 and £20, and 4d on higher payments. No opposition was offered to the proposal at first hearing, but the commercial community took alarm, assuming that the burden would fall upon the shopkeepers. Several towns, including London, attempted to petition against it, and many speakers in the debate on the third reading admitted that they had received instructions from their constituents to oppose it.[2] But Pitt refused to join in the attack, arguing that the tax was more likely to prove ineffective than harsh, and the third reading was carried by 145 votes to 40. Although discontent continued to smoulder for some time, it is doubtful whether the tax had any effect on the

---

[1] Debrett, xi, 159–80.

[2] London, Exeter, Westminster and Taunton petitioned while the measure was before Parliament, and Trowbridge and Ripon subsequently. The House of Commons adhered to its practice of not entertaining petitions against taxation. The boroughs of Tewkesbury, Stamford, Taunton, Honiton, Southwark, Pontefract, Guildford, Hertford and Preston sent instructions to their members.

general election result in 1784: Thomas Pitt's hope that the coalition would be rendered unpopular by the imposition of taxes was not fulfilled.[1]

The negotiation of the definitive treaties was a forlorn task. The leaders of the coalition had been obliged to pledge themselves to accept the preliminary articles when they had been debated in February in order to meet the charge that they courted a renewal of the conflict, but by doing so they had tied their own hands. They were able to obtain concessions for the better treatment of British citizens in Tobago, a clearer definition of British rights to participate in the gum trade, and a small modification of French fishing rights in Newfoundland, but the proposed commercial treaty with the United States foundered,[2] and in the provisional treaty with the Dutch they had to be satisfied with Negapatam instead of Trincomali.

By the time the definitive treaties were laid before Parliament in November the interest had gone out of the controversy, and the debate was routine and perfunctory. The king's attitude during the renewed negotiations was one of morose indifference. On 19 July he told Fox that the country had only itself to blame for the difficulties arising with Spain: 'after the extraordinary and never to be forgot vote of February 1782, and the hurry for negotiation that ensued, it is no wonder our enemies seeing our spirits so fallen have taken advantage of it.' On 7 September he expressed

---

[1] Cavendish's own position may have suffered as a consequence, and there is evidence of strong feeling in Yorkshire generally. *York Courant*, 6 January 1784; N. C. Phillips, *Yorkshire and English national politics 1783–4* (1961), 33–5. But reports that unstamped receipts were still legal led to so great a falling-off in yield that an explanatory measure had to be introduced later in the year. This in itself suggests that the burden was not severe enough to be politically damaging. Horace Walpole wrote that the taxes were 'popular beyond example', and that the receipt tax was 'in general much approved'. *Last journals*, ii, 627–8.

[2] The American Intercourse Bill, which had originated with the Shelburne ministry, had accorded the Americans certain privileges pending a general settlement. It was abandoned by the coalition after William Eden had attacked it as making 'gratuitous and endless concessions'. David Hartley, the member for Hull, was then sent to Paris to begin negotiations, but they broke down on the question of the American carrying trade. The subject is fully discussed in V. T. Harlow, *op. cit.*, ch. ix.

doubts whether the Dutch would be reconciled, and wrote, pointedly, to Fox: 'in states as well as in men, where dislike has once arose, I never expect to see cordiality.' To North, the same day, he declared that he was glad he would not be in town when peace was proclaimed 'as I think this completes the downfall of the lustre of this Empire . . . one comfort I have, that I have alone tried to support the dignity of my crown and feel I am innocent of the evils that have occurred, though deeply wounded that it should have happened during my reign.'[1]

The change of ministry in April 1783 made little difference in Irish affairs. The Shelburne cabinet and its successor were equally convinced that England had made sufficient concessions in 1782 and would contemplate no more unless forced upon them. Shelburne's attitude towards the warnings Temple had constantly sent him had been to play for time. In November 1782 he had told William Grenville: 'If we had peace, the advantages to government in Ireland would be great and almost infinite. Such an event would throw the Volunteers upon their backs, would bring the army to that country and to this, and would also bring the fleet into the channel.'[2] It was with the greatest reluctance that he had agreed to the introduction of the Renunciation Act— and then only because Temple insisted that the situation was getting out of hand. But when the Volunteers, in the course of 1783, turned to a new object and commenced a campaign for parliamentary reform in Ireland, the Castle government felt obliged to resist, lest the last vestiges of its power should vanish. In September the Volunteers decided to summon a national convention for 10 November in Dublin to discuss the means of procuring reform. The situation carried revolutionary implications. To Northington Fox wrote in considerable alarm:

With respect to the Volunteers and their delegates, I want words to express to you how *critical* in the genuine sense of the word I conceive the present moment to be. Unless they dissolve in a reasonable time, Government, and even the

---

[1] Fortescue, vi, nos. 4422, 4468, 4470.   [2] Buckingham, i, 68.

name of it, must be at an end . . . If they are treated as they ought to be, if you show *firmness*, and that firmness is seconded by the aristocracy and Parliament, I look to their dissolution as a certain and not very distant event . . . Immense concessions were made in the Duke of Portland's time, and those concessions were declared by an almost unanimous House of Commons to be sufficient. The account must be considered as having been closed on the day of that vote, and should never again be opened on any pretence whatever.[1]

Northington replied by stressing the unsettled state of the country and the difficulty experienced by the government in enforcing its wishes. But he did not share Fox's anxiety about the outcome of the national convention, believing that internal differences would render it harmless. The Lord-Lieutenant's judgement, in the event, proved correct. The deliberations of the convention were singularly confused, strong disagreements soon arose about the position of the Catholics, and there was rivalry between the moderate Charlemont and the flamboyant Lord Bristol, bishop of Derry. When the convention did agree to propose a plan of reform and Henry Flood moved for leave to introduce it in the Irish House of Commons, it was denounced as coming from an unconstitutional assembly, and defeated by a decisive majority. The convention had to be content with a loyal address begging the king for reform, while Northington, delighted with the success of his policy, hinted that an indication of the king's approbation would not be amiss. But by the time the letter arrived, nothing was further from the king's thoughts than to show approbation to any of the ministers.[2]

At Westminster the opposition made two challenges before the summer recess. The first was on a motion for parliamentary reform, moved by William Pitt on 7 May. The campaign to arouse support in the country had been coordinated by Christopher Wyvill during the winter months, but Pitt must have hoped

[1] Russell, ii, 163–4.
[2] Correspondence between Northington and the ministers is contained in his letter book, Add. MS. 38716. Temple's letter books are Add. MSS. 40733 & 40177–80. Biographies of two of the leaders of the Volunteers are W. S. C. Pemberton, *The earl bishop* (1925) and M. J. Craig, *The volunteer earl* (1948).

to embarrass the coalition by striking at the point where their lack of agreement was most apparent, and placing Fox, in particular, in an awkward position.[1] The debate attracted great attention; the public gallery was full several hours before the House was due to meet, and more than five hundred members were said to have been present. Pitt's speech was studiously moderate in tone, expressing great veneration for the constitution, but proposing three resolutions—to reduce bribery, to disqualify corrupt boroughs, and to augment the representation of the counties by a number of seats to be agreed later. The main effect of his proposal was to prepare a triumph for Lord North, the only leader whose following was united on the issue, and who dominated the debate with a speech that demonstrated all his arts and understanding of the House.[2] He denied that Pitt's main proposition would effect a reform at all: 'A gentleman behind me (Thomas Pitt) says, Give the people *fifty knights* and then make a stand. I oppose this idea; the addition of fifty county members would give a decided superiority to the landed interest over the commercial.'[3] His answer to Pitt's assertion that the secret influence of the crown was 'sapping the very foundation of liberty' was a skilful blend of personal apologia and public argument:

I trust the candid and discerning part of the House will see that the attack is most unjust. I was not, when I was honoured with office, a minister of chance, or a creature of whom Parliament had no experience. I was found among you when I was so honoured. I had long been known to you. In consequence, I obtained your support; when that support was withdrawn, I ceased to be a minister. I was the creature of Parliament in my rise; when I fell I was its victim. I came among you without connection. It was here I was first known; you raised me up, you pulled me down. I have been the creature of your

---

[1] The campaign is described in I. R. Christie, *Wilkes, Wyvill and reform*, (1962) ch. v.

[2] By comparing the lists in Robinson's state of 10 March (Melville MSS. 63a) with the supporters of Pitt's resolutions (C. Wyvill, *op. cit.*, ii, 255–6), it is possible to form some idea how the parties split. Of the 112 members classified by Robinson as favouring Fox, 53 supported reform (47 per cent); of 189 favouring Shelburne, 76 supported reform (40 per cent); of the 149 favouring North, only 9 supported reform (6 per cent).

[3] *Gentleman's magazine*, 1783, ii, 823.

opinion and your power, and the history of my political life is one proof which will stand against and overturn a thousand wild assertions that there is a corrupt influence in the crown which destroys the independence of this House. Does my history show the undue influence of the crown? Or is it not, on the contrary, the strongest proof that can be given of the potent efficacy of the public voice? If then, that voice is so powerful as to remove whatever may be displeasing to the opinions of the country, what need is there of this paraded reformation?[1]

Dundas's conversion to reform, announced later in the debate, provoked considerable sarcasm, but the Northites, with Eden and Robinson acting as tellers, carried the day by 293 votes to 149. 'My defeat', admitted Pitt ruefully, 'was much more complete than I expected.'[2]

The second challenge was more embarrassing to the coalition, and arose out of an action by Edmund Burke as Paymaster. There is no doubt that the period after the death of Rockingham was one of the most painful in his life; in July 1782 he complained to Loughborough of the 'innumerable, unspeakable vexations which I have suffered', and his excitability reached such a pitch that there were rumours of madness. His fellow members of Parliament, exasperated by his long and vehement harangues, treated him with scanty respect: in the debate on reform, in which North had so distinguished himself, Burke had not been able to gain a hearing. In April 1783, on returning to the Pay Office, one of his most pressing problems was to decide what attitude to adopt towards two of the senior officials, John Powell and Charles Bembridge, who had been dismissed by his predecessor on suspicion of corruption. On 17 April he wrote reinstating them, though warning each that if the charges were confirmed, 'however disagreeable it may be to me, I shall certainly remove you'. The decision did credit to his heart but not his head. What appeared to Burke as an act of elementary justice in preserving two conscientious officials from losing their livelihoods before proof had been produced seemed to the opposition a shady protection accorded

---

[1] Debrett, ix, 712–13.   [2] Pitt to Lady Chatham, 15 May 1783, Stanhope, i, 121.

to malefactors. The issue was the more delicate in that the balances of Fox's father, Lord Holland, a former Paymaster, were involved. When the matter was raised in the House of Commons on 2 May Pitt argued that the restoration of the two men 'seemed to cast no small reflection on those who had been the authors of their dismission', and James Martin, the out-spoken member for Tewkesbury, described it as a 'gross and daring insult to the public'. At this Burke fell into a violent rage and had to be restrained by Sheridan. The attack was resumed on 19 May when Sir Cecil Wray called Burke's action 'highly indecent'. Burke, though more moderate in tone, would make no concession: he felt a 'sunshine of content' in his mind, he assured the House. Fox and North both came to his assistance, but on the division the government scraped home by 161 votes to 137, the minority containing, as Burke admitted, 'some of his most respected friends'. All the danger signals were now in evidence, and two days later he was forced to give way. He defended his conduct in a rambling speech, went out of his way to pay tribute to Lord Rockingham, 'who, he said, was gone to a better place', and forgot the main point of his remarks, which was that Powell had resigned and Bembridge had offered his resignation. Fox then persuaded him to bow to the wishes of the House and accept Bembridge's offer. Burke's mortification was complete when, on 26 May, Powell committed suicide: two months later, Bembridge was tried and found guilty. 'Thank God Burke is quiet', wrote Lord Sheffield in June.[1]

---

[1] Auckland, i, 52. In October 1784 Burke wrote to a friend: 'You know that my enemies of all descriptions fastened upon my restoration of that unfortunate man as a point on which they thought me most vulnerable . . . they laid hold on my lenity as an indulgence to crimes; and you know how much trouble and vexation this business cost me.' The episode can be traced in full in *State Trials*, ed. T. J. Howell, xxii, 1–160; *The correspondence of Edmund Burke*, v, 87–91 & 169–74; Debrett, ix, 678–84; x, 17, 20, 33–58, 100–3; *Gentleman's magazine*, 1783, i, 454, 539; ii, 614 & 975–6. It is discussed in T. W. Copeland, *Edmund Burke* (1950), ch. ii, and J. E. D. Binney, *British public finance and administration, 1774–1792* (1958), 153–6.

It was apparent, however, to most observers that the fate of the ministry would be decided outside the House of Commons. 'The same *fixed aversion*, I believe, still continues', Pitt confided to his mother on 15 May: 'you will easily guess where.'[1] His conjecture was dramatically verified by the events of mid-June.

Among the problems inherited by the coalition was the question of an establishment for George, Prince of Wales, who would come of age on 12 August 1783; the arrangements made for him in 1780, whereby he lodged at Buckingham House with the royal family, could not long continue. The prince had for some years engaged in affairs of gallantry, and was now beginning to show an interest in politics, being on terms of close acquaintance with Fox and Sheridan. On both moral and political grounds the king had reason to disapprove of his son's conduct, and was unlikely to enter the negotiations in an open-handed spirit. When the matter was first discussed in cabinet Fox, as the prince's partisan, argued for an income of £100,000 p.a., including £12,000 from the revenues of the duchy of Cornwall. Lord John Cavendish and Lord North thought this excessive, but acquiesced, and the proposal was formally put to the king by the duke of Portland. The king replied that the sum might be thought unreasonable, and asked the ministers to reconsider it. On 6 June Portland repeated the proposal, and suggested that it could be made acceptable to Parliament, provided that there was no intention to augment it in the event of the prince's marriage. The king accepted without enthusiasm, and on 15 June drafted a letter to the prince's treasurer, Colonel Hotham, which concluded with the most stringent censures on the prince's conduct, 'his neglect of every religious duty . . . want of even common civility to the Queen and me . . . and his total disobedience of every injunction I had given'. The following day the king received a letter from Portland discussing the various ways in which the money might be raised, and revealing that the prince had accumulated debts

[1] Stanhope, i, 121.

to the amount of £29,000, which had to be included in the settlement.[1]

The king's reply to this was ferocious: 'it is impossible for me to find words expressive enough of my utter indignation and astonishment at the letter I have just received from the Duke of Portland.' He repudiated any suggestion that he might bear part of the expense of the debts, declared that unless Parliament provided the whole sum he would make the transaction public, and accused Portland of attempting to 'gratify the passions of an ill-advised young man.' In face of this onslaught, the duke retreated, explaining that the proposals had been put forward tentatively for the king's consideration: the ministers were perfectly prepared to ask Parliament to find the whole £100,000 p.a.

At this point the king changed his ground and denounced the grant of £100,000 p.a. as 'a shameful squandering of public money'; the most he was now prepared to give was £50,000 p.a. from the Civil List, with Parliament to provide a grant of £50,000 to pay the prince's debts and enable him to set up house. In addition, he wrote separately to North and Stormont, hinting that they could not have been aware of the proposals, and insisting that they should 'exculpate' themselves. Their reply, that Portland may have had reasons for submitting the alternative proposals for consideration, the king dismissed, not without justice, as far from explicit:

This whole business shows who has the interest of the public at heart and who has virtue enough to cast aside all private feelings where that interest is intended to be sacrificed . . . Believe me, no consideration can ever make me either forget or forgive what has passed, and the public shall know how well founded the principles of economy are in those who have so loudly preached it up . . . yet, when they think it will answer their own wicked purposes, are ready to be most barefacedly lavish.

[1] Fox to Northington, 17 July, Russell, ii, 115–21; *The correspondence of George, Prince of Wales*, ed. A. Aspinall, i, no. 79.

The ministers were in a most delicate situation. Notice had already been given that a statement would be made in Parliament on 17 June. Archibald Macdonald wrote to Lady Gower that evening:

You will wish to know what passed in the House of Commons this day, which was to have produced a message relative to a certain establishment. The House was surprisingly full for the season. Fox came in as dirty as a scavenger but *no message*, nor a word upon the subject. It was a good deal whispered about that there are objections *somewhere* . . .[1]

To add to their embarrassment the prince, alarmed at the turn events had taken, complained that with £50,000 p.a. he would be worse off than before.

Most of the coalition supporters assumed that the end of the ministry was imminent; there was talk of immediate resignation, and Fitzpatrick wrote to Ossory that the wish was 'to do something tomorrow, and at least to die handsomely'.[2] But those ministers aware of the misgivings within the cabinet counselled submission to the royal ultimatum, provided that the prince could be persuaded to waive his claim to the larger sum. 'The unpopularity of the ground we stood on', wrote Portland, 'was becoming so general that it was not thought advisable to support it and to risk the existence of administration upon so doubtful and questionable an event.' Consequently no reply was made to the king's counter-proposals, and on 18 June Portland braced himself for an audience on the king's return from Windsor. His reception was the very reverse of that he had anticipated: the king had had another remarkable change of heart, and, though not abandoning his position, had decided not to regard the disagreement as a *casus belli*. He was therefore overwhelmingly gracious:

On entering the closet I instantly perceived that everything was to be made up, and that what had happened was to be done away. For His Majesty expressed in the strongest terms his extreme concern at the unguarded expressions he had used, and on my observing to him that a copy of them *in his own writing* had

<hr>

[1] Granville MSS.   [2] Russell, ii, 113.

been transmitted by him to Lord North, with directions to communicate them to Lord Stormont, he made the fullest apology for them, begged me to forget them, assured me of his kindness, used every argument to persuade me of the sense he had of the injustice he had done me, and very handsomely repeated to Lord North the apology he had made me, and entered with him into reasons to palliate his own conduct, which he allowed to be in every respect unwarranted and perfectly unjustifiable, but to be attributed to the unfortunate event of the American War, which he told Lord North had so soured and ruined his temper that he was afraid there were moments when he was afraid Lord North would think very differently of him, from what his conduct before the acknowledgement of American independence had given him reason to do. I should say that I am perfectly satisfied with Lords Stormont and North. Throughout the whole of this business they have acted a firm and manly part, and contributed most essentially to convince his Majesty of the impossibility of breaking this or forming a new administration.[1]

It remained to be seen whether the prince could be induced to acquiesce, since Fox regarded himself as pledged to the larger sum. Fox appealed to him to bear it with 'calmness and constancy', and the duchess of Devonshire was brought in to smooth away ill-feeling. At length the prince accepted the king's proposals, provided that the sum for the payment of his debts was raised to £60,000. On the 21st the king despatched to him the letter drafted on the 15th, with the revised terms but the original reproaches. To these the prince replied with expressions of 'extreme concern' and assurances of dutiful reformation. Whatever his shortcomings, the prince had acquitted himself in the affair with a good deal more dignity than the king.[2]

There was much speculation about the king's motives and the part played by Lord Temple: 'this we suppose has been settled with the enemy', wrote Fitzpatrick on the 17th.[3] The king's letter of 16 June and his subsequent behaviour suggests a spontaneous outburst of rage, triggered off by the fresh revelations of

[1] Portland to Northington, 20 June, Add. MS. 38716, f. 66; Fortescue, vi, nos. 4384–6, 4388–93.
[2] *The correspondence of George, Prince of Wales*, ed. A. Aspinall, i, nos. 79, 91, 93, 94.
[3] Russell, ii, 113.

his son's debts. No doubt much of the indignation was genuine. But the account given by Lord Temple of an audience with the king affords ground for suspecting that the royal wrath may have concealed at least an element of calculation. On Friday, 13 June, before he went to Windsor, the king had a conversation on the subject of the prince's establishment with Portland, and listened 'with the same good humour that he would have heard me on any indifferent subject'. Immediately afterwards he granted an audience to Temple, who had just returned from Ireland, and expressed to him the 'resentment and disgust' he felt towards the ministers and his 'personal abhorrence' of Lord North:

He repeated that to such a ministry he would never give his confidence, and that he would take the first moment for dismissing them. He then stated the proposition made to him by the Duke of Portland for the annual allowance of £100,000 ... His Majesty declared himself to be decided to resist this attempt, and to push the consequences to their full extent, and to try the spirit of the Parliament and of the people upon it ...

Temple's advice was not to force a breach on this issue: he and his friends might be willing to form a new administration if the coalition ministers resigned, but their dismissal would be a very different proposition. It is therefore clear that the king had determined to resist before Portland's letter arrived at Windsor on Monday 16 June, and that he was biding his time; and it is possible that the violence of the royal reply, described by the editor of the king's correspondence as 'the strongest in language I have encountered among the whole of his papers', was a deliberate attempt to force Portland's resignation, and compel Temple and Pitt to come to the rescue.[1]

The episode revealed the weak points in the position of both sides. The core of the king's predicament was the absence of an alternative administration as long as Pitt remained aloof: his

---

[1] Add. MS. 38716, f. 66; *Gentleman's magazine*, 1783, i, 534; Buckingham, i, 303–5; Fortescue, vi, p. xii; Auckland, i, 54–5; Pitt to Lady Chatham, 14 June, Stanhope, i, 125. A straightforward narrative of the affair is in *H.M.C. Dartmouth MSS.*, iii, 268–9: the one given in H. Walpole, *Last journals*, ii, 628–31 is seriously inaccurate.

opponents took comfort from the solidarity in their ranks at the first serious test, but could hardly fail to be weakened by this fresh demonstration of the king's enmity. In public the ministers affected great confidence. 'Charles Fox is in high spirits', reported Sir William Gordon: 'he says everywhere that he is now perfectly satisfied with His Royal Master's reception and he thinks that the Closet is now more in their favour.'[1] His private opinion, revealed to Northington, was more sober:

As to the opinion of our having gained strength by it, the only rational foundation for such an opinion is that this event has proved that there subsists no such understanding between the King and Lord Temple as to enable them to form an administration, because if there did, it is impossible but they must have seized an occasion in many respects so fortunate for them . . . In this sense . . . I think we may flatter ourselves that we are something stronger than we were. In every other view I own I think quite otherwise. The King has certainly carried one point against us, and the notoriety that he has done so may lead people to suppose that he might be successful in others . . .[2]

Both sides began regrouping. The ministers, though they can hardly have been deceived by the king's protestations of regard, may have hoped to turn them to advantage by taking them at their face value and pressing for patronage concessions. Northington's reaction to the unexpected reconciliation was to urge his colleagues to seek a complete understanding with the king, rather than one which 'appears to me only to reserve your dismission to a more favourable opportunity, and that at no distant period'.[3] On 8 July a meeting at Portland's house considered means of strengthening the coalition: a memorandum drawn up by George North noted that Lord Clarendon wanted 'something', Lord Wentworth 'wants anything excessively', Lord Audley, more specifically, wanted £500 p.a., and Lord Paget wanted an Earldom.[4] A few days later Portland raised the question of peerages once more

---

[1] Gordon to Lady Gower, 21 June, Granville MSS.   [2] Russell, ii, 115–16.
[3] Northington to Fox, 23 June, Add. MS. 47567, ff. 5–6.
[4] Portland MSS., Pw F 7230 & 7231.

with the king and received a flat refusal. The coalition leaders chose not to make an issue of it. Fox, confident of his ability to command a majority when the House of Commons reassembled, was determined not to give the king the slightest pretext to dismiss them during the recess: 'if ever there was a situation in which it was becoming to bear all that can be borne without absolute dishonour or immediate detriment to the country, I think ours is that situation.'[1]

One of the politicians whose adherence to the coalition might tip the scales was Lord Thurlow. He had been dismissed the Lord Chancellorship in April, but the fact that the Great Seal had been put into commission suggested that the door was not finally slammed. Thurlow's was a complex character. Affecting the bold and truculent manner of one indifferent to the consequences of his actions, he was in reality anxious to be on the winning side, and could play a timid and vacillating role as he did at the time of the Regency crisis in 1789. 'He wishes most eagerly to be restored', wrote Temple in July 1783.[2] Negotiations with the coalition seem to have been inaugurated by Richard Rigby, Thurlow's ally, and on 17 July Ashburton told Shelburne that the ministers entertained 'great hopes' of enlisting his support.[3] In exchange for his restoration to the Woolsack, Thurlow engaged to persuade the king to grant some peerages. The proposition was serious enough for Fox to sound out Loughborough's reaction to the suggestion that he should stand aside for Thurlow. Loughborough's assessment was judicious and, under the circumstances, remarkably fair:

The accession of Lord Thurlow gives you, in the first place, the use of his abilities. It secures Lord Weymouth, and it must attract Lord Gower. It presents an appearance of influence in the closet, and you are offered a proof of it by the disposal of some peerages. The advantage of the last point seems to me very questionable; for his influence, though employed for you, is not your

---

[1] Fox to Northington, 17 July; Fox to Ossory, 12 August; Russell, ii, 115 & 199.
[2] *H.M.C. Fortescue MSS.*, i, 214. The letter should be dated 21 July.   [3] Bowood MSS.

influence; and peerages which the administration could only obtain by his aid, will not add to the reputation of their strength . . . You then bring into your cabinet a temper which you have never yet tried in business, and which hitherto has been mostly employed to perplex and to censure the measures of those he acted with. You gain a powerful and, of course, a formidable ally; but are you clear that you will gain a hearty and cordial friend? . . . I cheerfully give you my explicit assent to any course you may think most conducive to the full establishment of the administration . . .[1]

The ministers may have been sceptical of Thurlow's ability to procure peerages, which, in the light of the king's attitude, appears an extraordinary claim, or they may have been unwilling to alienate Loughborough, whose contribution in counsel and debate was important.[2] Whatever the explanation, the negotiation fell through, and within a few days Thurlow was sounding out Pitt and Temple.

Their inability to obtain favours made it all the more necessary for ministers to exploit those offices under their command. Henry Dundas had retained his post as Lord Advocate, and in July was reported to be encouraging the belief among his Scottish friends that the ministers dared not dismiss him. On the 24th William Adam warned Portland of the danger of leaving him unmolested, and on 1 August Fox informed him that his services were no longer required. Henry Erskine, his successor, was not in Parliament. The open breach with Dundas may have done the coalition little direct harm, but it decreased whatever slight possibility remained of reaching an understanding with Pitt. That Fox still retained some hope of this is clear from his letter to Ossory on 9 September: 'if Pitt could be persuaded (but I despair of it) I am convinced if he could he would do more real service to the

---

[1] Loughborough to Fox, and Portland to Fox, Russell, ii, 204–7. The letters are undated, but the reference in Portland's letter to Clements establishes that it must have been written before 20 September. Since Thurlow was abroad from the first week in August until late October, I conclude that the negotiations probably took place in mid-July.

[2] Lord Sackville wrote to William Knox, 4 July: 'Lord Loughborough's conduct appears very able, and if this ministry stands it will be owing to his support in the House of Lords.' H.M.C. Various Collections, vol. vi, H. V. Knox MSS., 191.

country than any man ever did.' Immediately after the opening of the new session of Parliament he made fresh approaches to Pitt, which were at once repulsed and reported to the king by Temple.[1]

Perhaps the greatest comfort the ministers could draw from the summer recess was the harmony with which they had worked together. Charles Jenkinson and John Robinson claimed to detect deep dissensions within the administration, and exchanged avidly every rumour of discord they could come by. 'I hear . . . that they are not in love with their situation', hinted Robinson on 13 September. 'I am not surprised to hear they are not in love with their situation', replied Jenkinson dutifully on the 17th. On 4 November Jenkinson submitted 'evident symptoms' of schism: 'Fox wants to be himself at the head of the whole and to get rid of the Duke of Portland and Lord North.'[2] But those disagreements that did arise in the ministry were settled without difficulty.[3] 'Nothing can go on as well as we do among ourselves', Fox told Ossory on 9 September, an opinion confirmed from the other wing of the coalition a month later by Eden, not the least suspicious of men: 'in the meantime the principal branches of the coalition flourish together perfectly well, and there is a real cordiality and confidence through the whole set.'[4]

The coalition's adversaries started the summer in almost total disarray. Shelburne left for Spa before the session was over, and on his return retired ostentatiously to Bowood, taking no further part in the struggle: the death of Lord Ashburton in August and

[1] Portland MSS., Pw F 37; Fox to Dundas, 1 August, Melville MSS.; Russell, ii, 208; Fortescue, vi, no. 4520.

[2] Add. MS. 38567, ff. 153–4; Abergavenny MSS. 514 & 518. More rumours were reported on 24 September, 31 October and 7 November. H.M.C. Abergavenny MSS., 60–1; Add. MS. 38567, ff. 162–3.

[3] These were over the dismissal of Dundas, the appointment of Thomas Pelham to replace William Windham as Chief Secretary in Ireland, and the appointment of Lord Derby as Ashburton's successor in the Chancellorship of the Duchy of Lancaster. North to Eden, 27 August, Add. MS. 34419, f. 254; Eden to Loughborough, 30 August, Auckland, i, 59–61.

[4] Russell, ii, 208; Eden to Northington, 10 November, Add. MS. 33100, f. 391.

the growing blindness of Colonel Barré deprived him of two of his most trusted lieutenants. Richmond, after an abortive attempt to convince the House of Lords that the appointment of judges to the commission for holding the Great Seal constituted a threat to the independence of the judiciary, contemplated a withdrawal from politics to supervise the education of his nephew on the grand tour.[1] Camden, confessing himself 'quite at a loss what part to take', resolved the dilemma by not attending Parliament at all.[2]

Two of the ex-ministers had no such misgivings. Temple and Pitt had taken steps to concert plans immediately after Temple's return from Ireland.[3] Supremely confident that they were the king's 'only resource', they were determined to dictate their own terms. On Saturday, 19 July, Thurlow called on Pitt to assure him that the king *'had not altered his sentiments with regard to his present ministry'*, but that he had 'no insight' into the means of forming an alternative government. Pitt's reply was cool and guarded:

I stated in general, that if the King's feelings did not point strongly to a change, it was not what we sought; but that if they did, and we could form a permanent system, consistent with our principles, and on public grounds, we should not decline it. I reminded him how much I was personally pledged to parliamentary reform.

Temple, with whom Pitt discussed the significance of the conversation, agreed that they could afford to be patient. While not doubting the genuineness of the king's wish to get rid of his ministers, he advised caution:

If this is to be a negotiation, let it be avowed . . . the particulars can be settled only personally with the King; and you sufficiently remember what passed between Lord Shelburne and Lord Rockingham in March 1782 not to be very cautious upon anything which may give that light which must be the consequence and not the cause of a negotiation . . .

[1] Debrett, xi, 210–35; A. Olson, *The radical duke* (1961), 197–202.
[2] Camden to Richmond, undated, Camden MSS. The letter was probably written on 1 June 1783.   [3] Lord Stanhope, *Miscellanies*, 2nd series (1872), 22–3.

In other words, even those champions who were to rescue the king from the bondage of the coalition accepted the Rockingham view of the proper constitutional practice between monarch and minister.

On Tuesday 22 July Pitt dined with Thurlow, expecting the conversation to be renewed, but nothing transpired, and a few days later Thurlow left for the continent. By 10 September, Pitt was convinced that no change would take place before Parliament reassembled, and embarked upon his own continental trip with Edward James Eliot and William Wilberforce. To Temple he explained:

I am still inclined to believe . . . that the King does not like to hazard dismissing the present ministry till he has found some ostensible ground of complaint, or till he sees the disposition of Parliament next session; and there is probably also some view, as we have for some time supposed, to the terms on which new arrangements would be formed. This will make the opening of the session of infinite importance and delicacy . . . I am just returned from St. James's . . . The King was gracious as usual, and he enquired as to the time of my stay in a manner which I rather thought significant.[1]

---

[1] This correspondence between Pitt and Temple is printed in Lord Stanhope, *Miscellanies*, 2nd series, 22–35. It is also included in *H.M.C. Fortescue MSS.*, i, 214–20, together with letters on the same subject to William Grenville.

CHAPTER 6

THE INDIA BILL:
1, THE HOUSE OF COMMONS

Although the ministers would have preferred to avoid contentious matters after their experience over the prince's establishment, there was one subject that demanded their attention as soon as the session was over—the condition of the East India Company, exercising responsibility for the government of more than twenty million people in an area five times the size of England and Wales. The previous reorganisation of the Company's affairs, undertaken by North's Regulating Act of 1773, had proved seriously defective. The Governor-General, Warren Hastings, had quarrelled bitterly with his council, and had defied several attempts to secure his recall; the working of the new Supreme Court had been far from satisfactory; and the most alarming convulsions in the Madras Presidency had resulted in the imprisonment of the Governor, Lord Pigot. At home, what control the government could exercise through the Court of Directors was vitiated by the Court of Proprietors, which retained the final power of decision and pursued an independent line.

In 1778 John Robinson, Secretary to the Treasury, drew up plans for a wide extension of the government's powers over the Company. But pressure of work and an understandable reluctance to add to his troubles induced Lord North to postpone any decision in 1779, and again in 1780. In the meantime the Maratha War, followed by the attack of Haidar Ali in 1780, as well as casting doubt on the ability of the Company to defend its possessions, threw its finances into complete confusion. In 1781 the government once more shied away from the problem, contenting itself with extending the Company's charter for ten years.

The initiative in Indian affairs, abandoned by the government, was taken up in 1781 by the two parliamentary committees, whose reports during the next two years focused attention on the problems and personalities involved. But the reports, and the prosecutions that followed in their wake, were no substitute for a thorough review of the administrative arrangements, and neither the Rockingham nor the Shelburne government undertook that. The king's speech at the beginning of the session in December 1782 expressed the hope that Parliament would 'frame some fundamental laws' for India, but the ministry expired before Dundas was able to present his proposals.[1] The inter-ministerium of March 1783 found the Company in a most parlous state, and emergency measures were rushed through as soon as the coalition took office to stave off immediate financial disaster.

The coalition was therefore obliged to grasp the nettle that previous governments had left alone. Fox was under no illusions about the magnitude of the task: it was, he told Northington in July, 'of a very delicate nature', and would produce formidable opposition.[2] Preliminary discussions began in August. 'Burke is to draw out on paper some sort of plan', reported Sir Gilbert Elliot, 'which Fox is to consider as soon as possible. Fox says he is determined to do the business immediately after the meeting of Parliament, but I think it may not be ripe.'[3] But Burke made rapid progress. By the beginning of September the proposal to replace the Court of Directors by a new commission was under active discussion,[4] and on 20 September Portland was able to communicate the main outline of the scheme to the duke of

---

[1] In April 1783 Dundas moved for leave to bring in a bill and outlined his scheme: its main feature was to strengthen the Governor-General's position against his council. Though leave was granted, Dundas did not pursue the matter. Debrett, ix, 608–13.

[2] Russell, ii, 119.

[3] Elliot to Lady Elliot, 20 August, Minto MSS., M. 17. Burke's collaborators in the business seem to have been Francis and Elliot. Arthur Pigot helped with the drafting.

[4] Fox replied on 3 September to an appeal from Sandwich that he could give no undertaking to support any candidate for the Court of Directors since the whole matter was under review. Sandwich MSS.

Manchester, inviting him to succeed Hastings as Governor-General.[1] Political control of the Company's affairs was to be vested in seven commissioners, members of Parliament, appointed in the first instance by Parliament and subsequently by the crown, and holding office for not less than three nor more than five years: commercial control was to be exercised by eight (later changed to nine) assistant commissioners. The ministers were determined that the measure should be bold:

It is so far advanced as that it may be considered as a measure upon which the existence of the present administration will be fairly staked, and may be risked with credit; for though it is strong and unprecedented, and may wear the appearance of violence and injustice, the evil which it is to remedy is grown so rank, all palliatives have proved so ineffectual, the cure is of so much importance to the existence and character of the nation, that I pant for the experiment, on the success of which the happiness of millions, and the restoration of our national character, seems essentially to depend.

It has been suggested that the main features of the bill derived from the Rockinghams' need to demonstrate consistency with their former declarations.[2] This seems to me doubtful. They had entered a protest in the Lords' Journals against North's Regulating Act of 1773 complaining of the violation of the Company's charter in such emphatic terms that a rigorous consistency would have tied their hands completely. In any case, politicians are often less sensitive to charges of inconsistency than commentators feel they should be: when the accusation was made by William Grenville on the first reading of the bill, it was turned aside by Lord John Cavendish and Fox without embarrassment on the grounds that too much had happened since 1773 to make the circumstances comparable.[3] It seems more probable that the main features of the plan were a direct response to the recent events in

---

[1] *H.M.C. 8th Report, appendix*, 132–3.

[2] L. S. Sutherland, *The East India Company in eighteenth-century politics* (1952), 398.

[3] Debrett, xii, 67–92. The argument about the 1773 protest was of course of no consequence to North, whose consent was necessary before the bill could be proposed. The evolution of Burke's views between 1773 and 1783 is studied by P. J. Marshall in *The impeachment of Warren Hastings* (1965).

India: it is impossible to read Burke's speech of 1 December, the most sustained defence of the measure, without recognising the tremendous impact that the revelations contained in the reports had had upon his mind. He believed that, with a change of personnel, the Indian side of the 1773 arrangements might yet work satisfactorily. But the inadequacy of the powers of the British government had been repeatedly demonstrated: ministers could hardly fail to be impressed by the inability of successive governments to secure Hastings's recall. In addition the harmful consequences to India of four British governments in just over a year was apparent to everyone. The basic proposal of the bill was therefore to transfer responsibility from the Company to the new commissioners in order to give direct control, while providing for some continuity of policy by granting the commissioners security of tenure for at least three years. The latter proposal had the additional advantage that it helped to rebut the charge that the bill would increase the influence of the Crown.[1] One objection to the proposal, advanced by Jenkinson, was that the commissioners might well find themselves out of sympathy with the government of the day,[2] but at the time the bill was framed Burke was more concerned with the danger that frequent changes of government would leave India with a fluctuating policy, or none at all.

Two other principles of considerable importance emerge from Burke's defence of the bill. The first is a clear statement of public accountability:

All political power which is set over men . . . ought to be some way or other exercised ultimately for their benefit . . . To whom, then, would I make the East India Company accountable? Why, to Parliament, to be sure; to Parliament, from whom their trust was derived; to Parliament, which alone is

---

[1] Loughborough commented to Eden before Parliament met: 'You will observe that the seven trustees are during good behaviour; that is a very favourite but a very difficult point . . . if it were carried it is a great point, but for that reason I think it will fail.' Auckland, i, 61.

[2] Quoted by L. S. Sutherland, *op. cit.*, 400–1.

capable of comprehending the magnitude of its object, and its abuse; and alone capable of an effectual legislative remedy.

Secondly, Burke strove to lift the level of debate from arguments about property and patronage to an examination of the welfare of the subject people: 'My sole question, on each clause of the bill, amounts to this: is the measure proposed required by the necessities of India? I cannot consent totally to lose sight of the real wants of the people who are the objects of it, and to hunt after every matter of party squabble that may be started on the several provisions.'

These statements of Burke's basic principles suggest that some of the criticisms levelled at his proposals have been beside the point. It has been objected that the bill was essentially negative in character, that it was more concerned to curb abuses than to provide for strong government. But that is what it was intended to do. Burke did not mean it to lay the foundations for a great and vigorous expansion of British power, but to ensure that those territories already in British hands were governed with some regard to the interests of the native population. Administrators criticised it as hampering the government in India. That was its intention. When the duke of Manchester suggested that what India needed was a 'temporary dictatorial power', Fox's reply was cool,[1] and in his speech of 1 December he repudiated any such solution, attacking Dundas's proposals for strengthening the position of the Governor-General:

The learned gentleman's bill afforded the most extensive latitude for malversation; the bill before you guards against it with all imaginable precaution. Every line . . . presumes the possibility of bad administration, for every word breathes suspicion. This bill supposes that men are but men; it confides in no integrity, it trusts no character; it inculcates the wisdom of a jealousy of power, and annexes responsibility not only to every *action*, but even to the *inaction* of those who are to dispense it . . .[2]

[1] *H.M.C. 8th Report, appendix*, 134, 136.
[2] Debrett, xii, 291.

It was not, therefore, that Burke failed to realise what was needed, but that his aims were different from those of his critics. Dr P. J. Marshall, in a notable phrase, has referred to the impeachment of Hastings as in some respects 'one of the most spectacular crises of conscience through which an imperial power has ever passed'.[1] The struggle over the India bill was an earlier manifestation of that crisis. It is certainly difficult to believe that Fox was insincere when he wrote to Mrs Armistead:

They are endeavouring to make a great cry against us, and will I am afraid succeed in making us very unpopular in the city. However, I know I am right and must bear the consequences, though I dislike unpopularity as much as any man . . . If I had considered nothing but keeping my power, it was the safest way to leave things as they are, or to propose some trifling alteration, and I am not at all ignorant of the political danger which I run by this bold measure; but whether I succeed or no, I shall always be glad that I attempted, because I know that I have done no more than I was bound to do, in risking my power and that of my friends when the happiness of so many millions is at stake. I write very gravely, because the amazing abuse which is heaped upon me makes me feel so. I have the weakness of disliking abuse, but that weakness shall never prevent me from doing what I think right.[2]

The accusation made against him during the debate, and repeated by historians, was that his main concern was to seize the patronage of the Company for his party. That it was no consideration would be difficult to credit: Burke, in the House of Commons, did not deny that there would be party advantage through the bill.[3] The shortage of places as a consequence of the economical reform campaign and the king's refusal to grant peerages meant that the patronage would be extremely welcome to the coalition. But there was nothing in the parliamentary situation to justify such a risk as the bill represented. The ministers' majority was ample for normal purposes: Fox, in July, had looked upon the House of Commons as their strong place, and later events

---

[1] *The impeachment of Warren Hastings*, 180. I must, however, acknowledge that Dr Marshall's interpretation differs from mine.
[2] Add. MS. 47570, f. 153. Part of the letter is printed in Russell, ii, 219–20, where the addressee is coyly described as 'a most intimate friend'.   [3] Debrett, xii, 263.

justified his confidence. The suggestion that they hoped to fortify their position and hold it against the king can hardly be seriously maintained[1]: the seven commissioners who were to be entrusted with power were already staunch supporters of the administration. Sir Gilbert Elliot, one of the nominated commissioners, put the matter in fair perspective when he wrote to his brother: 'There never was a measure taken so beneficial to so many millions of unhappy people as this one. This is one good reason for my liking a part in it. There are many lesser ones, amongst which a great patronage and probably a handsome salary are two . . .'[2] Although Burke had succeeded in instilling into his colleagues something of his own moral fervour, he had not turned them into angels.

The scheme, with its considerable political risks, was not adopted by the coalition without misgivings. Loughborough, on whose shoulders the burden of the defence in the House of Lords would fall, expressed grave doubts, and throughout November there were repeated rumours that Stormont would resign, or at least vote against the bill.[3] Lord North, consulted at an early stage, gave his approval, but continued uneasy: Loughborough found him 'seriously alarmed', but 'very little disposed to communicate that alarm to others'.[4] North's curiously passive role in the whole affair was much commented on at the time:

[1] It is put forward in Stanhope, i, 139. Richard Pares, *King George III and the politicians*, (1953), 127, commented that such a view 'exaggerated the importance of India or of patronage altogether', while Lecky, *History of England in the eighteenth century* (1878–90), iv, 292 dismissed it as 'grotesquely absurd'.

[2] 12 December 1783, Minto MSS., M. 1260.

[3] Auckland, i, 61; Baring to Shelburne, 20 November, Bowood MSS.; Macdonald to Lady Gower, undated, but probably 24 & 25 November, Granville MSS.; Chandos to Flood, 26 November, Add. MS. 22930, f. 133; P. Yorke to Hardwicke, 28 November, Add. MS. 35381, f. 168; Rachel Lloyd to Lady Gower, 29 November, Granville MSS.; Sir T. Dundas to Erskine, 4 December, quoted in A. Fergusson, *Henry Erskine* (1882).

[4] Portland, in his letter to Manchester of 20 September, emphasised North's concurrence. John Nicholls's evidence in *Recollections, and reflections* i, 54–6, that North did not see the bill until it was completed is obviously unreliable, though the remark he attributes to North has the characteristic flavour: 'he thought it a good receipt to knock up an administration.'

'you would be astonished', wrote Lord Midleton during the debates, 'to see him sit by and permit his colleagues to move the whole of this business which is in his department.'[1] North was, of course, never anxious to exert himself unless it was unavoidable, but on this occasion there is evidence that he was in very poor health and it may be doubted whether he would have been able to steer the bill through. He was absent through illness from the debate of 18 November, and was forced to leave the House in the middle of the debate on 1 December: a fortnight later he was reported to have a 'dangerous leg' which some thought might prove fatal.[2] But his approval of the bill, with whatever private reservations, was signalled by George North seconding Fox's motion for leave to proceed.

Very little information about the proposals seems to have seeped out to the opposition. During the last week of October Temple held a 'grand congress' at Stowe, but the key figure, William Pitt, was still absent, and no definite plans seem to have emerged.[3] Macdonald reported to Lady Gower on 31 October that 'nothing hostile to our present governors has been concerted in the course of the vacation', and three days later Robinson was still lamenting 'the want of *some head* with practicable principles'.[4] The greatest comfort to the ministry's enemies was fresh evidence that the king's detestation of the coalition was as strong as ever. To Temple he wrote on 7 November asking to be informed if any overtures were made towards Pitt, and on the 13th, he unburdened himself to Robinson, whom he passed on horseback, in a remarkable outburst:

'Mr. Robinson, you are always the same, you do not change with the times, you are always steady.' I bowed and answered, 'I hoped I should ever continue to

---

[1] Midleton to Thomas Pelham, 30 November, Add. MS. 33128, f. 238.
[2] Grantham to Hardwicke, 18 November, Add. MS. 35621, f. 197; Debrett, xii, 303; Orde to Shelburne, 16 December, Bowood MSS.
[3] Sir William Gordon to Lady Gower, 22 October, Granville MSS.; Pitt to Temple, 30 October, Stanhope, *Miscellanies*, 2nd series, 36.
[4] Granville MSS.; Robinson to Jenkinson, 2 November, Add. MS. 38567, f. 160.

be and act so.' His Majesty said, 'Yes, you always do,' and turning his head back to me as he was then riding on faster, His Majesty called out, 'These are bad times, bad times indeed,' and then bowed to me, and pushed on in a canter.[1]

The new session of Parliament opened on 11 November auspiciously for the coalition. The address of thanks passed *nem. con.* in both houses after nothing more than mild skirmishing. In the House of Lords only Temple ventured criticism, drawing attention to the depressed state of public credit and warning ministers that he would 'watch their conduct': Pitt, in the House of Commons, dismissed the definitive treaties as a 'mere transcript' of the provisional articles and demanded a deep and searching reform of Indian affairs, but was moderate in tone.[2] Neither Shelburne nor Gower made any appearance in the Lords, nor Henry Dundas in the Commons: 'the threatened opposition is disjointed', observed Walpole, 'and half of its expected leaders did not appear'.[3] People were 'hopeless of the future', thought Thurlow.[4] In short, only Pitt could fire the signal to attack, and he was biding his time.

Charles Fox did not altogether share the jubilation of his supporters. On 17 November he wrote to Burgoyne in the sombre mood that prevails on the eve of battle:

I have but too much reason to think that, upon our India measure . . . we shall meet with great embarrassments and difficulties. The variety of private interests that will militate against us can not fail of making it a most tempting opportunity to opposition . . . You will of course consider this as said to yourself only and not let it be known that I am holding croaking language . . .[5]

The following day, in an excited House, the public gallery filled to overflowing, he moved for leave to bring in the bill.[6] He made

---

[1] Fortescue, vi, no. 4520; Memorandum by Robinson, Add. MS. 37835, f. 203.

[2] Debrett, xiv, 6–9; xii, 7–11. Pitt's restraint may have prompted Fox to make him the offer two days later which was rejected.   [3] Walpole to Mann, 12 November.

[4] Thurlow to Gower, undated, Granville MSS. The letter refers to the address of thanks and was clearly written soon after the 11th.   [5] Add. MS. 47568, f. 206.

[6] There were, in fact, two bills. The first contained the main administrative provisions while the second proposed a reform of land tenure.

much of the need for reform, admitted on all sides—'the business forced itself upon him and upon the nation': unless the government intervened, the Company would be driven into bankruptcy. Pitt, in reply, professed to reserve judgement, but deplored the abrogation of chartered rights and dismissed Fox's plea of necessity as 'the argument of tyrants': 'the right honourable secretary was willing to secure to the Gentoos their natural rights, but let him take care that he did not destroy the liberties of Englishmen.' Fox's system he denounced as 'nothing more on one side than absolute despotism and on the other side the most gross corruption'.[1] He concluded by moving for a call of the House in a fortnight, a proposal passed *nem. con.* by the members already present, but received without enthusiasm in deepest Somerset, where India seemed remote indeed, and country gentlemen thought the new year soon enough to turn their attention to parliamentary affairs.[2]

The opposition was in no hurry to bring matters to a conclusion. They needed time to rally their supporters and to whip up opinion in the country. 'I do not see Lord Tyrconnel in town, nor

[1] Debrett, xii, 29–55. Lecky commented on the language employed by Pitt and Thurlow that there were 'few things in the history of political exaggeration more extravagant than these assertions, and it may very reasonably be doubted whether such men as Pitt and Thurlow can for a moment have believed them'. The charge has been repeated more recently by C. S. Philips, 'The East India Company Interest and the English Government 1783–4', *Transactions of Royal Historical Society*, xx, 88. But it is perhaps unfair. Fox's opponents were as vehement in their private correspondence as in their public utterances, and their indignation was shared by many others. Francis Baring told Shelburne it was 'the boldest and most artful effort ever attempted by any subject since the restoration', and Daniel Pulteney thought it 'the most barefaced violent act since the Act of Settlement'. 20 November, Bowood MSS.; *H.M.C. Rutland MSS.*, iii, 71. One must bear in mind the enormous respect that the century had for property, and its conviction that the security of property was one, if not the chief, object of government. That the state, instead of jealously preserving property rights, should itself infringe them seemed to many people subversive of the established order of society. I think they were right.

[2] John Acland wrote to William Dickinson: 'what the devil does the *stripling* mean by giving people the trouble to dance at his heels . . .' 23 November, Dickinson MSS. The call of the House to ensure attendance was a procedure dating back at least to the sixteenth century: the last call was in 1836. This call does not seem to have been followed up, and the House did not in fact meet on 2 December. *Commons' journals*, 39, 731; J. Redlich, *The procedure of the House of Commons* (1908), ii, 112–14.

Pochin, nor Sir Henry Peyton,' wrote Pitt to Rutland, 'can you apply to any of them?' Their adversaries were equally active. 'I wish you could speak with Frank Charteris', Sir Thomas Dundas asked Henry Erskine, 'as he is a little difficult to manage'.[1] The first reading of the bill on the 20th went through fairly quietly. William Grenville, Lord Temple's brother, leading for the opposition, criticised the violation of charters, reminded the Rockinghams of their protests against former measures, and begged for more time to consider the matter, but did not push it to a vote. Jenkinson's intervention against the bill caused some anxiety in coalition circles, not for its debating effect, for he was a notoriously poor speaker, muffled and contorted, but because it was assumed that he would reflect the true opinion of the king. One constitutional point of some significance emerged from the exchanges. Pitt's immediate response on the 18th had been to denounce the vast increase in the power of the crown that it would bring. This produced a good deal of confusion, since many people found it hard to understand how a measure that added dangerously to the power of the crown could also be said to render the king a cypher,[2] and subsequent speakers were at pains to point out that ministers would be endowed with powers that they might use against the crown. Fox, in the debate, deprecated any 'egregious' distinction between royal and ministerial power: while not, of course, denying that ministers alone could be censured or punished, he denied any division of powers. At most times, when ministers were approved of and supported by the crown the distinction was immaterial, but in moments of constitutional

---

[1] 22 November, *Correspondence between the Rt. Hon. William Pitt and Charles, duke of Rutland*, ed. Lord Mahon (1890), 4–5; 21 November, A. Fergusson, *Henry Erskine*.

[2] There is a nice specimen of political innocence in a letter from Rachel Lloyd to Lady Gower, 29 November, Granville MSS., relating a conversation with George Selwyn, a king's man *à l'outrance*: 'I have but one topic to write upon, the East India Bill—nobody talks of anything else . . . I told him I was for this bill passing, and supposed he would be so for the same reason I was, which was that it would restore to the crown some of the influence that these same gentlemen had taken away. He said if it would give influence to the crown he certainly should be for it, but it would not do that, it would only give power to the present set of men, and wondered that I should be for it.'

conflict, as over the question of peerages, it became of acute importance. Fox's claim that the ministers should exercise all the powers of the crown may seem bold, but it is hard to believe that even the eighteenth-century system could have functioned for long on the contrary assumption.

At this state the opposition in the House of Commons had had little success. Pitt still believed that the bill might be rejected by the House of Commons, but Archibald Macdonald, eager for the fray, was dismayed at the lack of vigour, and warned Lady Gower that the Commons would not save them. Fox was hoping for a majority of between 100 and 150.[1] But outside Parliament, the opposition's campaign was beginning to get under way. On 21 November there was a very full attendance at a Court of Proprietors of the Company. Sir Henry Fletcher, the chairman of the Company, and Jacob Wilkinson, who had supported Fox, were severely censured, and after a seven hour debate a motion by Governor Johnstone for a petition against the bill was carried unanimously. Fletcher was obliged to submit on the 24th the proprietors' petition, complaining that the bill authorised a 'total confiscation' of their property, and the following day a petition from the Directors declared that the financial position of the Company was by no means as desperate as had been implied. On the 26th Fletcher tendered his resignation as chairman, and was replaced by Nathaniel Smith, who had taken an active part against the bill.[2] Meanwhile the opposition began to enlist the aid of the press. The *Morning Herald*, 22 November, warned its readers that if the bill passed, Fox would be 'the most dangerous subject in Europe', and that his influence, even out of office, would be greater than that of the king and the whole administration. This was followed up by further attacks on the 24th, and in

---

[1] Pitt to Rutland, 22 November, *Pitt–Rutland correspondence*, 4; 21 November, Granville MSS.; Fox to Ossory, 21 November, Russell, ii, 215. Macdonald was perhaps still smarting from the fact that the House had refused to hear him on the 18th. *Gentleman's magazine*, 1783, ii, 1053.

[2] Debrett, xii, 95–9; *London Chronicle*, 20/22 and 25/27 November.

the *Whitehall Evening Post*, 22/25 November. The same week saw the first of James Sayers's remarkably effective series of caricatures: Fox was portrayed making off with the India House and trampling underfoot a list of the Directors; a fortnight later came the devastating 'Carlo Khan's Triumphal Entry into Leadenhall Street'—one of the most influential political caricatures ever published.[1] 'The thing begins to work very much beyond what I expected', confided Macdonald: 'we have taken all the pains that a few scattered people can to expose the true meaning of this plot. I think it is now understood pretty generally. Our spirits rise a good deal'.[2] Slowly the leaders of opposition coordinated their activities. Richmond, Temple and Thurlow dined with the duke of Chandos and agreed as a first step to try to protract the debates until after Christmas: although Pitt was prevented by a debate from joining them the significant thing was that he was now willing to cooperate.[3] 'Things are ripening very fast to overthrow the present administration', conjectured Francis Baring: 'if my information is true, the negotiations going forward must be with Pitt and his friends.[4]

On 27 November, the second reading came on in the House of Commons, and the bill's opponents could no longer defer a trial of strength. Their tactics for the debate were argued out in a meeting at Pitt's house in the morning, where the Lowthers and the Grenvilles were joined by Henry Dundas, just arrived from Scotland, Thomas Powys, an independent member and a valuable catch, Lord Apsley and Macdonald. It was agreed that they would get greater support on a motion for the adjournment than on a direct negative, and that they should reserve their grand onslaught for the committee stage.[5] The debate opened with the

---

[1] M. D. George, *English political caricature to 1792* (1959), 169 & Plates 65 & 66.
[2] Macdonald to Lady Gower, Granville MSS. It can be dated from internal evidence as written on 24 November.   [3] Chandos to Flood, 26 November, Add. MS. 22930, f. 133.
[4] Baring to Shelburne, 27 November, Bowood MSS.
[5] Macdonald to Lady Gower, 28 November, Granville MSS. The *Morning Chronicle*, 15 December, in a hit at Powys's somewhat ostentatious independency, suggested him for the place of 'Country Gentleman to the Court'.

presentation of a petition from the City of London expressing its fears of so unconstitutional a measure; next, counsel for the proprietors and directors addressed the House for some three and a half hours, calling witnesses to support their financial statement. A move by Sir James Lowther and Lloyd Kenyon further to protract matters by demanding that the evidence submitted should be read was quashed by the Speaker. When Fox was at length enabled to put his case, he professed surprise that the opposition had concentrated its attention on the Company's financial position, which he regarded as the weakest part of their case. He challenged Dundas, as the author of the previous measure presented to the House, to explain how any effective reform could be instituted without in some way infringing the Company's charter—a challenge that Dundas prudently declined to meet. Pitt, in reply, reiterated that the bill was 'one of the boldest, most unprecedented, most desperate and alarming attempts at the exercise of tyranny that ever disgraced the annals of this or any other country', accused Fox of trying to impose upon the House a financial statement 'every way absurd and erroneous', and moved the adjournment. One feature of the debate was the return to active service of Lord North, not perhaps at his best, but still formidable: the constitution of the Company, he argued, was admitted on all sides to be defective, while talk of 'confiscation' was ridiculous when the Company was to retain its commercial monopoly and the profits thereof. Dundas took no part in the debate, and the best supporting speech on the opposition side came from Archibald Macdonald, who declared that the bill 'left the Crown indeed where it was, but placed the sceptre in another hand'.[1] But when, at 4.30 in the morning, the House divided, the motion for the adjournment was defeated by 229 votes to 120.[2]

[1] The *Whitehall Evening Post*, 27/29 November also thought highly of his speech, calling it 'by far the ablest . . . for the adjournment'. But it may not have been unsolicited testimony.

[2] Debrett, xii, 112–203.

Fox had won a splendid triumph. 'Mr. Pitt did not succeed so well as he usually does in contradicting Mr. Fox's observations upon the Company's accounts', admitted Philip Yorke, who had from the beginning taken a decided stand against the bill, and Macdonald agreed that 'the debate was not well managed according to my humble opinion on our part'.[1] Fox's friends were correspondingly jubilant. Rigby was 'in raptures' with his speech, and Burgoyne, who had come over from Ireland to give his vote, reported to the Lord-Lieutenant:

He went through a dissection article by article of this complicated and artful statement in a manner that did wonderful service to his cause, mingling the most convincing reasoning with a knowledge and accuracy of figures that would have made strangers believe he had been educated in the bank . . . The debate was really ill supported on the other side . . . Our friends are in the greatest spirits, the most sanguine not having expected so great a majority; the opposition are much depressed and seem now to place their whole hopes in the House of Lords.[2]

There were good reasons for the satisfaction which Fox felt. He had demonstrated his superiority in a field where Pitt was reputed to be most expert—in the command and exposition of financial detail. He had got the majority of over one hundred that he had hoped for. He had received strong support both from the independent members of the House of Commons,[3] and from the members in the India interest, influenced perhaps by the news received a few days before of serious defeats sustained by British forces in India at the hands of Tippoo,

[1] Yorke to Hardwicke, 28 November, Add. MS. 35381, f. 168; Macdonald to Lady Gower, 28 November, Granville MSS.

[2] Rachel Lloyd to Lady Gower, 29 November, Granville MSS.; Burgoyne to Northington, 28 November, Add. MS. 33100, f. 423.

[3] Macdonald told Lady Gower: 'The Cocoa-Tree people, such as Sir William Dolben, were chiefly against us.' The Cocoa-Tree was a club in Pall Mall with Tory-Independent associations. B. Lillywhite, *London coffee houses* (1963), No. 262; *Survey of London*, ed. F. H. W. Sheppard (1960), xxx, 461–3. Twenty-seven county members voted with the coalition, twenty against.

who had just succeeded his father Haidar Ali as the ruler of Mysore.[1]

The opposition in the House of Commons never recovered from the disaster of the second reading debate. For the 1st December they had planned a 'great battery' on the motion to go into committee on the bill, and Powys opened for them with an effective speech, insisting on the dangers to the constitution. But they were confronted on the other side by an even greater battery, Edmund Burke in full spate, dwarfing all other contributions in an enormous three-hour survey of India and her problems and culminating in a sustained panegyric on Fox. Even Fox's summing-up of the debate, itself a good example of his brilliant technique, paled into insignificance beside this gigantic oration.[2] Government increased its majority to 114, dividing 217 against 103.

The committee stages of the bill went through uneventfully.

---

[1] *Morning Chronicle* and *Morning Herald*, 22 November contained accounts of Tippoo's successes. See also *Fort-William–India House Correspondence*, ed. C. H. Philips and B. B. Misra, xv, 197–8.

Well over half of the 'India interest' supported the bill. The precise definition and extent of this interest is, of course, difficult to decide. C. H. Philips, *The East India Company 1784–1834* (1940), appendix i, identified fifty-eight members of Parliament as belonging to the interest. This is probably too high, though the estimate of thirty-two members, made in the *House of Commons 1754–1790*, i, 152 seems to me a little low. Another estimate is made by Gerrit P. Judd IV, *Members of Parliament 1734–1832* (1955), appendices 17 & 18. My own calculation is thirty-six, thirteen of whom were or had been Directors of the Company.

Nor can one achieve complete accuracy in the matter of voting. There is a division list for the second reading in the *Political magazine*, 1783, 5–7, which includes further details of the opposition vote on the second and third divisions. But the most complete list of voting on all three divisions was compiled by John Robinson and is in the Abergavenny MSS.; it is referred to in Laprade, 54. The lists need to be compared carefully. My calculation of the division on the second reading is Government 19, Opposition 9, absent 8, as follows: GOVERNMENT: Cockburn*, P. Cust*, G. Graham, G. Dempster*, H. Fletcher*, R. Gregory*, Hotham, Purling*, E. Monckton, T. B. Rous*, C. W. B. Rouse, J. M. Smith, R. Smith, Stephenson*, Strachey, G. Steward, R. Walpole, J. Webb, J. Wilkinson*; OPPOSITION: J. Baring, G. Johnstone, J. Macpherson, Pardoe, S. Smith*, F. Sykes, Townson*, R. Palk, Wraxall; ABSENT: Barwell, Benfield, Durand, Farrer, James*, Stratton, T. Rumbold*, W. R. Rumbold. Those marked with an asterisk were or had been Directors of the Company.

[2] Wraxall, an opponent, wrote: 'If I were compelled to name the finest composition pronounced in the House of Commons during the whole time that I remained a member of that assembly from 1780 to 1794 I should select this speech of Burke.' Wraxall, iii, 173.

On 3 December Fox revealed the names of the directors and the assistant directors, and it was agreed that they should hold office for four years.[1] None of the main opposition speakers took part in the discussions. 'The opposition in the House of Commons were so humbled by their two defeats', wrote Walpole, 'that though Mr. Pitt had declared he would contest every clause in the Committee . . . he slunk from the contest, and all the blanks were filled up without obstruction'. Francis Baring, too, found Pitt's absence remarkable 'as I understood that every means was to have been taken to prevent the Bill from getting through the Lords before the holidays'.[2]

The final debate, on the third reading, was vigorous but unsensational, being left mainly to the supporting speakers. John Wilkes emerged to testify to the respect he had always felt for the ancient constitution, now threatened by this monster; John Scott, later Lord Eldon, ransacked history and literature in defiance of the bill; and John Lee, the Attorney-General, com-

---

[1] The Directors were to be Lord Fitzwilliam, Frederick Montagu, Lord Lewisham, George North, Sir Gilbert Elliot, Sir Henry Fletcher and Robert Gregory. The names of the 9 assistant Directors are given in Debrett, xii, 323: they had all been Directors of the Company.

Fox has been much criticised for not attempting to disarm his opponents by nominating persons other than supporters. Indeed, J. H. Rose, *William Pitt and national revival* (1911), 146, argued that 'the appointment of seven pronounced partisans . . . wrecked the measure'. I am very sceptical whether, at this late stage of the controversy, Fox's opponents would have declared themselves disarmed. In point of fact there was hardly any criticism of the nominations either in the House or in the newspapers, though there was a little ribaldry at the expense of George North. Since the point of having Directors in Parliament was to ensure direct responsibility, it would have been quixotic to have appointed persons hostile to the proposed reform, and had he done so Fox would certainly have been accused of proselytising. Rose added that Fox's four supporters were 'better known at Brookes' Club than at the India House'. Since Fletcher and Gregory had both been Chairmen of the Company, this is a little hard to believe. Fitzwilliam's character was admitted on all sides, and Montagu was a respected Lord of the Treasury: North's three supporters included a future President of the India Board and a future Governor-General; George North himself was a perfectly competent man. Thurlow dismissed them as 'four gentlemen to be named by Mr. Fox and three persons whom nobody calls gentlemen by Lord North', but Sir Joseph Yorke, a less violent partisan, told his brother that 'the choice of Directors meets with pretty general approbation'. Thurlow to Gower, undated, Granville MSS.; 8 December, Add. MS. 35372, f. 344.

[2] Walpole to Mann, 5 December; Baring to Shelburne, 4 December, Bowood MSS.

mitted a monumental indiscretion: his nonchalant description of a charter as 'a skin of parchment with a waxed seal at the corner' provided the opposition with ammunition for weeks.[1] The division, 208–102 in favour of the ministry, was the smallest on the bill, and suggests that some members were already weary of the arguments.[2]

The *Morning Chronicle*, 4 December, found the collapse of the opposition strange:

> There scarcely ever has occurred, in our acquaintance with parliamentary business, an instance of a bill that had been so violently opposed in the House on its first and second reading as the India Bill, being treated in the Committee with such candour and moderation on all sides. It seemed yesterday to be a kind of honourable contest between the Minister and Opposition, which should act most fairly . . .

But the conduct of the opposition was neither so generous nor so unintelligible as the *Morning Chronicle* believed. After their early disappointments in the House of Commons, they had turned their attention to more hopeful ways of overthrowing the coalition.

---

[1] The best answer to Lee's gaffe came from Boswell, who was reported to have asked: 'what was the great harm of hanging an Attorney-General? an hanged Attorney-General was only a carcase dangling at the end of a rope.' Debrett, xii, 415.

[2] Debrett, xii, 352–404.

CHAPTER 7

THE INDIA BILL:
2, THE HOUSE OF LORDS

As it became increasingly clear that the India bill would not be defeated in the House of Commons, the ministry's opponents began to ponder alternative lines of action. Many suggestions were canvassed. There was the possibility of employing the royal veto, in abeyance since 1707. But apart from the obvious constitutional objections, such an action would leave the ministry in power, and undoubtedly enraged: 'nobody who prefers a calm to a storm' would advise that policy, thought Lord Clarendon.[1] A better possibility was the dismissal of ministers as soon as the bill passed the House of Commons, followed by an immediate dissolution of Parliament. But there could be no guarantee of success. Although governments won eighteenth-century elections, time was needed to make the necessary arrangements: if the new ministers waited to allow patrons to be closeted and their terms ascertained, the old ministers would certainly throw obstacles in the way of a dissolution. 'If defeated, no worse than before', argued one opponent cheerfully; but to most of the others the prospect of a new lease of seven years for the coalition was a sobering thought.[2]

Best of all would be for the bill to be rejected by the House of Lords. But under normal circumstances, this was distinctly improbable. The coalition had strong support in the Lords, in numbers if not in eloquence, and had been assiduous in rallying its forces: nor would their lordships lightly reject a bill that had been carried in the House of Commons by such handsome

---

[1] Clarendon to Alvensleben, 4 December, MSS. Clarendon dep. Bodleian, f. 603.
[2] Memorandum on the India bill, Granville MSS., Box 3.

majorities. It was, in fact, unknown for the government to be defeated in the House of Lords. According to theory, the House of Lords was a balancing factor in the constitution: 'a body of nobility', in Blackstone's celebrated analysis, 'to support the rights of both the crown and the people, by forming a barrier to withstand the encroachments of both'.[1] In practice, it was an adjunct of the crown, and the Scottish representative peers, the bishops and the household peers, augmented by the ministers and their friends, constituted an automatic majority for the government of the day.[2] The only hope of defeating the bill lay in a direct intervention by the king against his ministers.

This possibility had always haunted the coalition. The Rockinghams considered that they had been betrayed by the king over the repeal of the Stamp Act in 1766, and were on guard against a repetition.[3] In September 1783, before any details of the bill were public, the duke of Manchester had replied to Portland's communication with a friendly warning: 'His Majesty perhaps might be induced to acquiesce without being thoroughly convinced of the fitness of the measure, and should he coldly support it in the outset, means at the same time might be found to thwart it before it could be brought to maturity.'[4] There was nothing in the king's behaviour over the prince's establishment to set coalition fears at rest.

There has been much discussion whether the king was adequately informed of the provisions of the bill. After the dismissal of the ministry, Fox and his colleagues maintained that the bill had been explained to him clause by clause, and that he had given

---

[1] Blackstone, *Commentaries*, book i, ch. 2. Blackstone's observations were certainly not based on contemporary practice. They seem to have been derived from Charles I's 'Answer to the Nineteen Propositions' in 1642, which described the House as 'a screen and bank between the Prince and People, to assist each against any encroachment of the other'. J. Rushworth, *Historical collections*, 3rd part, 731.

[2] D. Large provides an admirable analysis of 'the party of the crown' in 'The decline of "the party of the Crown" and the rise of parties in the House of Lords, 1783–1837', *English Historical Review*, October 1963.

[3] The episode is discussed in R. Pares, *King George III and the politicians*, 108.

[4] *H.M.C. 8th Report, appendix*, 134.

no indication of disapproval. Although this has been questioned, it is unlikely that ministers would have attempted to push through a measure which they knew to be highly contentious without some sign of royal acquiescence, nor is it easy to believe that a politician of the king's experience could have failed to understand the significance of the proposals. Some evidence does survive which suggests that the main features of the bill were certainly known to the king. On 30 November, before the issue became of any importance, Lord Midleton told Thomas Pelham that Portland had had conversations with the king about the commissioners and their salaries: it would have been strange if the king had not taken the opportunity to enquire what the commissioners were to do.[1]

The opposition's first task was to discover to what lengths the king was prepared to go to get rid of his ministers. On 1 December, Thurlow was granted an audience, and submitted a memorandum drawn up in collaboration with Temple. After describing the bill as a plan to appropriate 'more than half the royal power', it continued:

An easier way of changing his government would be by taking some opportunity of doing it when, in the progress of it, it shall have received more discountenance than hitherto.

This must be expected to happen in the Lords in a greater degree than can be hoped for in the Commons.

But a sufficient degree of it may not occur in the Lords if those whose duty to His Majesty would excite them to appear are not acquainted with his wishes, and that in a manner which would make it impossible to pretend a doubt of it, in case they were so disposed.[2]

Thurlow's audience was soon known, and the inference drawn. Fox, in the debate that night, remarked pointedly on attempts to injure ministers 'through a certain great quarter'.[3] Emboldened by

---

[1] Add. MS. 33128, f. 238. The account is a fairly detailed one, and Midleton is a good witness, since there was at that time a suggestion that he might serve as a commissioner himself. [2] Buckingham, i, 288–9. [3] Debrett, xii, 307.

the king's reply, Henry Dundas wrote at once to the duke of Gordon not to send his proxy to the ministers, for 'to be in opposition at present is no wise hostile to ——', and on the 3rd Atkinson told Robinson that 'everything stands prepared for the blow if a certain person has courage to strike it'.[1] 'You may be assured', wrote Jenkinson, 'that the King sees the bill in all the horrors that you and I do.'[2]

Confirmation that the king disliked his ministry and would take action to remove it, though gratifying to the opposition, was not in itself decisive. The king's hostility had not been sufficient either to resist the coalition in the spring or to eject it in June. The need was still for a viable alternative ministry. Temple could certainly head such a ministry, but in the House of Commons only Pitt had the stature and ability to confront the coalition's array. Since any royal ministry would be formed in the teeth of a substantial majority of the House of Commons and would without question face the most turbulent debates, the situation was if anything more difficult than it had been in the spring, and Pitt's position more critical. But Pitt had been distressingly irresolute during the spring crisis, and one more fiasco would place the coalition out of reach of its enemies. To Gower, Thurlow wrote: 'The danger of relapsing into that situation must prevent any step being taken without having prepared an arrangement which promises, and that pretty confidently, a different upshot from the former.'[3] The nearer the coalition's adversaries came to forming their own ministry, the more important became the differences in their own ranks. The administration envisaged, built around Temple, Pitt, Thurlow and Gower, would have two protagonists of parliamentary reform and two antagonists.

[1] Gordon to Dundas, 6 December, Melville MSS.; Abergavenny MSS., 520. Gordon was kept in Scotland by debt. He replied that Portland had written to him on 30 November for his proxy but that Dundas had 'given me a new light totally in political matters which I confess I was ignorant of'. [2] *H.M.C. Abergavenny MSS.*, 61.

[3] *H.M.C. 5th Report, appendix*, 210–11. The letter is undated, but from internal evidence was written between 11 and 18 November.

Thurlow hoped that Pitt and Temple would not prove too stubborn: an intransigent position would produce 'a degree of reluctance in others to coalesce in a system which may possibly end so very contrary to their public opinions . . . this end, however, seems to be the object of few, and they seem to be growing sensible both of their need of assistance and of the necessity of conforming in some degree to the publick and genuine sentiments of those whom they are looking to'.[1]

Pitt's part in the negotiations that led to the king's intervention in the House of Lords has been for many years a matter of speculation. His earlier biographers could not bring themselves to believe that he could have had any share in transactions the propriety of which they themselves doubted. 'Whatever bolts of party indignation have been, or may be, hurled against the king, or against Lord Temple, they at all events fall short of Pitt', wrote Lord Stanhope: 'he had taken no part in these transactions. So far as we can trace, he had not even been apprised of them beforehand'.[2] J. H. Rose went further. Not only did he presume that Pitt was innocent of all knowledge of the plot, but he suggested that, on discovering Temple's part in it, Pitt was so pained that he broke off his alliance with that nobleman.[3] Later commentators have been more judicious. Pitt's most recent biographer concedes that he probably knew of the plan, but was 'not directly involved in the fall of his predecessors, and . . . did not concern himself with the means by which Fox had been driven from office'.[4] But evidence in the Bodleian Library allows the matter to be established beyond doubt.

Negotiations at this stage between the king and Pitt were bound to be delicate: neither fully trusted the other, and the utmost secrecy was essential. Most of the prominent politicians of the day were watched, and their activities reported within a

---

[1] *H.M.C. 5th Report, appendix*, 211.
[2] Stanhope, i, 155.
[3] *William Pitt and national revival*, 152–3.
[4] J. W. Derry, *William Pitt* (1962), 38.

matter of hours. The court's intermediary therefore needed to be discreet and obscure. The person chosen was a superannuated diplomat, Lord Clarendon.[1] His early life, traced by Sir Lewis Namier in a mordant little biography, reveals immoderate anxiety for recognition and employment, coupled with protestations that he never sought favours.[2] He did not change. He held office as Chancellor of the Duchy of Lancaster while North was first minister, despite occasional attempts to shunt him on, and was mortified in April 1782 to find himself dismissed: 'I regard the office as . . . in no sense political', he lamented to Shelburne. When Shelburne replied with polite condolences, Clarendon immediately asked for posts for his son, Lord Hyde, and himself: the Postmaster-Generalship or the Duchy of Lancaster would, he explained, 'satisfy my expiring ambition'. Nothing was forthcoming for either candidate, but during the Shelburne administration his younger son, George, was appointed a Groom of the Bedchamber. Acknowledging the favour on 10 January 1783 Clarendon once more drew attention to his own merits, and a fortnight later wrote suggesting a naval post for Lord Hyde. On the news of Shelburne's overthrow, Clarendon abandoned him with indecent haste, and wrote to beg office of Portland, who had his 'ardent wishes': of the retiring minister he declared melodramatically, 'I was his first victim'. The news of the illness of his successor as Chancellor of the Duchy, Lord Ashburton, filled him with fresh hope: on 17 July, anticipating Ashburton's death by more than a month, he begged Portland to restore him. Portland's answers proving unsatisfactory, Clarendon remembered that he had really been a follower of North all the time, and wrote: 'as I was turned out with your Lordship . . . I submit

---

[1] Thomas Villiers, 1709–86; employed on diplomatic service 1738–46; M.P. Tamworth 1747–56; Cr. Baron Hyde 1756; adv. earl of Clarendon 1776; Lord of the Admiralty 1748–56; Joint Postmaster-General 1763–5; Chancellor of the Duchy of Lancaster 1771–82 and 1783–6; Joint Postmaster-General September-December 1786. He seems to have been something of a favourite with the king, and was employed on similar political negotiations in 1766: see *The Grenville papers*, ed. W. J. Smith, iii, 353–4.

[2] *The House of Commons 1754–90*, iii, 587–8.

whether restoration . . . would not be an act of justice.' He
buttressed his request with an appeal to the king, explaining that
he would get peculiar satisfaction from the thought of receiving
patronage from His Majesty alone. In December his chance came.
He was entrusted with the negotiations, and when they proved
successful, was restored to his old place. The *Morning Chronicle*,
29 December, in a paragraph of singular untruthfulness, even for
a newspaper, remarked that Lord Clarendon's appointment had
been obtained 'without the smallest application on his part'.
Delighted at employment once more on a confidential and
important mission, he obligingly made careful notes of all his
negotiations with Pitt.[1]

For extra security, the negotiation was provided with a double
link, Clarendon reporting to the Hanoverian ambassador, Count
Alvensleben, who had access to the king. Pitt's attitude to the
first direct approaches on 9 December was encouraging but
watchful. To Alvensleben, Clarendon wrote:

Being yesterday authorised to enquire if there were good grounds to form
what is much desired, application was immediately made to know the sentiments of him, who must from the superiority of his talents and the purity of his
character be a leader in this important business. He was found well disposed to
the work and not deterred from the situation of things and the temper of men.
He concurred in the opinion that there should be no dismission till a strong
succession was secured, that the future plan should be well formed before the
present was dissolved. He prudently asked if this overture proceeded from
authority, and could be carried on through a proper and safe channel to the
fountain head. Those judicious questions being answered in the affirmative, he
said he would consider and consult on the matter . . .[2]

On the 11th, Clarendon informed Pitt of the reception of his
report by the king:

---

[1] All references to Clarendon's letters are from MSS. Clarendon dep. Bodleian, Letter
Book, ff. 470, 472, 473, 552, 557, 562, 568, 570, 572, 576, 581, 587, 589. The exchange
with the king is in Fortescue, vi, nos. 4458 & 4459.
[2] f. 604. The identification is completed by a letter from Clarendon to Pitt on 11 December,
f. 618, referring to 'what passed between us on Tuesday last'.

It met with approbation and it was further said, we must now wait to see what Mr. Pitt can do. I am happy that such a leader in the negotiations is established and trust that Prudence will admit of despatch; for it is apprehended that the contested bill will pass the House of Lords if Power remains where it is.

A second interview with Pitt took place almost immediately:

His opinion is to see by a division the force on each side in the House of Lords, previous to any determination, excepting that the great Patriot's sentiments should be known and enforced to all who, from their situation, affection or regard for his honour and for the constitution, ought to be attentive to them, no one who can be directly or indirectly influenced to do right should be left unreminded of the necessity to appear in numbers whenever the bill now depending is agitated. The passing it may change the nature of government, the rejecting it may lessen even to dissolution the power of those who formed it; so far opinions were settled. It was afterwards submitted whether the petitions from the East India Company and from the City of London to the Throne should not be presented before any division in the House of Lords, as such objections as they would express and imply might have on that occasion a good effect and as the tendency of this bill would then appear to fill important corporations as well as individuals with apprehensions and disgust, it might be given not only as a plausible but as solid reason for the dismission, that seems to be desired. It was likewise mentioned for consideration whether, should a dismission take place, a dissolution of Parliament would or would not be necessary and whether the dismission should be general or only of the particular authors of the bill, leaving it to their followers to resign or to desert from their old standard . . . no positive answer was given on these sudden questions . . .[1]

It is therefore clear that Pitt was not only fully acquainted with the use to be made of the king's name, but insisted upon it as a *sine qua non* before agreeing to take office. It had a double significance. It was necessary to ensure the defeat of the bill; it was also a pledge of the king's absolute and unreserved support. There could be no turning back. Richard Atkinson heard the news from Dundas, and passed it on to Robinson:

A *direct* communication has been had, and all goes right. As far as I understand, the case is, that on Wednesday a letter was written declaring the readiness of

[1] Second report, 12 December, f. 605. This meeting was probably in the morning of 11 December.

certain persons to receive the burden, to which a reply was made full of assurance that he would go every length they desired him. He afterwards wrote commanding Lord Temple to go to the levee . . . and has given authority to say (when it shall be necessary) that whoever votes in the House of Lords for the India Bill is not *his* friend.[1]

In the meantime every endeavour had been made by the organisers of the opposition to ensure that Pitt would not have second thoughts as he had done in the spring. On that occasion the stumbling block had been the probable support in the House of Commons. In the search for assurance on this point, Dundas asked Robinson on 5 December to prepare an analysis of party affiliation as a matter of urgency. For two whole days, working long into the early hours of the morning, his pen 'constantly driving', Robinson made his calculations, feeding them through to Pitt, Dundas and Thurlow as each section was completed.[2] The result, based largely on the India bill voting, was not particularly encouraging. The proposed ministry's certain supporters Robinson estimated at 149, their certain adversaries at 231: even the 104 hopefuls against 74 doubtfuls did little to redress the balance. But there was a considerable number of members who, holding office or wishing to remain on good terms with government, could be expected to change their allegiance as soon as the new ministry was formed,[3] and Dundas, on the 7th, was able to point out several members who were more friendly than Robinson had assumed. 'The result has been', wrote Richard Atkinson, 'that although at the first blush it had not appeared quite so favourable as had been expected, yet on fuller consideration . . . it was

---

[1] 12 December, *H.M.C Abergavenny MSS.*, 62.

[2] This is the well-known analysis printed in Laprade, 66–105. It is clear from the comments that it was compiled before the change of ministry. It is a difficult estimate to make use of because Robinson combines three different analyses: (1) the situation before any change of ministry (2) after the change (3) after a general election. But he does not always adhere to these categories, and his forecasts are far from correct.

[3] Robinson's comments are too indeterminate to permit a numerical computation, but examples may be seen under Oxfordshire, Radnorshire and Irvine burghs.

admitted . . . that there was no *manly* ground for apprehension.'
Nevertheless, it was apparent that, without a dissolution, the new
ministers would face a very difficult situation. Robinson next
turned his energies to an analysis of the House of Lords, while
Pitt, Temple, Richmond and Thurlow met at Gower's house on
the 10th to concert final plans.[1] The following afternoon Temple
was granted an audience, from which he emerged empowered by
the king to declare that 'whoever voted for the India Bill were not
only not his friends, but he should consider them as his enemies;
and if these words were not strong enough, Earl Temple might use
whatever words he might deem stronger or more to the purpose'.[2]

The news of this extraordinary intervention burst on the political scene like a bomb. Supporters of the coalition were stunned
and bewildered. Without exception they had assumed that the
bill would have a comfortable majority in the House of Lords.[3]
Now everything was in the melting pot. Their first reaction was
incredulity. 'The Duke of Portland', wrote George North, 'did
not believe this report for some time as his Majesty had never
expressed to him the slightest disinclination to give the bill his
full support and even on the Friday when the Duke was with him
did not give him the least hint of what had passed with Lord
Temple'.[4] William Eden, writing to Northington on the 12th,
was still inclined to dismiss it as a ruse on Temple's part, 'probably
for the purpose of gaining some pretext which the loose conversation of such an audience might furnish, for holding a language

---

[1] Robinson to Jenkinson, 7 & 9 December, Add. MS. 38567, ff. 167–8 & 169–70; Atkinson
to Robinson, 8 December, Abergavenny MSS.; Temple to Gower, 9 December,
Granville MSS. I do not know of any record of Robinson's sketch of the House of
Lords, which would be of considerable interest. The item listed in *H.M.C. Abergavenny
MSS.*, 61, no. 524 as a canvass for this division has been incorrectly identified, and
relates to a division during the Rockingham ministry, probably for the debate of 1 May
1782 on the Contractors' Bill.

[2] This is the version quoted by Fox in the House of Commons. His opponents did not
challenge it. Debrett, xii, 430.

[3] Of the ten estimates made by supporters that have come to my knowledge, not one
expressed doubt that the bill would pass: the average majority envisaged was 25–30. See
also the testimony by Lord John Townshend in Russell, ii, 24–8.

[4] George North to Thomas Pelham, 16 December, Add. MS. 33100, f. 471.

likely to gain five or six recruits'.[1] But the following day Loughborough admitted that he could not disbelieve the story, and by Sunday 14th the coalition leaders were almost certain of the exact expressions used at the audience.[2]

It was impossible to calculate the effect the intervention would have. The first reading of the bill in the House of Lords on the 9th had been unremarkable: Temple and Thurlow delivered forthright condemnations, but had not attempted to divide the House. The coalition's tactics at this stage seem to have been to treat the matter lightly, since expostulation might increase the effect of the message. Should the bill, notwithstanding the royal appeal, be carried, there would be time for explanations. The bill's opponents were also in a delicate position. From mere prudence they could not speak too openly. Pitt, on the 9th, had tried through Thomas Orde to persuade Shelburne to attend the second reading, explaining, in guarded terms, that he could see means, if used, to make the decision in the House of Lords doubtful. Orde considered such a vague invitation unbecoming to Shelburne's 'situation and dignity', and Shelburne seems to have agreed with him, for he remained at Bowood throughout the crisis, nursing his resentments.[3] Proselytising was not easy. Lord Sydney received a terse answer when he tried, on the day of the debate, to induce Lord Onslow, one of the Lords of the Bedchamber, to withdraw his proxy from the coalition:

I thought I had made you understand the resolution I had come to in the few words I said to you this morning, *viz.* that having taken a part in favour of the bill from the beginning I could not change my conduct till I knew from better *authority* than vague report and opinion that which alone could make me do so . . .[4]

The key to the situation was the attitude of the twenty-six

---

[1] Add. MS. 33100, f. 456. Another letter in which the coalition's bewilderment is apparent is William Windham to Northington, 12 December, Add. MS. 33100, f. 522.

[2] Auckland, i, 67; Burgoyne to Northington, 15 December, Add. MS. 33100, f. 464.

[3] Fitzmaurice, ii, 270–1.   [4] 15 December, Brotherton MSS.

bishops. If the great majority of them voted with government, as they almost invariably did, the bill would go through.[1] William Markham, archbishop of York, was a dedicated courtier, and would certainly follow the king's lead, but John Moore, the new archbishop of Canterbury, had expressed approval of the bill and had connections with the coalition: he held the bishop of London's proxy for the debate, and much depended on his decision. Summoned for private audience with the king, his vote remained in doubt until the last moment. 'If he and the rest of the bench are steady', wrote Loughborough, 'there is no danger'; and Eden, the archbishop's brother-in-law, assured his allies on the eve of the debate that the Archbishop was still *'more than friendly'*.[2]

The whole position was still uncertain on the day of the second reading. Fox, Burke, Sheridan, George North and Pitt watched the proceedings from the bar of the House. Lord Abingdon, an eccentric and unbalanced peer, launched the debate with a characteristically wild speech, in which he denounced Fox's ambition as 'ten times more violent' than Cromwell's, and proposed summoning the judges to give their advice on the bill. There was no enthusiasm in any quarter for this bizarre suggestion. The opposition won its first success when Richmond presented a petition from the City of London, declaring that the bill was 'a heinous act of injustice, oppression and absurdity', and a 'gross perversion of the high powers' of the legislature. The duke of Manchester, brought over from Paris to give his vote and inadequately briefed, promptly plunged headlong into the trap: rising in indignation to denounce the language of the petition as extravagant and unbecoming, he was told that it was an exact copy of the Rockinghams' protest in 1773. Counsel for the Company then devoted several hours to the presentation of evidence.

---

[1] A bishop in opposition was a very rare bird. The *Parliamentary history* records 11 minorities in the House of Lords between 1770 and 1780: of the total of 375 votes cast in opposition, the bishops provided 11. Another illustration of their loyalty to government between 1801 and 1812 is given by D. Large, *op. cit.*, 683.

[2] Auckland, i, 67; Russell, ii, 25.

Not until eleven at night did the debate flare into life, when counsel requested more time, and the duke of Chandos moved the adjournment. Fitzwilliam opposed it as an attempt at prevarication, and Portland, rising to support him, drew attention to rumours 'of a very extraordinary nature' that had been circulated. Richmond at once demanded that Portland should be more specific, while Temple, declaring his readiness to face a direct charge, did not deny that he had been granted an audience, nor that his advice had been hostile to the bill. Portland seems to have been bewildered by Temple's counter-attack and made no reply, but Temple then overplayed his hand. Pointing out that Portland had not substantiated his allegations, he 'begged the conduct of the noble lord might be marked': as for himself, he was 'proud in the recollection of having acted the part of an honest man'. This gave Fitzwilliam an opportunity to take charge of the debate, which the rest of his colleagues had conducted so lamely. He expressed pleasure that Temple had publicly declared the rumours unfounded. This placed Temple in an awkward position. If he allowed Fitzwilliam's remark to go unchallenged, a few waverers might seize the chance to support government. He therefore accused Fitzwilliam of misinterpreting his speech: he had merely said that the rumour 'in the loose and vague manner in which it had been stated', did not affect him: he had neither said what the advice had been, nor what had been the outcome of his audience. Fitzwilliam rejoined issue:

The noble earl has positively evaded giving any precise answer to the notice which has been taken of the most alarming rumours. With regard to the assertion of a noble duke (Richmond), that the minister who should advise the Crown to support a bill depending in Parliament, and endeavour to influence the Crown in its favour, would act unconstitutionally, I deny the doctrine. If I know anything of the British constitution, the reverse is the fact. The crown can do no wrong. The minister alone is responsible for every measure of government while he is in office. He has a right, therefore, constitutionally, to exert his influence with the crown, and indeed it would be impossible for any government to go on without such exertion. The case is widely different . . . to which the noble duke has alluded. Thinking, as I do, that a rumour of so enormous a tendency ought to be minutely investigated, I do beg leave to call the attention of the House to it directly. I do not mean, my lords, the paragraph which has been read: I do not mean the rumour in the newspapers merely, but the rumour which they must all have heard, and which is, that the noble earl in my eye, had declared, that he was empowered by a great person, whose sacred name should never be heard, as interfering in the progress of a bill, to say, that that person was hostile to the bill.

Temple resorted to bluff and moved that Fitzwilliam's words be taken down, but after strangers had been cleared from the bar, he withdrew his demand, and amid considerable heat and confusion, the House proceeded to vote on the adjournment. Nearly three-quarters of the total peerage of the realm cast votes in the division. Led by the archbishop of Canterbury, the bishops divided 12–8 against government, and the adjournment was carried by 8 votes.[1] The fate of the bill was sealed.[2]

For Fox the debate must have been a torment and the result a devastating blow. There could be few more painful experiences for a man of his debating talent than to stand on the sidelines and watch his noble colleagues make a hash of their case. Even Loughborough had been less effective than usual; Portland had been useless, and Manchester worse than useless. The king's refusal to create peerages for the coalition, by depriving them of the services in the House of Lords of North, may have contributed to their defeat: it is possible that his vast experience could have turned the

---

[1] The voting was: *for the adjournment*, 69+18 proxy; *against the adjournment*, 57+22 proxy. There is a division list in the *Political magazine*, 1783, 404–5. There were 235 members of the peerage at the time, some of whom were, of course, minors, some Catholics, some aged and infirm. The Prince of Wales cast his first vote in the House with government. The Lords of the Bedchamber, most susceptible to royal influence, divided 5–6 against government: the rest of the Household peers divided 4–4. The Scottish representative peers divided 7–6 in favour of government, Lord Stormont supporting the ministers on this question. The *Lincoln, Rutland and Stamford Mercury*, 25 December, quoting the *English Chronicle*, reported that 27 peers had changed sides. This is perhaps a high estimate, as it would have given the coalition a potential majority of 46.

[2] Debrett, xiv, 36–69. There is a good description of the debate in a letter from George Aust to Hardwicke, 16 December, Add. MS. 35621, f. 246.

few votes needed. Thomas Orde's description of the scene, though lurid, is not unconvincing:

Charles Fox was behind the throne during the whole time of the business yesterday, and seemed to be in great agitation at every turn, particularly on the admission of evidence. He however earnestly cried out for a division on the question of adjournment and expressed the fullest confidence of victory. I am told that his countenance, gesture and expressions on the event were in the highest degree ludicrous from the extremity of distortion and rage, going off with an exclamation of despair, lugging George North along with him and calling out for Sheridan. So Caliban, Stephano and Trinculo reeled off after the disappointment of their similar project, for as Sir Richard Hill would say, these three certainly meant to commit a rape upon poor Miranda (the Constitution) and to knock out the brains of her poor father . . .[1] I understand that some of the bishops seemed to feel very awkward, and that those who still voted with administration cast a sad look of contrition towards those who might 'tell tales of them to high-judging Jove'.[2]

Fox's bitterness was apparent in his hasty note to Mrs Armistead: 'we are beat in the House of Lords by such treachery on the part of the King and such meanness on the part of his *friends* in the House of Lords as one could not expect either from him or them.' North's comment was more laconic: 'I own I never quite liked this awkward phrase, "*more than friendly*".'[3]

There was little chance for ministers to retrieve their defeat. On the morning of the resumed debate Portland had an audience and asked for authority to contradict the rumours: the king refused to grant it, 'having never approved the bill'.[4] Lord Rivers, one of the bedchamber peers, took his proxy out of the hands of Sandwich, explaining with candour that although he approved the bill on its merits, 'I now find it is no longer the *measure* that operates on the minds of men'.[5] Lord Hardwicke did the same. Lord Dacre, Camden's invalid brother-in-law, sent his proxy against the bill.

[1] Sir Richard Hill, the member for Shropshire, was fond of larding his speeches with literary metaphors. [2] Orde to Shelburne, 16 December, Bowood MSS.
[3] Add. MS. 47570, f. 156; Russell, ii, 25.
[4] William Windham to Northington, 18 December, Add. MS. 33100, f. 473.
[5] 16 December, Sandwich MSS.

The Prince of Wales, reminded of his filial duty, resolved to stay away.[1]

The second debate, on 17 December, was of a higher standard than the first. Lord Gower opened for the opposition, repeated the charge that ministers were interested only in patronage, and could see no reason for 'the annihilation of a Company which had maintained its credit as the first commercial company in the world for upwards of two centuries'. The main defence of the bill was undertaken by Gower's son-in-law, Carlisle, who took issue with the Company's counsel for suggesting that there was a right to be ruined if one chose: 'be it so, as long as he pulled down destruction only on his own head. But who were implicated in this ruin besides himself? Every inhabitant of India subject to the European government . . .' The bill's opponents, for the most part, reiterated their indignation at the violation of charters. But Walsingham offered a genuine criticism of the main principle of the bill: 'the friends of this bill contend, that the government of India should be in this country. It is impossible, my lords; you must govern India in India, and from the moment a contrary system is adopted, the loss of India will not be very distant.' On the division, opposition pushed up its vote by 8, Stormont, one of the cabinet, and his uncle Mansfield joining it, while the ministerial vote dropped by 3. By a majority of 19 the bill was rejected.[2]

While the Lords were engaged in their deliberations, the coalition's counter-attack was launched in the House of Commons by William Baker, the member for Hertford. After the serjeant-at-arms had been sent to require the attendance of members, he called upon the House to express its abhorrence of the rumour that had been spread and to resist as jealously as they always had

---

[1] *The later correspondence of George III*, ed. A. Aspinall (1962), i, 3. This is referred to hereafter as Aspinall.

[2] Debrett, xiv, 69–106. The voting was: *for the commitment* 57+19 proxy; *against the commitment*, 75+20 proxy. As far as I know this was the largest division in the House of Lords in the eighteenth century.

done any attempt to bias their votes. He then moved two resolutions, the first that to report any opinion of the king in order to influence debates was 'a high crime and misdemeanour', the second that the House would hold an enquiry into the state of the nation the following Monday. The opposition retorted by laying an elaborate smokescreen. Lord Nugent expressed astonishment that anyone should question the right of peers, as hereditary counsellors, to advise the king, while Pitt poured scorn on the solemn proceedings, declared that the rumour was but 'the lie of the day', and could not believe that such importance had been 'ever before imparted to mere rumour and hearsay'. Baker had argued that if persons not holding responsible offices influenced the king's actions, the ministers would be placed in an impossible situation. Pitt explained that his advice to them in that position would be to resign: 'the servants of the crown were worse than useless whenever they were without responsibility ... their duty, in a situation thus dishonourable and inefficient, was therefore obvious and indispensable.' North had no difficulty in ridiculing this disingenuous and puerile argument in a speech admitted to be 'great' even by his antagonists.[1] 'The responsibility of ministers', he warned the House, 'was the only security which Englishmen had against the abuse of the executive power.' Pitt's mode of reasoning was 'peculiarly proper' to his situation: 'it was only that one member, in one house, should publish such a rumour as has been so frequently mentioned, and another, in the other house, push ministers home. The game thus managed was sure, and the play required no very uncommon dexterity. He would presume, however, to advise the honourable gentleman to act with a little more patience and decency.' William Grenville, on behalf of his brother Lord Temple, challenged ministers to bring a specific charge. Fox at once accepted the challenge, quoted the exact words reported to have been written down, and denounced Temple's reply in the Lords as 'mean, insidious, equivocal and

---

[1] Atkinson to Robinson, 18 December, *H.M.C. Abergavenny MSS.*, 63–4.

temporising . . . to preserve the effect without boldly and manfully abiding by the consequences of the guilt'. On the broad issue, he contrasted the behaviour of the two Houses towards the measure:

> I dare anyone to mention a single argument brought against it (in the Commons) which has not been candidly and fairly tried . . . No bill was ever more violently and systematically opposed, investigated at greater length, or by more ability; passed the House under the sanction of a more respectable and independent majority, or had more the countenance and patronage of the country at large . . . What was the reception which, thus circumstanced, it received from their lordships? . . . It is the victim not of open and fair reasoning, but of that influence that shuns the light and shrinks from discussion . . .

Grenville, on the authority of Temple, denied that the words quoted had been used, but when Fox invited him to say whether words to the same effect had been used, he remained silent. Baker's resolutions were then carried by 153 votes to 80. A third resolution, moved by Thomas Erskine, was designed to forestall a dissolution of Parliament: in view of the urgent need for some provision for the government of India anyone advising the king to prevent it was 'an enemy to this country'. This, too, was carried comfortably, by 147 votes to 73, despite arguments that it trenched upon the prerogative of the crown.[1]

There seems no doubt that the king's intervention caused widespread uneasiness. Windham told Northington that 'people in general speak of it with much indignation', George Aust reported that many members who had opposed the India bill had supported Baker's resolutions, and Thomas Orde believed that had Fox not been too precipitate 'there could have been no ground which would have made the royal interference tolerable'.[2] Even

---

[1] Debrett, xii, 420–49.

[2] Add. MS. 33100, f. 473; Add. MS. 35621, f. 274; Orde to Shelburne, 18 December, Bowood MSS. Sir George Cornewall, the member for Herefordshire, who had voted for Shelburne's peace proposals and had taken no part over the India Bill, wrote to Sir Gilbert Elliot: 'after the bill had been carried in our house with so high a hand, I hardly conceived the King would venture to play this trick: what opinion can one have of any man who will submit to such usage . . . surely even the enemies of the Bill, and such

Jenkinson had misgivings. 'It would have been well', he told Orde, 'after His Majesty had made up his mind upon it if he had sent for the Duke of Portland and explicitly declared to him his disapprobation and the consequences. Perhaps Lord Temple should have advised it'.[1]

No constitutional defence of the king's action is possible, nor was any attempted at the time by his supporters: they either dismissed the allegations as false, or engaged in a different controversy over the right of peers to advise their sovereign. The convention against the intrusion of the monarch's name into parliamentary debates was long established: as far back as 1576 Peter Wentworth had protested against 'a rumour that runneth about the House . . . Take heed what you do, the Queen liketh not such a matter.' There was, of course, a tacit assumption that the king supported his ministers, but to appeal directly to his authority was regarded as a violation of the freedom of debate. But the action of December 1783 went further than that. Secret lobbying against his ministers was bound, as the coalition pointed out, to destroy the basis of responsible government: ministers could only be answerable for policy if it were their own. The argument that the king had not been adequately informed, even if it were true, was beside the point: he was under no illusions after 1 December, when Thurlow had shown him the memorandum, yet for a fortnight he gave the ministers no hint of his opinion. The only possible defence of the intervention was the one offered by Wraxall, which assumed that the constitution had virtually broken down, and that the king was entitled to use any means to defend his position: 'he was not bound to observe any measures of scrupulous delicacy with men who had entered his

men as Powys, will take the alarm, and join in checking such unconstitutional interference. I hope you have passed strong resolutions on it. I would heartily join you in them, as would Knight (the member for Leominster) who, though an enemy to the coalition, says this conduct makes him a convert.' Minto MSS., Box 43 B.
[1] Orde to Shelburne, 16 December, Bowood MSS.

cabinet by violence, who held him in bondage, and who meditated to render that bondage perpetual.' Such, no doubt, was the way the king saw it, and such had been the feeling of Charles I when he tried to arrest the five members. But this defence depends on the view taken of the previous use the king had made of his prerogative. It is true that the coalition had, in effect, deprived him of his choice of ministers, but he had tried to use that power in order to place certain politicians under a permanent ban. Unless they retired altogether from political life, or staked everything upon the reversionary interest, their only retort could be by 'storming the closet'.[1]

It was not the last time the king played this particular card. In 1801, after the Act of Union with Ireland had been passed, Pitt was urging the necessity of Catholic Emancipation to complete the measure. On 28 January, at the levée, the king declared to Dundas, loud enough for bystanders to hear, that he would 'consider every man who supports that measure as my personal enemy'. Pitt at once protested, reminding the king of the 'indispensable necessity of effectually discountenancing . . . all attempts to make use of Your Majesty's name'. His resignation followed, and Catholic Emancipation was deferred for twenty-eight years, with consequences to Anglo-Irish relations that some historians have seen as disastrous. Sympathy for Pitt on that occasion does not come easily: it is difficult to believe that the king would have been emboldened to make such a declaration had his previous intervention been less successful.[2]

The ministers were in an odd position, living on borrowed time. They were determined not to resign: constitutional convention did not require it, nor did the circumstances of their defeat in the Lords put them into a mood to be obliging to the king. Their dismissal was hourly expected throughout Thursday,

[1] Wraxall, iii, 191–2. He admits that the royal action 'appears at first sight subversive of every principle of political freedom'.
[2] R. I. W. and S. W. Wilberforce, *The life of William Wilberforce* (1838), iii, 7; *The diaries of Sylvester Douglas, Lord Glenbervie*, i, 147; 31 January 1801, Chatham MSS.

18 December. Pitt and Temple had audiences with the king in the afternoon, and were followed by Portland and Fox, neither of whom was given any indication of a change. But Portland presumed from the king's 'composure and serenity' that Pitt had agreed to serve, while Soame Jenyns, witnessing the king's very friendly manner towards his ministers at the levée, was convinced that it betokened a 'sudden change'.[1] At midnight, while Portland, Fox and North were in conference, messengers arrived from the king asking them to deliver up their seals of office. 'I choose this method', he wrote to North, 'as audiences on such occasions must be unpleasant'.[2]

---

[1] Portland to Sandwich, 18 December, Sandwich MSS.; Jenyns to Hardwicke, 19 December, Add. MS. 35631, f. 193.

[2] Fortescue, vi, no. 4546. There are various versions of the coalition's dismissal. The most reliable seems to be that by Lady Sarah Napier in *The life and letters of Lady Susan Lennox, 1745–1826*, ii, 43–4.

CHAPTER 8

THE 'MINCE-PIE' ADMINISTRATION

The coalition was convinced that its opponents had over-reached themselves. 'We are so strong', wrote Fox immediately after the division in the House of Lords, 'that nobody can undertake without madness: if they do, I think we shall destroy them almost as soon as they are formed'.[1] For the first week his optimism seemed to be justified. There was a marked reluctance among experienced politicians to commit themselves to the new venture. The day after the dismissal the appointments of Pitt as First Lord of the Treasury and Chancellor of the Exchequer and Temple as Secretary of State for the Home Department were announced: Gower, ever willing, answered the call, and was recruited as Lord President of the Council, but there the construction of the ministry halted. Lord Shelburne was not approached—it would be scarcely more alarming to bring forward Lord Bute, confided Sydney—an opinion that Orde thoughtfully conveyed at once to Shelburne.[2] Jenkinson was also too unpopular to be invited, though he made it clear that he was willing to serve and his administrative experience would have been of great value to the ministers: 'fears and doubts make difficulties to your having office at the moment', explained Robinson cryptically. The duke of Grafton, offered the post of Lord Privy Seal, 'could see nothing to encourage me to come forward'. Nor could Mahon, Pitt's brother-in-law, Camden, his father's old friend, Sackville, Grantham, Cornwallis, Beaufort or Richmond. It would be a 'mince-pie administration', thought Mrs Crewe, fit only for the festive season.[3]

[1] Fox to Mrs Armistead, 16 December, Add. MS. 47570, f. 156.   [2] Fitzmaurice, ii, 284.
[3] Jenkinson to Robinson, 24 December, *H.M.C. Abergavenny MSS.*, 64; Robinson to Jenkinson, 25 December, Add. MS. 38567, ff. 177–8; Grafton, 387; *The life of William Wilberforce*, i, 48.

On the 19th, the coalition's supporters attended the House of Commons in force, confident and jocular. Fox moved Dundas over from the opposition benches, where he had seated himself from force of habit: Pepper Arden, Solicitor-General presumptive, was greeted with banter and sarcasm when he rose to move the writ for Pitt's re-election at Appleby. The first brush came when William Baker moved the adjournment until Monday, 22nd, when the state of the nation was to be debated. Dundas appealed to the House to meet on the 20th in order that the Land Tax Bill should not be held up. Fox, rejecting Dundas's suggestion, spoke strongly against a dissolution, which he believed to be imminent. Though he did not dispute the royal prerogative, it should not be employed to suit the convenience of an ambitious young man; ministers were accountable for any 'wanton or imprudent' use of the prerogative, and, after the election, he would move for an enquiry. North ridiculed Mulgrave's comment that they ought not to carry on business in the absence of the minister: 'did the noble lord seriously think that if they were to sit there doing nothing until the minister should be re-elected, that they had any chance of ever seeing him again in the same House of Commons? . . . there was not a man in the House who was not sure that a dissolution was at hand'. Dundas seems to have decided that to press his amendment would only expose the weakness of his support, and Baker's motion went through unopposed.[1]

Fox's handling of the situation at this stage has been condemned by historians with singular unanimity. Lecky described his attempt to prevent a dissolution as a 'fatal error of tactics', an opinion which has been echoed down the ages with more or less elegant variation.[2] A rare exception to the general attitude is provided by D.

[1] Debrett, xii, 450–61.
[2] P. E. Roberts, writing in the *Cambridge history of India*, called it a 'terrible tactical mistake', to C. H. Philips it was a 'tactical error', and to Richard Pares a 'tactical imprudence'. G. M. Trevelyan wrote that Fox made 'one mistake after another'. A. S. Turberville and P. Magnus concur. Historians are not overfond of losers.

G. Barnes, who, though agreeing that Fox 'threw away every advantage with almost incredible recklessness', contrives to attack him from the opposite point of view.[1] Few of the commentators seem to have taken account of the realities of eighteenth-century electioneering: they wanted Fox to 'appeal to the country' in a way that was quite impossible in the conditions of the time. Fox had nothing to gain from a dissolution and everything to lose. In December 1783, he had a majority in the existing House of Commons of almost two to one, according to all the divisions of that session. By no stretch of the imagination can it be argued that a general election, conducted against the full weight of government influence, would have improved his position. Even if they were fortunate enough to retain a majority, they would still be faced by the hostility of the king and of the House of Lords, and those factors that wore down their majority in the spring of 1784 would have operated against them. But by taking a stand against any dissolution, they made a bid for the support of the independent members, to whom the expense of an election was distressing, and who were disconcerted at the prospect of a dissolution before the parliament had run half its term. In any case, Fox's critics have assumed that he had some choice in the matter. He had none. The power of dissolution rested solely with the king, and the more Fox 'demanded' an immediate dissolution, as Trevelyan thought he should have done, the less chance there would have been of the king granting it. There is one further point. The tactics adopted by Fox secured him an unexpected victory that came close to ending the contest at the very outset. They forced Temple's resignation.

Pitt and his supporters do not seem to have been in the best of spirits at the beginning of their enterprise. In addition to the difficulties they had experienced in filling up places, they were

---

[1] *George III and William Pitt, 1783–1806* (1939), 108. 'It should have been clear to the Whigs that they could not win a general election.' It was.

dismayed by the vigour of Fox's counter-measures, and the degree of support he had received. Lord Carmarthen, invited to a grand political dinner on the 20th, found the principal characters 'remarkably thoughtful', and the duke of Dorset confided to him that he 'feared a want of resolution in the new ministers'.[1]

There is some evidence to suggest that Pitt was uneasy about his position. Many people after the dismissal of the coalition were appalled at the possibility of months of fierce political warfare and unsettled government: one alternative put forward was a fresh regrouping, perhaps at the expense of Lord North's following.[2] On 20 December Lord Beauchamp mentioned the suggestion to James Grenville, Temple's cousin, who reported the conversation to the ministers. Pitt and Temple interpreted it as a peace-feeler, and immediately sought permission from the king to open negotiations through Lord Spencer. The following morning Pitt called on Spencer and explained that he was 'ready to go as far as he creditably could in the way of accommodation; that he had only two things to stipulate for himself . . . first, that it would be impossible for him to be in the cabinet with Lord North, and secondly, that he could not accede to the India Bill in the extent in which it was proposed'. Although North offered at once to stand aside, Fox, Portland and Lord John Cavendish rejected the proposals out of hand, declaring that the moment was inopportune for any negotiation and that the suggestion about North was 'perfectly inadmissible'. Pitt then apologised to Spencer for the trouble he had given him, especially since it had been based on a complete misunderstanding of Beauchamp's remarks.[3]

Temple's resignation, announced on 22 December, has attracted

---

[1] Leeds, 90–1.

[2] Eden to Morton Eden, 16 December, Auckland, i, 68–9; Clarendon to Sir James Harris, 15 December, Letter book, f. 616; Orde to Shelburne, 16 December, Bowood MSS.

[3] Pitt to Spencer, 21 December; Spencer to his mother, 22 December; Temple to the king, 21 December; the king to Temple, 21 December: these letters are printed in Aspinall, i, 4, note 9. An undated letter from North to Guilford in the Waldeshare MSS., probably written early in January 1784, describes his response.

much comment. Nineteenth-century historians, misled by an incorrect date given to one of Temple's letters, maintained that it was the result of a quarrel with Pitt over his claim to a dukedom. Contemporary evidence, however, was unanimous that it was connected with the decision not to dissolve Parliament, and there seems little doubt that this was the case.[1]

All observers had assumed that the dismissal of the coalition would be followed by an immediate dissolution because they did not see how any ministry could stand in defiance of a large majority in the House of Commons. Temple spent his first morning as minister on the 19th discussing election arrangements.[2] Every post carried letters into the country warning friends and agents to make ready. Some newspapers even declared that a dissolution had taken place.[3] Nevertheless, there were obstacles in the way of a dissolution that, on reflection, began to seem substantial. It would mean flouting the resolution of the House of Commons against any delay in dealing with Indian affairs; it would place the government in an awkward situation on 5 January when large repayments fell due if the Land Tax bill had not by then been made law. There had been little time to prepare election plans, and though a government majority was probable, it could not be guaranteed. But the decisive factor seems to have been the effect a dissolution might have on the independent

---

[1] The episode is discussed by Dr E. A. Smith, 'Earl Temple's resignation, 22 Dec. 1783', *Historical Journal*, 1963, pp. 91–7, and by Aspinall, i, pp. xxvii–xxviii & 6. Dr Smith clears up the error about dating, but I cannot accept the rest of his argument. He rejects the suggestion that Temple acted out of fear, and argues that Pitt sacrificed him to maintain his own reputation for integrity. But this does not square with Pitt's friendly letters to Temple on the 23rd, nor with what we now know of Pitt's own involvement in the use of the king's name. It is clear that, far from regarding Temple's resignation as politically advantageous, he thought it a severe blow: in a letter to the king the following morning he referred to the 'accumulated difficulties of this moment'. Indeed, Temple's resignation could hardly have been worse timed. Professor Aspinall accepts that Temple 'panicked at the very thought of impeachment proceedings', but does not connect it with the decision not to dissolve Parliament.

[2] Lord A. Percy to G. Rose, Add. MS. 42774A, f. 35. It is dated 18 December, but labelled 'Friday night'. I have presumed that the date is more likely to be wrong than the day.

[3] *Felix Farley's Bristol Journal*, 20 December, reported the *St James Chronicle* as having announced the dissolution.

members of Parliament. This was the point stressed by Lord Clarendon in a memorandum on the subject:

It seems worthy of deliberation whether an attempt should not be made, during recess, to gain a sufficient number of the present members to support the cause of government and avoid so early a general election, a measure that would certainly be inconvenient and disgustful to many well disposed to the change and would be called taken precipitately by the opponents, wanton and violent, which epithets could not with reason be given if on the failure of the trial, the opposition obstructed the business of state and rendered a dissolution absolutely necessary . . .[1]

There were not ten independents, considered Daniel Pulteney, 'who do not think of the £1,000 or £2,000 which it will cost them to be re-elected'.[2] Gower, Thurlow and Richmond were reported to have been against a dissolution, and their advice carried the day.[3]

The change of plan put Temple into a position he had not foreseen and did not in the least relish. He had presumed that he would never be held responsible for his action because the new House of Commons would not be inclined to press the issue. He was now confronted, at least in his own mind, by the possibility of impeachment at the hands of Fox's outraged majority. There seems little doubt that he genuinely considered his life to be in danger. The coalition was not unwilling to encourage such a belief, and the latest squib by Horace Walpole was handed round:

---

[1] 'Advice on a Dissolution', MSS. Clarendon dep., f. 614.

[2] Pulteney to Rutland, 28 December, *H.M.C. Rutland MSS.*, iii, 73.

[3] *Sherborne Mercury and Western Flying Post*, 9 February 1784. The decision seems to have been reached on Sunday 21st, and was perhaps connected with the 'information' Temple was to bring the king at 10 a.m. Temple's decision to resign was communicated to Pitt late that night, according to Pitt's biographer, Tomline. Pitt told Dundas early next morning. The timing has an important bearing on the argument. Dr Smith rightly points out that if Temple was influenced solely by respect for the House of Commons' resolution of 17 December, he would not have taken office at all. 'What', wrote Dr Smith, 'had so changed the political situation between 19 and 22 December that an appointment that seemed proper on the first date should be considered inexpedient on the second?'

> Master Billy you are silly
> Master Temple you are simple
> Thus to risk your heads in vain.
> But a greater fool than you
> Is he (to give the Devil his due)
> Whom God grant long to reign.[1]

More than a year later Temple wrote to his younger brother, Thomas Grenville, a supporter of the coalition, reproaching him for having 'joined in a vote which impeached my honour, and possibly my life'.[2] The breakdown of the negotiation with Fox, and the uncompromising attitude on the part of the coalition that it revealed, seems to have been the last straw, and he formed the conclusion that prudence demanded instant retirement. Pitt was in no position to object, since there had clearly been a change in the conditions on which they had taken office. But Dundas, informed by Pitt on the morning of 22 December, had no inhibitions in his remarks to Orde:

He now very frankly told me that Lord Temple was a damned dolter-headed coward, full of rashness, obstinacy and timidity by fits . . . He was now frightened out of his senses at what was likely to happen in the House today, and ready to advise a submission without further trial . . . there could hardly be a hope of any steady arrangement with such an uncharged blunderbuss in company . . .[3]

Accordingly, when the House of Commons met in the afternoon of the 22nd to discuss the state of the nation, William Grenville at once declared that, before there should be 'any farther proceeding' against his brother, he was authorised to announce his resignation, so that his ministerial position should not shelter him from enquiry or justice.[4] Fox brushed aside the explanation with

---

[1] Add. MS. 47579, f. 125.   [2] Buckingham, i, 308–10.
[3] Orde to Shelburne, 22 December, Bowood MSS.
[4] Fox used the expression 'Temple's cowardice' in a letter to Northington, and John Scott told Hastings that Temple was 'frightened at the violence of the House of Commons'. Russell, ii, 224; Add. MS. 29161, f. 246. The *Sherborne Mercury*, 9 February 1784, reported: 'it is an undoubted fact that Earl Temple accepted the seals of office on the express condition that the Parliament was to have been dissolved.' The account given

contempt—Temple best knew why he had accepted office and then resigned—and the Land Tax Bill was given its third reading without opposition. Erskine followed up his previous resolution by moving for an address to the king pointing out the 'inconveniencies and dangers' that would stem from a dissolution, and begging him to listen to the advice of the House of Commons rather than to the 'secret advices of particular persons who may have private interests of their own'. Fitzpatrick, seconding the motion, said bluntly that Temple had been 'terrified by bugbears', and that the nation had no cause to lament the loss of 'so timid a minister'. Dundas and Henry Bankes, Pitt's friend, declared themselves authorised to say that no dissolution was intended, and that the motion was therefore superfluous. North then intervened with what Orde described as a 'triumphant and sarcastic speech with a good deal of wit', and defended the coalition from attacks delivered on it during his absence from the House. What was the administration, that could boast only two cabinet ministers, but a coalition between persons who had differed on essential points? As for his own junction with Fox, he recalled how the members of Lord Shelburne's administration had fallen off, one by one:

It appeared necessary for the good of the state that a permanent government should be formed, and it was clear that it could not possibly be formed unless a coalition should take place among those, who although once enemies upon points that could no longer come into debate, might act together very cordially in every other respect: such a coalition was formed; but then it was charged with having seized upon government: this is, indeed, a charge that I do not understand, for the public waited for six weeks for a ministry; and every means were tried for a new one, without the assistance of the coalition; but failing in every attempt, the ministers all quitted the cabinet before the coalition was sent for . . . and who, as they were going out, cried, 'What a terrible cursed thing is this coalition, that is driving us from our situations.' But, if we

---

by Wraxall, a much maligned writer, appears to me perfectly correct: 'Lord Temple insisted on the immediate dissolution of Parliament as a step necessary to their ministerial preservation, if not even to their personal safety.' Wraxall, iii, 199.

became possessed of government, we are at worst charged with having carried it by storm . . . we carried on our advances regularly, and above ground, in view of the foe; not by mining in the dark, and blowing up the fort before the garrison knew there was an intention to attack it . . .

Henry Beaufoy, a new member, restored the balance a little with some shrewd thrusts at North: 'the friends of the noble lord applaud his good humour and his classic wit; and it must be acknowledged that the sorrows of his country have not reached him; while she laments the loss of half her empire . . . he himself possesses the utmost hilarity of temper'. But the tide was still flowing strongly for the coalition, and the address was carried.[1] On the 24th the king replied briefly that he would not use his prerogative to interrupt their meeting.[2]

Temple's defection was a shattering blow to the coalition's adversaries. Pitt suffered a sleepless night, for the only time in his life, while the king described himself as 'on the edge of a precipice', and took refuge once more in dark hints of abdication.[3] Most observers assumed that the attempt to form a ministry would have to be abandoned. But Pitt adopted Dundas's advice to 'die with harness on his back', though dubious whether an administration could now be constructed.[4] In the course of the 23rd, a cabinet took shape. Thurlow became Lord Chancellor once more, Sydney and Carmarthen were persuaded to take the

---

[1] Exactly what happened is not easy to establish. The *London Chronicle*, 20/23 December, reported that the friends of Pitt had not ventured to divide the House, and this is confirmed by Lord Palmerston's diary in B. Connell, *Portrait of a Whig peer*, 146–7. But Laprade, 54 suggests that there was a division on the address, and the *Morning Chronicle*, 24 December, declared that 'no less than 25 of the most respectable country gentlemen' previously opposed to Fox had joined him in the debate. Orde wrote to Shelburne that the House was very full, 'and the increase much in favour of the former majority'. 22 December, Bowood MSS. I think the explanation is probably that there was a division in committee on the address, but no division when the committee's findings were reported to the full House for confirmation.

[2] Debrett, xii, 461–86; xiii, 11–14.

[3] G. Tomline, *Life of Pitt* (1821), i, 231–3; the king to Pitt, 23 December, Add. MS. 42772, f. 3.

[4] Orde to Shelburne, 22 December, Bowood MSS.; Pitt to Temple, 23 December, morning, Chevening MSS., printed in Aspinall, i, 6, note 2.

Secretaries' seals, Rutland became Lord Privy Seal, and Howe went to the Admiralty—'for how many days or weeks remains to be seen', wrote Pitt candidly.[1] Even his friends had little confidence in the new cabinet. It reminded Camden of 'a forlorn hope, who for the hope of fame and so much a head are tempted to march up to the front of an open battery'.[2] Thurlow, the only one of Pitt's colleagues with real political weight, was moody and unpredictable: Gower, the other senior member of the cabinet, was more amiable, but indolent and reluctant to take a prominent part in debate. Sydney, given the lead in the House of Lords, had never been a politician of the front rank: the two young peers, Rutland and Carmarthen, were short of experience, and Howe, though respected in his profession, confined himself to naval affairs. Apart from the preponderance of peers, the most remarkable feature of the cabinet, according to Wraxall, was its collective capacity for drink.

There was greater talent in the rest of the administration. Dundas, who resumed his place as Treasurer of the Navy, had established himself as one of the most effective debaters in the House and a useful man of business; William Grenville, Burke's successor as Paymaster, developed into a valuable supporting speaker; Lloyd Kenyon, the Attorney-General, had a reputation for prickly integrity, though he was ill at ease in political life; Pepper Arden, Solicitor-General, was new to Parliament, but made up in pugnacity and determination for any deficiencies in legal knowledge he possessed. In the House of Lords, Richmond, who accepted office once more as Master-General of the Ordnance was a ready speaker, and when Rutland went to Ireland in January as Lord-Lieutenant was promoted to the cabinet.

Politically the ministry was a complete mixture, as its opponents were fond of pointing out. Four of the cabinet had opposed

---

[1] Pitt to Temple, 23 December, 5 p.m., *op. cit.*, i, 6, note 2.
[2] Camden to Thomas Walpole, 7 January 1784, Lullings MSS. J. H. Addington wrote to his brother Henry, 28 December: 'surely the nation can derive but little hope from those (excepting one) already appointed?' Sidmouth MSS.

the American War, three had supported it.[1] Thurlow and Dundas had been as prominent against parliamentary reform as Pitt and Richmond had been in advocating it. In this the ministry reflected the shattered state of political life. Of the 195 members supporting Pitt in the spring of 1784 who had been in the House during the war, 109 had been in favour of prosecuting it, and 86 against. In the new alignment, George Selwyn, the king's man *par excellence*, voted side by side with John Wilkes, the friend of liberty.

In one respect the new ministers were fortunate. Called into office just before the Christmas recess, they did not have to face an immediate parliamentary attack, and they had time both to prepare their own proposals on India and to seek to detach supporters of the coalition from their allegiance. Consequently, when the House discussed the matter on the 24th, Fox moved for a short adjournment until 8 January. But when country gentlemen complained that there would not be enough time to look after their business, he agreed to postpone it until the 12th. At the same time the majority sought to tie the hands of ministers more effectively by forbidding them to accept India bills for payment until the affairs of the Company had been put in order.

The engines of patronage, stopped during the coalition's tenure of office, were now given full throttle. The earliest indication of the new order was the signing by the king within the first week of the ministry of a warrant for a peerage to Thomas Pitt, doubtless *pour encourager les autres*.[2] Before the year was out, aspiring candidates were rehearsing their claims: 'I was a true and faithful follower in Parliament of the Pitts and Grenvilles during all their Opposition', Sir Hew Dalrymple wrote to Dundas, begging for an Irish peerage.[3] During the whole of the recess, the

[1] Thurlow, Gower and Howe had been supporters.
[2] Sydney to the king, 29 December, Aspinall, i, 14. It can scarcely have been to engage his borough interest at Old Sarum, since Thomas Pitt had taken a decisive part against the coalition from its inception.
[3] 29 December, Scottish Peerage Papers, MSS. 1026, f. 144, National Library of Scotland. The opposition referred to was in the 1760s, but all was grist to the mill.

political world buzzed with rumours of offers made, conversions effected, and temptations resisted. 'All the powers of the Crown', wrote Portland, 'have been let loose without reserve'.[1]

In this situation the key figure was John Robinson, North's former patronage secretary, a man of charts and computations. Full of zeal to be of service, he had moved, step by step, from assisting Shelburne's government, with North's complete approval, to supplying the opposition with the information they needed to overthrow the coalition administration.[2] His conviction that, during the recess, the coalition's majority could be effaced must have been an important factor in Pitt's decision not to dissolve. For a few days, while the orators were silent, his room was the centre of political life: under the name of 'Jack Renegado' the newspapers followed his activities day by day, printing lists of the 'Ratcatcher's' reputed successes.[3]

From his many estimates it is possible with reasonable accuracy to reconstruct the situation as he saw it developing. The basis of his calculations were the divisions on the India bill and the subsequent address of the 22nd: a total of 259 members, he believed, had cast votes for the coalition, 139 against, and 159 had been absent. To reverse this position would be a most formidable task, even though the figures may have flattered the coalition to some extent, since the obvious need for some action on India made a division on that subject a strong point for any administration. The first problem was the absentees. Robinson could be certain that at least forty members could never be induced to vote under any circumstances. Paul Benfield, the member for Cricklade, was in India amassing a fortune; Thomas Walpole was in Paris, a refugee

---

[1] Portland to Sandwich, 30 December, Sandwich MSS.

[2] His career is discussed by I. R. Christie, 'The political allegiance of John Robinson, 1770–1784', *Bulletin of the Institute of Historical Research*, xxix, 108–22. Wraxall is probably right in suggesting that Robinson's reward was the Earldom given to Lord Abergavenny, to whose heir his only daughter was married.

[3] Elliot told Harris that Robinson had promised to find sixty converts. Minto MSS., Box M 43, 29 December. For newspaper comment on Robinson's progress see *Public Advertiser*, 1, 2, 3, 7 January 1784.

from his creditors; Richard Hippisley Coxe was insane; Edward Gibbon had retired to Lausanne to complete *Decline and Fall of the Roman Empire*; Sir Merrick Burrell was eighty-four, and had not attended during the whole of the Parliament. Of the remaining 120 members, it might reasonably be assumed that they would split 2-1 in favour of the new ministry. This would give the coalition 299 votes against 219, leaving Robinson to make at least forty converts before he could hope for a majority.

Several members, such as Thomas Johnes, Glyn Wynn and John Anstruther, held minor office, and could be expected to change sides without further inducement. Others were in such close relation to the court that they would almost certainly switch their allegiance as soon as it was clear how committed the king was to his new ministers: Sir George Osborn was a Groom of the Bedchamber, John Peachey's father was a Groom of the Bedchamber, and George Pitt's father was Lord Rivers, one of the Lords of the Bedchamber, who had switched his vote between the 15th and the 17th. Sir James Cockburn, the member for Linlithgow Burghs, was in acute financial difficulty and received a royal pension through his wife: he was one of the first to be reported to have changed sides. Henry St John, a Groom of the Bedchamber, who stayed with the coalition, found himself deprived of his post.[1]

Robinson's main reliance was on the influence that the great patrons might be persuaded to exert on their members. Some successes came early and easily. The duke of Bridgwater, who had allowed his two members a loose rein in November, jerked them into a reminder of their duty as soon as the king's views were known.[2] Lord Weymouth abandoned the coalition and continued to hold office as Groom of the Stole: he was rewarded

[1] *History of the Westminster election*, 265, confirmed by the *Court and City Register*. The *House of Commons*, iii, 399 appears to be in error.
[2] The duke's borough was Brackley. Timothy Caswall had voted for the India bill; John William Egerton had been absent. See Macdonald to Lady Gower, 28 November 1783, Granville MSS.; and *The House of Commons 1754-90*, ii, 198.

in January by a peerage for his brother, Henry Frederick Thynne, with special remainder to Weymouth's younger sons. Although he was unable to detach Rigby from the coalition, his defection may have been worth four votes to Pitt's cause.[1] The duke of Northumberland's allegiance was also confirmed by the promise of a peerage to which his second son, Lord Algernon Percy, would succeed: six of the seven members under Northumberland's influence voted with Pitt when Parliament reassembled.[2] Two other great borough patrons received peerages. The support of Edward Eliot, who was created a baron in January, was of more consequence for the future than the immediate present: although he influenced seven seats, his members were returned for the most part as a straight commercial transaction, and he had in consequence little command over them. His son, Edward James Eliot, was a Lord of the Treasury in the new administration, and Eliot's successor for Cornwall was a supporter of Pitt, but the other five members were all friends of the coalition and continued to be so. Not until the general election could Eliot requite the honour granted him.[3] Another aspirant for the peerage to receive his reward was Sir James Lowther, the disagreeable and irascible member for Cumberland, who was promised an earldom. This represented no gain in voting strength, since Sir James had had

[1] One of his members, John Calvert, junior, sitting for Malmesbury, changed sides; John Calvert, senior, and Andrew Bayntun, who had been absent from the divisions over the India bill, attended in the spring and supported Pitt; John Scott, the lawyer, had opposed the bill from the beginning. Weymouth himself was created marquess of Bath in 1789.

[2] The duke controlled Newport (Cornwall), Launceston and Bere Alston, and Lord Algernon Percy sat for the county of Northumberland. Laurence Cox came over from the coalition; Lord Algernon, Sir John Coghill and Lord Feilding, who had been absent, attended and voted with Pitt; C. G. Perceval, who had contemplated resignation because of his obligations to Lord North, was persuaded to continue, and took office as a Lord of the Admiralty; Sir John Jervis continued to support Pitt. The seventh member, Lord Maitland, stayed with Fox with whom he was on terms of close friendship, though Robinson was said to have declared that he would be the first of the converts. Elliot to Harris, 29 December, Minto MSS., Box M 43. It is perhaps scarcely necessary to add that it is impossible to estimate the precise degree of dependence between members and patrons.

[3] The five coalitionists were Sir John Ramsden, Thomas Lucas, Dudley Long, Wilbraham Tollemache and Samuel Salt.

his nine members on parade during the passage of the India bill, but it was a comforting insurance against defection, and it allowed the new first minister to pay off old debts.[1]

Not all the borough patrons succumbed to temptation. Before Christmas Robinson had hopes of Lord Hertford, Lord Clive and Sir Francis Basset: between them they commanded at least ten votes.[2] All three were mentioned by Sir Gilbert Elliot as persons to whom offers of peerages in some form had been made, and Robinson, in an early list of borough prospects, included Hertford and Basset's seats as 'supposed to be partly accessible'.[3] Of Basset in particular Robinson must have been hopeful, for he was known to entertain strong ambitions of a peerage and had just quarrelled violently with Portland. But none of the three came over, and Basset's zeal for the coalition seems to have prompted him to force the resignation of J. P. Bastard, who sat for Truro, in order to bring in a more reliable member.[4] Another disappointment to Robinson was Lord Lisburne, who was worth four votes in the Commons, his own, his brother's, and two for his brother-in-law's borough of Downton. Anxious to convert his Irish peerage into a British one, and described as feeling himself neglected by Lord North, Lisburne was a promising target. At the end of the year, Sydney wrote to enquire whether his support for Fox's India bill had been merely because of the need for some action, and assured him that Pitt 'would be happy to know if

---

[1] It was perhaps significant that Lowther's peerage was delayed until May 1784: even then, there was a last-minute dispute. The other eight members of his group were Pitt himself, sitting for Appleby; James, John and William Lowther, cousins; Sir Michael le Fleming, J. B. Garforth, W. S. Stanhope and Edward Norton.

[2] Lord Hertford had four sons in this Parliament, and could exert some influence over Whitshed Keene; Lord Clive had his own vote, being an Irish peer, that of his brother William, and influenced Henry Strachey, who sat for Bishop's Castle; in addition to his own vote, Basset could probably influence the conduct of R. P. Carew and J. P. Bastard and possibly that of his relative, Francis Basset, who sat for Barnstaple. Bastard and Carew had been absent from the divisions before Christmas: the other ten had voted with the coalition, so conversions would have been of double value.

[3] Elliot to Harris, 29 December, Minto MSS.; Laprade, 107.

[4] *The House of Commons 1754–90*, ii, 65.

there are any wishes of yours that he can meet or promote'.[1] But the invitation was declined. 'They are crying peerages about the streets in barrows', wrote Horace Walpole, not without justice.[2]

The king himself followed up his intervention with the utmost vigour. On the 23rd, Lord Fauconberg, one of the Lords of the Bedchamber, wrote to express his 'great concern' that his proxy vote should have been used in the House of Lords contrary to the king's wishes. Another recantation came from the duke of Marlborough. On 18 December he had written to Eden: 'this measure of sending about personally to influence people's votes can not but be wrong.' But on the 29th he received a letter from the king calling upon him to engage his friends to support government. Marlborough replied that he would not have given his proxy in favour of the bill had he not thought it 'calculated to increase rather than to diminish the power of the Crown'. Though the king described this answer as 'very satisfactory', the duke did not find it easy to mobilise his troops. His two brothers, Lord Robert and Lord Charles Spencer, together with William Eden, who sat for Woodstock, had taken too prominent a part on behalf of the coalition to change sides. Lord Parker, the other member for Woodstock, who had been absent at the time of Fox's bill, resolved to remain absent, and in this prudent decision he was joined by the fifth member of the duke's force, Francis Burton, who had already voted against the bill. Marlborough was forced to confess in January 1784 that he had found it 'impracticable' to obey the royal commands completely.[3]

The king's first big success was the capture of the duke of Newcastle, which he announced to Pitt on 1 January. This was more than a paper victory. Newcastle had command of six seats and was prepared to use his power to the full. Five of the six members had voted with the coalition on the India bill, the

[1] 31 December 1783, Egerton MSS., 2136, f. 237.
[2] Walpole to Countess of Upper Ossory, 30 December 1783.
[3] Aspinall, i, 6–7, 14–15, 16, 24–5; Add. MS. 34419, f. 314. It is of course possible that the duke was not trying too hard.

sixth, Newcastle's son, being absent. Two members, Charles Ambler and Sir Samuel Brudenell Fludyer, changed sides without delay, and Lord Lincoln made his appearance in support of Pitt when Parliament reassembled. Charles Mellish, the member for Aldborough, developed scruples and was forced to resign. Sir Henry Clinton and Anthony Eyre deserted the coalition, but could not bring themselves to vote for the new ministry: to Newcastle Eyre explained that he had taken a decisive part in favour of the bill without knowing it was contrary to his patron's wishes. Neither of the recalcitrant members was rechosen at the general election. Sir Samuel Fludyer's brother, George, also changed sides, at the instigation of his uncle, George Bridges Brudenell, so that the operation deprived the coalition of six votes and added four to the ministry.[1]

The king was also involved in determined efforts to enlist the support of Lord Sackville, who had taken offence at the inclusion of Lord Carmarthen in the government.[2] Pitt, Sydney and Thurlow collaborated in a mass bombardment by post on 29 December, and Nathaniel Wraxall was commissioned to make a flying visit to Drayton to add his voice to the entreaties. When Sackville continued to return frosty answers, the duke of Dorset took up the matter on behalf of the king: 'my *master* asked me a good deal about your opinion of things . . . he has *empowered* me to mention *his* name to *you* and to assure you how much he has at heart the success of his present servants in the present struggle'. This appeal from on high appears to have been successful.[3]

By the end of December Robinson had accumulated enough fresh information to justify a second edition of his estimate. This promised Pitt a majority, with 222 votes against 204: there were 61 hopefuls and 45 doubtfuls. 'Things go well and favourably *for the whole*', he reported on 5 January, 'altho' difficult and with

1 The king to Pitt, 1 January, Chatham MSS.; *The House of Commons 1754-90*, ii, 409; iii, 129.
2 Carmarthen had called Sackville's peerage a 'disgrace to the House' in the debate of 7 February 1782.   3 *H.M.C. Stopford-Sackville MSS.*, i, 80-4; Wraxall, iii, 251-3.

vengeance to me.' On the 10th, two days before the House of
Commons met again, he declared that 'days, nay hours' were
making great alterations in his list. The second edition was revised
to read 240 supporters against 196 opponents, and a further
thirty-six members were described as 'very hopeful'. In Robinson's judgement, therefore, Pitt could anticipate a substantial
majority when the House assembled.[1]

The frenzied activity on the government side was matched by
the coalition. Lord North gave excellent dinners to keep the
troops in good spirits, while the subalterns chased round after
doubtful votes. 'For God's sake, send Frank Charteris up', wrote
Sir Thomas Dundas to Henry Erskine: 'we have lost but one
member, and that is a Scots one, Sir J. Cockburn. Sir Robert
Herries was thought to be off, but he is as firm as flint. Pray,
where is Sir Robert Laurie? . . . We must not lose him . . .' The
younger members of the coalition, like Eden and Elliot, were full
of confidence, but North and Loughborough, with greater
experience, were less sanguine. North's opinion was that the
coalition would have a majority on most questions, 'but that the
amount of that majority will vary much upon the particular
state of the question'. Loughborough concurred, telling Eden on
the 2nd: 'I do not feel the same confidence that you and most
people do upon the result of the first weeks. I expect to find more
coldness and backwardness in the bulk of your friends to adopt
any strong measure, much inclination in many to accommodate,
and a general disposition to allow the ministers to produce their
plans. During the interval . . . offers will be privately and openly
made which will divide men's opinions'.[2]

---

[1] Dorset to Sackville, 3 January 1784, *H.M.C. Stopford-Sackville MSS.*, i, 84; Robinson to
Jenkinson, 5 & 10 January, Add. MS. 38567, ff. 179-80 & 181-2. Robinson's second
edition is in two parts. The estimates for English counties and for Wales were printed
separately in Laprade, 51-3: the rest are to be found in the Abergavenny MSS. The day
to day changes referred to are printed in Laprade, 54-5.

[2] A. Fergusson, *Henry Erskine*, 253; Elliot to Harris, 31 December, Minto MSS.; Eden
to Morton Eden, 30 December, Auckland, i, 70; Loughborough to Eden, 1 January,
Add. MS. 34419, f. 330.

Loughborough's caution was well advised. Not all members were eager for the fray. Of Glyn Wynn, who held office and was expected to change, a friend wrote: 'it would be an act of great kindness if he could be permitted to trim a little and temporize, till it is more clearly to be discerned how majorities are likely to be . . . possibly he may not be wanted . . .'[1] Benjamin Keene, the member for Cambridge, explained his own decision not to attend on the 12th to Philip Yorke:

I have never yet been a partisan . . . I never was a friend to the coalition and very much disliked the means by which it came into power, but as it afterwards seemed to have strength, ability and firmness I by no means wished its removal . . . The present ministry, not having the prospect of a long continuance, can hardly expect the support of persons unconnected as I am who may think its immediate dissolution would be preferable to its existing in a weak and lingering state during a great part of the session . . .[2]

Among the militants, however, excitement ran high. The king took the opportunity afforded by the bishops' annual address on the New Year, normally an innocuous occasion, to deliver himself of a declaration of intent. He regarded the era as one 'of the most critical importance to this country', and though he would never interfere in the rights of the legislature, he was determined 'to maintain in full vigour and effect all the prerogative to which by the constitution he was certainly entitled'. Lord North, appealing for Lisburne's assistance, described the situation as 'one of the most extraordinary scenes that we have beheld in our time', while Thomas Coutts, with a banker's sensitivity, thought that 'there is no saying how soon civil commotions may be kindled'. Worked upon by Gallic imagination, the rumours and alarms took dramatic shape. From Paris, Lady Clermont reported: 'They are all sure there will be a revolution, and that Fox will be king'.[3]

---

[1] *The House of Commons 1754–90*, iii, 669.   [2] 11 January, Add. MS. 35641, f. 70.
[3] Orde to Shelburne, 1 January, Bowood MSS.; *General Evening Post*, 6/8 January; Egerton MSS., 2136, f. 241; Coutts to Charles Stuart, 8 January, *A Prime Minister and his son*; Letters of the duchess of Devonshire, printed *Anglo-Saxon Review*, September 1899, 71.

CHAPTER 9

THE PARLIAMENTARY STRUGGLE:
THE EARLY STAGES

Despite private computations and bets confidently laid, neither side had any clear idea what would happen when the House of Commons met on 12 January. The more sanguine members of the coalition hoped that if Pitt found himself in a minority he would at once resign, and obviate the need for extreme measures. The ministers placed their trust in a new India bill, which Dundas and Atkinson had been working on during the recess, arguing that the House could not reasonably refuse them a hearing after all that had been said in the previous session about the urgency of the problem. But Pitt still held in reserve the possibility of a dissolution should the coalition command an insuperable majority. The king was reported to have Treasury riders at the ready, and to have assured Pitt that 'he should not think of repose till he knew the division'. The coalition, on its part, was fortified by the presence of the Prince of Wales, seated under the gallery.[1]

Two themes dominated the first part of the debate, secret influence and the question of a dissolution. Fox gained possession of the floor by rising at 2.30 p.m. to move the order of the day for a committee on the state of the nation, though the debate was held up until 4 p.m. by the swearing-in of re-elected members. Pitt then countered by asking for leave to bring in his India bill. Erskine and Fox, opening for the opposition, demanded to know whether the House could deliberate in freedom, or whether the threat of dissolution was still held out against them should they prove uncooperative. Not since the days of the Stuart kings, declared Fox, had there been resort to a dissolution during a

---

[1] *Morning Herald*, 13 January.

session with parliamentary business still unfinished. His own India bill had been thrown out in the House of Lords not by fair examination, but by secret influence, unconstitutionally exerted. To the latter charge, Pitt replied in tones of outraged virtue:

He knew of no secret influence, and his own integrity would be his guardian against that danger . . . Little did I think to be ever charged in this House with being the tool and abettor of secret influence. The novelty of the imputation only renders it so much the more contemptible. This is the only answer I shall ever deign to make on the subject, and I wish the House to bear it in their mind, and judge of my future conduct by my present declaration: the integrity of my own heart, and the probity of all my public, as well as my private principles, shall always be my sources of action . . .

It was the lie of a master, perfect of its kind, superb in its insolence, and totally successful; its very unctuousness carried the war into the enemy's camp, smearing them as the purveyors of shabby slanders and cheap rumours. On the matter of a dissolution, he was decidedly unforthcoming: his only comment on the pledge made on his behalf by Bankes was that 'such at the time had been his real sentiment: he could not at present say more'. General Ross then injected a little reality into the debate by revealing that he had been warned by a lord of the bedchamber not to vote against the ministers unless he wished to be considered an enemy of the king. When the order of the day was put, at 2.30 in the morning, the coalition carried it by 232 votes to 193, a majority of 39, and the House moved on to discuss the state of the nation. The opposition drove home its advantage with a string of resolutions designed to hamper and embarrass the ministers—against the payment of any money after a dissolution, for an immediate statement of all payments since the ministry began, for a postponement of the second reading of the Mutiny bill until 23 February, and for an administration having the confidence of the House and of the public. To these the ministers offered only token resistance. The last resolution, however, condemning the 'unconstitutional abuse' of the king's name in order to influence the deliberations of Parliament, provoked more excitement. Governor Johnstone poured scorn on the assertion of secret influence: it was 'a fine catch-word . . . to amuse the credulous vulgar . . . I would as soon believe in witchcraft or the Cock-Lane ghost as think that the late administration was dissolved by secret influence.' Dundas argued that it was too late for an adequate discussion of the resolution, and moved the adjournment. On this motion the second division took place, the coalition majority rising to 54. The resolutions were then carried, and the House adjourned at 7.30 a.m.[1]

Lord Palmerston's assessment of the outcome was sober and judicious: 'this majority of 39 shewed on the one hand how diligent the ministry had been, in the interval of Parliament, in getting over proselytes, or in the fashionable phrase, *Rats*. On the other hand, it presented such an unpromising prospect as was sufficient to have made prudent men despair of their undertaking.' The general opinion, however, was that the honours of the day had gone to Fox and his friends. They had managed '*ably* and *boldly*, the others *weakly*', thought Lord Hardwicke and for once Philip Yorke was obliged to agree with him. The king received the news with 'much uneasiness', but was resolved never to surrender: 'if they in the end succeed, my line is a clear one, and to which I have fortitude enough to submit'. In the meantime he would hold himself in readiness to hear any suggestions the ministers had to make.[2]

The ministers however had depressingly few suggestions to make. A cabinet meeting at Rutland's on the 13th, augmented by Richmond, Dundas, Weymouth, Pepper Arden and George Rose, appears from Carmarthen's account to have been gloomy and unproductive:

---

[1] Debrett, xii, 492–540.
[2] B. Connell, *op. cit.*, 148; Add. MS. 35381, ff. 214 & 215; the king to Pitt, 13 January, Stanhope, i, appendix, iv.

We endeavoured to find out some method to surmount the obstacles thrown in the way of a dissolution by the opposite party; this however seemed extremely difficult, and at the same time it appeared impossible to go on with the public business with the House of Commons against us, no matter by what means. Mr. Pitt even hinted at giving the thing up; this however was represented to him by us all as betraying both the Crown and People, as well as highly disgraceful to ourselves personally . . .[1]

The only outcome of the meeting was that Richmond volunteered to join the cabinet and was accepted. Though this was gratifying proof that someone thought the ministry might last, Richmond's support for Pitt had been long declared, and he did not carry enough political weight to be in himself an adequate retort to the menaces of the opposition.

The most substantial hope left to the ministers was that the new India bill would gain widespread approval and afford them a rallying-point. When Pitt outlined his proposals in the House of Commons on 14 January, he was at pains to emphasise that they had been prepared in close consultation with the Company. Two of his most active supporters, Governor Johnstone and Richard Atkinson, had succeeded in the course of December in taking over the lead in the Company's affairs, replacing in the Directorate Sir Henry Fletcher and Jacob Wilkinson, who had been forced out. On 20 December, at their instigation, the Company declared its readiness to negotiate with the new administration, and there were frequent discussions during the parliamentary recess. The basis for negotiation was Dundas's earlier plan, and though the Directors had strongly condemned it at the time, they now accepted it in general, lest worse befall. In this respect Pitt profited from Fox's abortive measure which, by threatening their very existence, rendered the Directors more docile. In India, the main feature of the bill was a considerable increase in the powers of the Governor-General, both in relation to his council and to the subordinate Presidencies. At home, the Court of

Directors and the General Court of Proprietors were retained, but the latter was stripped of most of its powers. On the other hand, Dundas was unable to carry his favourite proposal for a third Secretary of State in charge of Indian affairs, presumably because Pitt considered it would be politically damaging.

The most obvious difference between Pitt's scheme and that put forward by the coalition was the intention to separate the political and commercial activities of the Company, vesting the first in a new Board of Control, but leaving the second in the hands of the Directors. The Board was to consist of the Secretary of State for the Home Department, the Chancellor of the Exchequer, and certain privy counsellors, the number to be decided subsequently, all serving without salary.[1] It was therefore in no way independent of the government, as Fox argued that his commissioners might have been, and the opposition was enabled to assert that the power of the crown was greatly increased. However questionable in terms of eighteenth-century political theory, the arrangement was realistic, and met Jenkinson's criticism of Fox's bill. But the division of responsibility between the Board and the Directors was left ill-defined, in C. H. Philips's opinion deliberately so.[2] Pitt's explanation to the House that while the Board would have powers of supervision over commercial activities the administration would be left 'as far as possible' with the Directors gave great scope for demarcation disputes. Although he gave prominence to the proposal that the Directors should retain the powers of appointment, including that of the Governor-General, in practice the senior positions were filled by the government, which was also accorded a share in the lesser patronage. In case of dispute, the Directors were to have a right of appeal, but since it was to the Privy Council, in which all the members of the Board sat, the opposition might be justified in

---

[1] When the measure became law later in the year, the number of privy counsellors was fixed at four. The Charter Act of 1793 instituted salaries.

[2] *The East India Company 1784–1834* (1940), chs. i & ii.

considering it no more than a paper safeguard. The ultimate beneficiary of the measure proved, in fact, to be Henry Dundas, who acquired in the course of the following decade a control which his colleagues, preoccupied with departmental problems, could not or would not contest. The Directors had to content themselves with the appearance of power, while in most important respects command passed to the government. For this reason C. H. Philips has called it a 'clever, dishonest bill', though this perhaps exaggerates the extent to which its framers could foresee how it would develop.

It was not to be expected that much attempt would be made to discuss the bill on its merits. Fox launched his attack the moment Pitt sat down. Nothing in the bill, he objected, met the desire of the House to see justice done to the native population or to restrain corruption and abuses. Reserving his detailed criticism for a later stage, he complained of the identification of the Board with the government, and the increased power which it gave to the executive. The House showed little wish to debate the matter further at this stage, and fell into a noisy and unprofitable exchange about fresh allegations of proselytising at home. Leave for Pitt to bring in the bill was granted without a division.[1]

The second reading of the bill, proposed by Pitt for the 21st, was postponed by the majority until the 23rd, partly as a demonstration of strength and partly to embarrass still further the ministry's timing in case of a dissolution. In the meantime, on the 16th, Lord Charles Spencer moved that the appointment of the ministry had been accompanied by 'circumstances new and extraordinary', and that its continuance was 'contrary to constitutional principles and injurious to the interests of His Majesty and his people'. This provoked some of the country gentlemen to argue that the prerogatives of the crown were being challenged, though Fox himself was careful to maintain that he questioned not the legality but the wisdom of the royal policy. The main

---

[1] Debrett, xii, 541–570.

defence of the administration on this occasion fell to Dundas, who took the opportunity to improve upon Pitt's rejection of the charge of secret influence. Granting for the sake of argument the truth of all the rumours that Temple had made an unconstitutional use of the king's name, how did that affect the present ministers?

Is my lord Temple a minister? . . . lords of the bed-chamber are no ministers; who therefore are those men that your resolution means to slander? . . . Sir, I defy any man even to insinuate that any one of his Majesty's cabinet has ever had the least share of that secret influence upon which this motion is founded . . . The throwing out of the India Bill was a matter previous to their appointment, a matter in which they had no concern, and for which they can share no blame, even if I allow, for argument's sake, that blame is due anywhere . . .

This appeal for fair play from men who had themselves broken every rule in the political game made some impression on the House.[1] Sir William Dolben and General Murray, both of whom had supported Fox on the India bill, agreed that the new ministers should at least be given the chance of presenting their measure, and the majority of 21 by which the resolution was finally passed, even taking into account the smaller attendance, revealed a distinct falling-off in support for the opposition.[2] The king certainly was well satisfied with the result which demonstrated, in his opinion, that the majority would soon be 'in favour of decorum instead of siding with anarchy'.[3]

This shift of opinion was confirmed by the debate on the second reading of Pitt's India bill. By this time the House was weary of Indian affairs, and the debate was neither long nor animated. Even Fox seems to have been affected by the general torpor, and

---

[1] The full version of the letter from Atkinson to Robinson, 12 December 1783, printed in part as no. 526 in *H.M.C. Abergavenny MSS.*, makes it clear that Atkinson's information came from Dundas, who was therefore well aware both of the use of the king's name and of Pitt's implication in it. Since Pitt's declaration of innocence on the 12th had gone unchallenged, it was apparent to Dundas that the coalition had no evidence that it could use.

[2] Debrett, xii, 585–605. The figures were 205 to 184. Thirty-six fewer voted than in the first division on 12 January.

[3] The king to Pitt, 17 January, printed in J. H. Rose, *Pitt and Napoleon* (1912), 202–3.

his speech, though cogent, was unremarkable. Pitt, however, excelled himself. The main purpose of his plan, he explained, was to ensure the greatest possible political control to the government with the least opportunity for the corrupt use of patronage. It was idle to pretend, as Fox did, that an effective administration for India could be maintained independent of the home government: such an arrangement could lead only to chaos:

Earl Fitzwilliam, Sir, by that bill, had power to involve this country in war with France or with Holland, not only without the direction, but without the privity of the government of this country . . . What an *imperium in imperio* was this! . . . When the right honourable gentleman therefore calls his system permanent, because his commissioners were thus separated and insulated from the Crown, I should lament such permanency if it were possible; but I deny the possibility; for all our dependencies cannot continue to exist unless in our Asiatic and European politics there be some unity of action.

But despite his plea to the House to regard his bill as a basis for reform, to be adapted and improved in committee, it was rejected on the division by 222 to 214.[1]

At first glance it might appear that the ministers should have been delighted at whittling down the adverse majority to a mere 8 votes. But they were well aware that the success was deceptive. It had been their best chance of gaining a majority in the existing House of Commons and they had failed to do so. They had used up two of their most compelling arguments—the need to take immediate action on India, and their right to be heard. The opposition could now recapture the initiative and turn the discussion once more to the constitutional issue, on which the ministers were least comfortable. The division on the second reading, therefore, instead of convincing the cabinet that with a little patience it might acquire a majority, provided a renewed inducement to seek a dissolution.

As soon as the vote on the bill had been taken, Fox pressed for

---

[1] Debrett, xii, 618–37.

assurances that there would be no dissolution: the royal answer to the address in December appeared to rule out any such possibility, but the House was entitled to some explanation. For more than two hours Pitt was subjected to a most uncomfortable barrage. Conway denounced his 'sulky silence', and termed his conduct an insult and indecency to the House, but more damaging was the intervention of James Martin, an independent whose detestation of the coalition was notorious, and who warned Pitt that he would abandon him unless some answer was forthcoming. Called upon from all sides, Pitt remained seated, and at length Fox suggested an adjournment of a few hours to give the ministers a chance to reflect. When they resumed, the attack was taken up by Thomas Powys, another independent, but whose recent votes had all been with Pitt. Weeping copiously, a facility which seems to have come easily to him, he declared himself haunted by the previous night's scene: surely the House had some right to know whether it would be in existence on Monday 26th? To this Pitt, fresh from cabinet deliberations, was obliged to pledge himself, though with obvious reluctance.[1]

Behind the scenes the most frantic consultations were taking place, as ministers saw time running out. The shortest return of Parliament since the Act of Union was fifty-two days,[2] and, according to Loughborough, the minimum was fifty days.[3] If a dissolution took place on 26 January, without previous prorogation, the new House could not meet until Thursday, 18 March. Some days would be taken up by the king's speech, the election of a Speaker, and the swearing-in of members, yet the new Mutiny Act had to be law by 25 March. If the government missed this opportunity of calling a general election, they would put into the hands of their opponents the power to prevent any dissolution for two months by postponing consideration of the Mutiny bill.

[1] Debrett, xii, 638–44; *Morning Herald* and *Morning Chronicle*, 24 & 26 January.
[2] Between 8 April and 31 May 1754.
[3] Loughborough to Eden, 1 January 1784, Add. MS. 34419, f. 330.

The week-end of the 24/25th was therefore critical, and the strongest rumours of a dissolution circulated.[1]

The most ardent advocate of dissolution was the king. On the 23rd, he wrote that the Chancellor should be asked whether a prorogation was strictly necessary, and the following day urged Pitt to dissolve: 'if not, I fear the constitution of this country cannot subsist.' Later that evening he wrote again to ask for a cabinet to be summoned on the matter at once. It seems to have been found impossible to assemble the ministers at such short notice, but most of the following day was spent in conference. After several hours in the morning, the ministers were still not in a position to offer advice, and Pitt had to postpone his audience. The king interpreted this as further evidence of irresolution, and his reply was addressed to the timid and legalistic: 'we must be men; and if we mean to save the country, we must cut those threads that cannot be unravelled. Half-measures are ever puerile, and often destructive.' But despite this brave attempt to put heart into them, the ministers remained in an agony of indecision.[2]

At the outset, Gower, Carmarthen and Sydney favoured a dissolution; Richmond thought they should persevere with the existing House of Commons; Pitt and Rutland were still concerned about the pledge that had been given not to dissolve; and Thurlow 'seemed perplexed'. Five hours discussion persuaded Richmond to give way, and they adjourned for dinner determined to dissolve. But with the port, doubt crept in, and a further six hours were needed. Carmarthen objected that it was possible to get the Mutiny bill passed in time by the new Parliament only by ignoring the normal forms of procedure. Eventually the decision

---

[1] See T. Pelham to Lord Pelham, 24 January, Add. MS. 33128, f. 278; John Horne Tooke to Sir Robert Bernard, 24 January, Manchester MSS.; Loughborough to Eden, Add. MS. 34419, f. 346; North to Lord Guilford, 26 January, Waldeshare MSS.; the *Sherborne Mercury*, 26 January, assured its readers, on the authority of a London correspondent 'whose intelligence we have every reason to depend upon', that a dissolution had taken place.

[2] Aspinall, 26–7; Stanhope, i, appendix, iv–v; J. H. Rose, *Pitt and Napoleon* (1912), 203.

of the morning was reversed, and Pitt was left to break the news to the king.[1]

Since the cabinet's decision not to dissolve seems to have been unaccompanied by any suggestion how business was to be carried on in a hostile House of Commons, the king suspected that it was a preliminary to surrender. He therefore summoned the ministers to attend him the following day which, observed Carmarthen, 'we all did, and not without great anxiety':

His Majesty in a well conceived speech of some length, and in different parts of which he appeared much agitated, expressed his wish upon all occasions to observe the true principles of the constitution as the sole rule of his conduct . . . and declared a fixed and unalterable resolution on no account to be put bound hand and foot into the hands of Mr. Fox, that rather than submit to that he would quit the kingdom for ever . . . We assured him we would by no means desert him in his gracious endeavour to preserve our constitution inviolate.[2]

Pitt did his best to derive some advantage from the situation when the House met on the 26th. Although he insisted that the royal message of December could not be interpreted as an indefinite postponement of a dissolution, he assured members that he had no intention of advising an immediate dissolution. This conciliatory answer did not prevent the tide of opinion from running strongly against him. The independents once more took a prominent part in the debate. Charles Marsham, the member for Kent, who had voted with opposition on Fox's India bill, now seconded a motion which interpreted the royal message as a guarantee against dissolution while Indian business was still

[1] I find the explanation of these events given by D. G. Barnes, *George III and William Pitt 1783–1806*, 79, totally unconvincing. 'What explanation can be offered for failure to "cut those threads", that is, to dissolve Parliament, when the King was anxious to do so. The obvious one is that Pitt was unwilling at this time to break definitely with the Rockingham Whigs . . . He saw in Fox, Portland, Burke, Sheridan and their followers his natural allies . . . In no other manner can the failure to dissolve Parliament after the defeat of Pitt's India Bill on January 23 be satisfactorily explained.'

[2] Leeds, 95–7. Richard Pares, *King George III and the politicians*, 151, cited this as a rare example of the king attending a cabinet meeting. I do not think it can be described as a cabinet in any real sense. It lasted only a few minutes and, apparently, only the king and Pitt spoke. The atmosphere was that of a commander haranguing his reluctant troops.

undecided, and Powys once again was highly critical of the minister. Admitting that he had opposed the original resolutions against the administration, he argued that the case was 'very materially altered' since the rejection of Pitt's India bill.[1] Fox demanded to know why Pitt clung to office in defiance of the wish of the House: it was totally without precedent. Pitt, in reply, was cautious, admitting the novelty of his situation, but claiming that, since the appointment of ministers did not belong to the House, he was doing nothing illegal: 'he considered himself as performing an act of necessary duty to his king and country, and so long as that continued to be the case he should persevere.' This, Fox retorted, was to prefer his own opinion to the collective view of the House, and must lead to 'universal anarchy'. But although Fox's language was strong, his advice was temperate, and after the resolution had been passed without opposition, the House adjourned until the 29th.[2] The situation was stalemate. The moderation of the two chief protagonists could not disguise the fact that the balanced constitution, admired by generations of English and foreign observers, had broken down.

It was not accidental that the independent members were beginning to take a more active part in debate. The crisis presented them with a unique opportunity. They had always considered themselves to have a special responsibility for the preservation of the constitution: now, as they had for decades prognosticated, party faction had brought about its destruction. With the parliamentary situation so nicely balanced, both sides must heed their advice and adopt their remedies.

The possibility of a fresh alignment of parties to bring together Pitt and Fox had been mooted on 16 January by Powys, the doyen of the independents, together with 'an admirable disquisition on the constitution'.[3] Such a conjunction could only be at the

---

[1] This important speech is not given in Debrett or *Parlt. Hist.*, but is printed in the *Morning Herald*, 27 January.   [2] Debrett, xiii, 4–11.   [3] Debrett, xii, 587.

expense of North, who intervened at once to say that he would not stand in the way of a general pacification. This gesture was enough to kindle the hopes of the country gentlemen, and in the debate of the 20th the suggestion was ventilated more fully. Fox's reaction was cool: the proposal was 'easier to recommend than to effect', the principles of the two sides were 'almost irreconcilable'. But it was taken up with great fervour by the independents, and the defeat of Pitt's India bill three days later gave fresh impetus to the movement.[1]

While the cabinet was holding its protracted meeting on the 25th, the country gentlemen were busy issuing summons for a meeting at the St Albans Tavern at twelve o'clock the following day.[2] From the names of seventy-eight of the members attending, it is clear that Pitt's supporters were in a considerable majority.[3] 'I do not find that there are above ten or twelve of them that have ever voted with Fox, and those whimsical and uncertain, the rest are composed of Pitt's friends', wrote Cornwallis: 'I do not see how a number of Pitt's friends can make a fair and equal treaty between him and Fox.'[4]

The outcome of their first meeting was the election of a committee to lobby Pitt and Portland, and the adoption of a resolution to support 'the party who should, in the present distracted moment, manifest a disposition to union'.[5] The two party leaders gave bland replies, but Portland added that Pitt's retention of office, after the House's declaration of 16 January, was a barrier to

---

[1] Debrett, xii, 605–17.

[2] The St Albans Tavern was a favourite haunt of the country gentlemen, and had been used from time to time for meetings of this nature. Sir William Dolben, Sir Henry Hoghton, Thomas Gilbert, John Sinclair and others had discussions there in the spring of 1782 on ending the American War. *The correspondence of the right honourable Sir John Sinclair, bart.* (1831), i, 80, and *The House of Commons 1754–90*, sub Sinclair.

[3] Of the fifty-two members who had taken part in the divisions on Fox's India bill, thirty-three had voted with Pitt and only nineteen with Fox. It should be remembered that Fox had a 2–1 majority on the bill. A list of the members who attended the St Albans Tavern meetings is given in the *Annual Register*, 1784/5, 268.

[4] *Correspondence of Charles, first Marquis Cornwallis*, ed. C. Ross, i, 164.

[5] *Morning Chronicle*, 28 January.

further discussion. The view of most of the party militants was summed up by Lord John Cavendish, who thought them 'a very absurd sort of people, yet everybody is obliged to compliment them as the greatest men in the world'.[1]

Two more meetings followed, on the 27th and 29th. After thanking Pitt and Portland for their replies, they placed on record their hope that some expedient for overcoming the obstacle might be found: the general opinion seems to have been that Pitt should resign.[2] Later that week, when the House of Commons met, there was much skirmishing for position. Fox remarked acidly that the only activity left to the government seemed to be the granting of honours, while North professed astonishment that the minister would not retire without putting the House to 'every degree of exertion'. Pitt retaliated by pressing once more for specific charges to be brought: they should either impeach him or address the crown for his removal. He took the opportunity to pay yet another tribute to his own virtue: 'His heart, his principles, his hands were pure; and while he enjoyed the conscious satisfaction of his own mind, no language . . . no clamour, no artifice of party, no unfounded imputations should affect him.'[3]

The ministers were by no means happy at the turn events had taken. Carmarthen complained that the St Albans Tavern group soon revealed 'the most barefaced predilection for the late ministers', while the king, although in theory the anti-party group should have delighted him, found their attitude incomprehensible: 'I cannot say the meeting . . . seem as yet to have taken the only step which ought to occur to them; the cooperating in preventing a desperate faction from completing the ruin of the most perfect of all human formations—the British constitution.' In the meantime Pitt and Portland exchanged sentiments on

---

[1] Lord John Cavendish to Lord Spencer, 26 January, Spencer MSS.
[2] The *Morning Herald*, 29 January, says that the meeting agreed to recommend it. This is unlikely. The *Gentleman's Magazine*, 1784, i, 71 reports that the 'general sense' was that Pitt should resign.
[3] Debrett, xiii, 15–27.

whether some mode of resignation might be found acceptable to them both, and, not surprisingly, failed to find one.[1]

The king was undoubtedly right in believing that the group would be of consequence only if they acted boldly and in unison. Instead they took refuge in pious platitudes and fell out among themselves. On 2 February Thomas Grosvenor rose in the House to move on their behalf a motion for 'a firm, efficient, extended, united administration'. This was as far as their unity held. When James Luttrell seconding the motion insisted that there was no reason for Pitt to resign, he was sharply reminded by Sir George Cornewall that such had not been the view of the meeting. James Martin and Sir Edward Astley disliked the old coalition too much to welcome another, while Benjamin Hammet boasted that he had been the first to moot the idea. Neither Pitt nor Fox found the slightest difficulty in concurring with the motion, which passed without opposition.

Deference having been shown to the mediators, the real business commenced with a motion from Thomas William Coke, a staunch Foxite, condemning the continuance of the ministry as an obstacle to a settlement. Dundas countered with an adroit speech. He agreed without hesitation that the House had a right to advise the king on the appointment or dismissal of ministers, but it was a right to be used with discretion: it was certainly imprudent to exercise it when addresses from all parts of the country were beginning to testify to the popularity of the new government. Powys, admitting that he found great difficulty in deciding which course to follow, voted for the motion: though he had not approved of the resolution of 16 January, the ministers should act upon it. Pitt devoted much time to a refutation of Powys's argument. He was determined not to resign: 'could it be expected that he should consent to march out . . . with a halter about his neck, change his armour, and meanly beg to be readmit-

[1] Leeds, 98; Stanhope, i, appendix, vi; *Annual Register*, 1784/5, 267–70; Fox to Portland, 29 January, Add. MS. 47561, f. 66; Aspinall, 28.

ted as a volunteer in the army of the enemy?' But the motion was adopted by 223 votes to 204, and the following day a further resolution to place it before the king was passed by 211 to 187, a majority of 24. 'Our majority last night increased considerably,' wrote Sir Thomas Dundas to Henry Erskine, 'and that upon a personal question . . . The *Country Gentlemen* of the Congress at the St Albans begin to be out of humour with Pitt, and what is of more consequence, they speak of the Duke of Portland in the highest terms'.[1]

The debate of 2 February was in reality a debacle for the independents. Two days later they declared that they would 'steadily persevere' whatever the outcome, and spasmodic attempts to effect a union sputtered throughout the rest of the month: they were still treated with respect, at least outwardly, but their hour had passed. Portland had handled the negotiations well. In point of numbers, neither side gained any advantage. Of the nineteen members who may be classified as initially favourable to Fox, five went over to the government; of the thirty-three favourable to Pitt, nine went over to opposition: the proportion of converts was about the same.[2] But Portland's converts included the two leaders of the group, Powys and Marsham, both ready

---

[1] Debrett, xiii, 27–72; A. Fergusson, *Henry Erskine*, 254. Jenkinson told Robinson on 30 January that the coalition hoped for a majority of 16: the support of some independents was probably a bonus. Abergavenny MSS.

[2] There is of course no exact way of estimating the outcome of the St Albans Tavern manoeuvres, but one can make a rough guess by comparing members' voting on Fox's India bill with their final position as shown in Stockdale's list just before the general election. This is certainly inexact—e.g. it suggests that John Sinclair, who abandoned Fox as early as December 1783, was a convert through the outcome of the group. The proportion of converts in each case was 26–7 per cent. Pitt's five gains were Goddard, Gough, Berkeley, Sinclair and Hoghton; Fox's nine were Bouverie, Marsham, Powys, Honywood, Lawley, Scott, Sloper, Tempest and Thistlethwayte. Some confirmation of this analysis comes from *An authentic list of the whole House of Commons*, presumably published in a newspaper, copies of which are in the Bond and Abergavenny MSS. It gives the following list of members who 'quitted Mr. Pitt on account of his resisting the resolutions of a majority of the House of Commons': Bouverie, Honywood, Powys, Sloper, Marsham, Ridley and Thistlethwayte. I do not include Sir Matthew Ridley as a convert. He was not a member of the St Albans Tavern group, and had been absent from the divisions on Fox's India bill: immediately on his arrival in London (reported in the *Morning Herald*, 23 January) he took a decisive part with opposition.

speakers and men of high reputation. Powys's change of front, in particular, rankled with ministerialists, and he was subjected to the most bitter attacks. The coalition news-writers, proud of their acquisition, lauded him to the skies as 'a most independent and upright man, of great fortune . . . who knows and loves the constitution'.[1]

Buried with the hopes of a union was the old doctrine of independency, caught in a trap of its own making. Lord Hardwicke, in a letter of 4 March, exposed their weakness: 'they . . . are not enough united to carry real weight, which mediators can only do by turning the scale.' But how could they unite without sacrificing their precious independency? While they debated this dilemma, events passed them by.[2]

The king, greatly affronted at the news that the House of Commons proposed to address him again, now recalled that the House of Lords had also claims to be the custodian of the constitutional balance. Since their vote on Fox's India bill, their lordships had been remarkably unobtrusive, possibly because ministers feared a clash between the two Houses. But on 3 February the king wrote that the time had come for the Lords to 'throw off

[1] *Morning Chronicle*, 24 February. For an attack on him see the squib entitled 'The Sale of Opposition's Household Stuff', Granville MSS., Box 5. 'Here's old Goody Powis's tongue, Hot or cold as may best serve your end; You will find it will never do wrong, Except to your party or Friend.'

[2] Add. MS. 35382, f. 3. For a most interesting discussion of the doctrine of independency, see B. Kemp, *Sir Francis Dashwood, an eighteenth century independent* (1967). I am sure Miss Kemp is right in suggesting that the basic independent attitude was to criticise rather than support government. Yet this definition seems to me to reveal that the doctrine was essentially a survival from the seventeenth century when parliaments were still intermittent. Practical politicians had long recognised that if Parliament was to be annually summoned and armed with executive powers, somebody had to support government. Miss Kemp dislikes the suggestion that the 'logic of events' was against the independents, though she confesses to being 'perplexed to see what effect their programme would have had'. I think the probable result would have been to divorce the House of Commons from a responsible share in government and to encourage the introduction of devices to enable a ministry to carry on in the face of capricious defeats. Superficially captivating and undoubtedly flattering to the vanity of country gentlemen, the doctrine of independency continued to be a constitutional aspiration long after it had ceased to be a political possibility.

their lethargy', and the following day he repeated his advice, together with the customary threat of abdication.[1]

At this hint, their lordships moved into action, and Lord Effingham proposed two resolutions condemning as unconstitutional the actions of the House of Commons.[2] Most of the leading speakers took part in the debate that ensued. Fitzwilliam and Manchester opposed any move that might lead to a breach with the other House. Richmond thought that the Commons had acted in a most unprecedented fashion on the strength of a rumour, 'which had no proof, and which only circulated, as it would seem, at random'; Thurlow declared that had he been a Lord of the Treasury he would certainly have disregarded the Commons' instructions as illegal. Stormont, Mansfield and Loughborough all delivered long speeches on behalf of the coalition. Stormont's speech, which Loughborough greatly admired, put the opposition's case on the use of the prerogative with great clarity, insisting that it was the prudent use of the power that was at issue, not its legality:

Nothing can be more absurd than to assert that His Majesty from capricious choice, or in direct insult and avowed opposition to the sentiments of Parliament or of his people, can appoint an administration . . . With respect to the election of ministers, there have been frequent examples and precedents of the interference of Parliament . . . There are, I believe, no instances from the era of the Revolution in which an administration has survived the reprobation of Parliament.

The examples of Walpole, Granville and North demonstrated beyond doubt that Parliament possessed an 'unquestionable right'

[1] The king to Pitt, 3 & 4 February, J. H. Rose, *Pitt and Napoleon*, 203; the king to Pitt, 4 February, Stanhope, i, appendix, vi. See also the exchange with Sydney on 3 February printed in Aspinall, 29.

[2] The first resolution attacked the Commons' vote of 24 December warning the Lords of the Treasury not to accept India bills, and declared that any attempt by one branch of the legislature to assume to itself a discretionary power which had been vested in others by an Act of Parliament was unconstitutional. The second resolution was directed at the motion of 16 January, insisted that the appointment of ministers was 'solely vested in His Majesty', and professed 'the firmest reliance in His Majesty's wisdom in the exercise of this prerogative'. Debrett, xiv, 114–18.

to comment on the use made of the royal prerogative. Stormont's view appears to me a good deal closer to the constitutional reality of his day than that of some of his adversaries[1]: the weakness in his position was the assumption that 'Parliament and the people' were opposed to the new ministers. This was true of only one House of Parliament, and the accumulating evidence, day by day, demonstrated that it was untrue of the people. The first resolution was carried by 100 votes to 53, and the second passed *nem. con.*

Relieved no doubt to have some fresh matter to discuss the coalition majority in the House of Commons seized upon the challenge. Fox expressed surprise that their lordships had allowed nearly six weeks to elapse before noticing that a daring assault on their rights had been perpetrated on 24 December. The situation was the very reverse—'the life of the House of Commons was aimed at'; there was a 'settled design to insult and trample upon them'. Pitt retorted that Fox should be less fond of 'general insinuation'; Fox replied with the wish that Pitt would desist from 'challenging proofs when he knew from the offence no proof could be adduced'. It was agreed to appoint a committee to search the Lords' Journals for any reference to the actions of the House of Commons.[2]

The intervention of the House of Lords turned out to be a doubtful advantage to the government. True, it established the point that the House of Commons did not speak for Parliament, but it resurrected old jealousies, and enabled the coalition to repeat its vote of 24 December by passing resolutions reaffirming the rights of the Commons. Those members who had voted for

---

[1] Debrett, xiv, 118–47. He might even have buttressed his argument by appeal to Pitt's father, whose objection to Bute's elevation to the Treasury in 1762 had been that 'favour and honours might be allowed, but not within the walls of the Treasury'. Quoted by L. B. Namier, *England in the age of the American Revolution*, 2nd edition, 122. Loughborough's comments on this debate are to be found in an undated letter to Eden, Auckland, i, 74/5. His own view was: 'the use of any prerogative is liable to be questioned, and unlimited as the choice of ministers is by any direct control, Prudence will necessarily confine it to such men as possess the means of executing their office'. Add. MS. 34419, f. 332.
[2] Debrett, xiii, 73–80.

the original motion found it difficult to withdraw, and the coalition's majority, when Pitt moved the previous question in the debate of 16 February, rose to 31. Their lordships showed no enthusiasm to take the contest further.[1]

---

[1] Debrett, xiii, 111–34. The voting was 187 to 156. The matter was briefly debated once more in the House of Lords on 19 February and allowed to drop. Debrett, xiv, 148–50; *Gentleman's magazine*, 1784, i, 224.

CHAPTER 10

THE PARLIAMENTARY STRUGGLE: THE LATER STAGES

At what point the majority in the House of Commons began to lose heart is hard to determine. On 9 February they were still exuding confidence. 'Tis said the new ministry totters very much today', wrote John Milbanke: 'the present glorious ministers begin to droop most piteously', thought Sir Thomas Dundas. But a fortnight later Cornwallis detected signs that success might elude them.[1]

The first factor in this changing situation was tactical. Fox's supporters, with few exceptions, had assumed that the only problem was to retain a majority during the Christmas recess: that the ministry might be defeated but not resign seems scarcely to have occurred to them. When week followed week and the king paid no attention to their resolutions and addresses, dismay and frustration set in. As early as 30 January North had recognised that the coalition's new problem was to keep its troops usefully occupied: 'it is difficult to stand still without great danger', he warned Eden.[2] Yet action was also difficult for Fox could not afford to appear impetuous. On 29 January he had moved to adjourn the committee on the state of the nation, and again on 9 February. But the morale of his forces could hardly be sustained by repeated adjournments. Although the majority in the division of 16 February was satisfactory, the attendance was not: there were more than ninety members fewer in the House than had been present on 25 January for the second reading of Pitt's India

---

[1] Milbanke to Lord Pelham, Add. MS. 33097, f. 122; Dundas to Henry Erskine, A. Fergusson, *Henry Erskine*, 257; *Correspondence of Charles, first Marquis Cornwallis*, i, 167–8.
[2] Auckland, i, 72–3.

bill. Sir James Harris, Elliot's friend, decided in the course of February that a visit to Bath could no longer be deferred, and although he paired off, others might not be so punctilious.[1] Moreover, the time was drawing near when Fox and his friends would have to decide how far they were prepared to go in postponing the Mutiny bill and withholding supplies. Their measures against a dissolution had won them a stay of execution, not a pardon.

The second factor to discomfit the coalition was the growing evidence of its unpopularity in the country at large. The weapon of Pitt's admirers was an address to the king. The corporation of London set the tone on 16 January with an address congratulating His Majesty on dismissing the coalition administration, and thanking him for 'so salutary and constitutional' an exercise of his prerogative.[2] This was followed by a steady stream of addresses from all parts of the country, at the rate of fifteen or sixteen a week, throughout the following months. The coalitionists, as a matter of course, dismissed the addresses as the contrivances of small cliques, but the evidence was overwhelmingly against them. In only one or two places were they able to produce counter-addresses advocating union or begging the king to appoint a ministry that possessed the confidence of the House of Commons.[3] For the most part, when they attended meetings and offered resistance, they were swept aside. At Plymouth, on 24 January, the friends of Sir Frederick Rogers and George Darby, the coalitionist members, seem to have moderated the official address, but a well-attended meeting immediately afterwards complained that the wording was 'not sufficiently expressive of our sentiments', and went on to approve a declaration assuring Pitt of 'our respect for his great abilities and integrity'.[4] At the

[1] *Diaries and correspondence of James Harris, first earl of Malmesbury*, ed. Lord Malmesbury (1845), ii, 13.　　　　　　　　　　　　　[2] *Gentleman's magazine*, 1784, i, 70.
[3] Byng was able to produce one from the first Middlesex meeting, another came from Lancaster, and Sir Francis Basset seems to have had some success in Cornwall, producing counter-addresses from Tregony and Redruth.　　　[4] *Exeter Flying Post*, 12 February.

county meeting for Cornwall on 18 February, after an address had been adopted supporting the crown's undoubted right to choose its ministers, 'a pretty general murmur was heard of "*Not strong enough*" '.[1] Winchcombe Henry Hartley, the sitting member, spoke in vain against an address at the Berkshire meeting in Reading; at St Albans a 'very strongly expressed' resolution was signed by nearly 180 persons, despite the exertions of the Spencer family, whose member refused to present it; Lord Sandwich's attempt to promote a counter-address from Huntingdon had to be abandoned.[2]

One of the most remarkable demonstrations of the strength of public opinion came from Buckinghamshire, where the sheriff called a county meeting at Aylesbury for 20 March. The Rev. Edward Stone, rector of Horsenden, wrote to Sir William Lee of Hartwell that many leading gentlemen of the county were 'determined to make a constitutional stand in opposition to so unprecedented a measure', and assured him of the support of the dukes of Portland, Bedford, and Marlborough, Lords Lewisham, Dartmouth, Spencer, Hampden, Inchiquin and Verney, and many members of the House of Commons. On the day, the freeholders ignored a speech by Lee, listened with great impatience to Burke, shouted down Coke when he declared himself a supporter of Fox's India bill, and proceeded to vote an address in favour of Pitt 'by a great majority'. Even in a county where they possessed great influence and property, the supporters of the coalition were helpless, and were obliged to content themselves with a protest.[3]

The scale of the movement in support of Pitt was unprecedented. Demands for the repeal of the Jewish Naturalisation Act of

[1] *Sherborne Mercury*, 1 March.

[2] Debrett, xiii, 179–80; Lord to Lady Spencer, 19 February, Spencer MSS.; Add. MS. 35629, f. 20–20b, quoted in Mrs E. George, 'Fox's Martyrs: the General Election of 1784', *Transactions Royal Historical Society*, 4th series, xxi, 152.

[3] Stone to Lee, 17 March, Lee MSS.; *Gentleman's magazine*, 1784, i, 228; *Jackson's Oxford Journal*, 27 March. Public opinion in Yorkshire is examined by N. C. Phillips, *Yorkshire and English national politics 1783–4*.

1753 have been estimated at about a dozen[1]; the Cyder Tax of 1763 called forth twenty-three petitions to the House of Commons[2]; the Supporters of the Bill of Rights mustered thirty petitions in response to their campaign in 1769[3]; Lord George Gordon's attempt in 1780 to secure the repeal of the Roman Catholic Relief Act was supported by fifteen petitions[4]; the movement for economical reform in 1780 produced thirty-eight petitions, and that for parliamentary reform in 1783 forty-one petitions.[5] The support for Pitt in the spring of 1784 dwarfed them all. Indeed, with more than 200 addresses, the campaign was a greater manifestation of public opinion than the six mentioned put together.[6] Nor was the number of signatories inconsiderable. More than 8,000 people signed the two addresses from Westminster, Fox's own constituency; nearly 5,000 signed the two addresses from Bristol; more than 4,000 signed the second address from Glasgow, and addresses with more than 1,000 signatures came from Devon, Leicestershire, Wolverhampton, Staffordshire, Buckinghamshire, Oxfordshire, Coventry,

---

[1] T. W. Perry, *Public opinion, propaganda, and politics in eighteenth-century England* (1962), 111.

[2] *Commons' journals*, vol. 29. An account of the campaign is to be found in B. Kemp. *Sir Francis Dashwood, an eighteenth-century Independent.*

[3] I. R. Christie, *Wilkes, Wyvill and reform*, 39.

[4] *Commons' journals*, vol. 37.   [5] Christie, *op. cit.*, 169 & 173-4.

[6] The total for the six campaigns referred to is 159. In 1784 the *London Gazette* printed 195 addresses, and on two occasions several were reported to have been omitted for want of space. There were addresses from 18 English counties; 5 Welsh counties; 11 Scottish counties; 113 English towns (several of them twice and some three times); 24 Scottish burghs (Glasgow and Aberdeen three times each); 1 Welsh borough; 1 from Belfast, and 1 from the Grand Synod of Ulster. An ominous sign for the coalition was that addresses came from 92 English parliamentary boroughs.

In estimating the extent of public interest and participation, one must also take into account places where, after a discussion of the issues, it was resolved not to address. These can be gleaned only from casual references in the provincial newspapers. Decisions to this effect are reported from the corporation of Salisbury, the Grand Juries of Kent and Hampshire, and the freeholders of Flintshire and Denbighshire. The Flintshire meeting at Mold on 28 February attracted a good deal of attention. It was decided by 212 votes to 82 that addresses could 'have no other tendency but to widen the breaches between contending parties', and to thank the member of Parliament, a coalitionist, for his services. *Drewry's Derby Mercury*, 4/11 March. Some of Fox's supporters inferred from this that the tide would turn. It did not.

Berkshire, Dorset, and Newcastle-upon-Tyne. Even the smaller towns, like Trowbridge, Sudbury, Ripon and Taunton produced dozens of signatures; at Rotherham 200 persons were said to have signed within an hour.[1]

Almost all of the provincial newspapers reproduced from the *London Gazette* the names of the places submitting addresses, and frequently quoted in full addresses from their own locality. Discussions at county meetings were also reported at considerable length: at Leicester the local newspaper devoted nearly two columns to the speeches.[2] The corporation of Wakefield ensured wide publicity for its views by sending four representatives to London in a coach on the front of which was 'a large blue flag . . . upon which is emblazoned in letters of gold, THE KING! THE CONSTITUTION! THE PEOPLE! AND PITT FOR EVER!' One observer drew attention to the oddity of the scene on 25 February when the members of the House of Commons attending the king to present their address demanding the dismissal of the ministry could 'with difficulty pass through the throng of delegates, crowding round the throne from Corporations, Counties and respectable bodies of men from all quarters, assuring their sovereign of their entire and unlimited confidence in and highest approbation of his new appointed ministers'. Some confirmation of this account is to be found in North's complaint to the House that he had been hissed while carrying up the address.[3]

In the face of this massive demonstration of public disapproval, denounced from the Orkneys to Penzance, the confidence of the

---

[1] Hunter to Fitzwilliam, 5 March, Wentworth Woodhouse MSS.

It is not possible to arrive at a precise estimate of the total signatories. The *London Gazette* gives the numbers for 119 addresses—i.e. just over half. Many of the others were signed merely by the Mayor and burgesses, or by the Grand Jury of the county. The address from Paisley was signed by 766 individuals, and by the Deacons of the Guilds of Weavers, claiming to represent 4,000 members: a similar address from Kilmarnock claimed to represent the views of more than 1,300. Ignoring such claims, the total of signatories of the 119 addresses is 59,828. This is roughly comparable with the number of persons voting in the general election of 1784.

[2] *Leicester and Nottingham Journal*, 20 March.

[3] *Leicester and Nottingham Journal*, 28 February, 6 March; Debrett, xiii, 228.

supporters of the coalition began to wilt. The pressure exerted on some members can be gauged from events in Bristol. The sitting members, George Daubeny and Matthew Brickdale, were both coalitionists, belonging to North's wing of the party. When a meeting to declare support for Pitt was summoned for 3 February, their friends were able to hold opinion in check: the attendance was poor and the members shrugged off the subsequent address as of no importance, refusing to present it. But a second meeting on 26 February could not be treated in the same way. A unanimous resolution thanked the king for dismissing ministers who had been 'desperate enough to sacrifice every public good which stood in the way of their unbounded ambition', and hints were thrown out to the members for the city that their conduct was under close scrutiny. Daubeny replied with a most respectful letter to the chairman of the meeting, assuring him of every attention: the members trusted that their constituents would recognise that their political behaviour was based upon principle and would put 'the most favourable construction on our conduct'. After this they seem to have decided to play safe. On 3 March Sydney drew attention to the fact that 'the members for Bristol . . . thought it inadvisable to vote for the last address of the House of Commons. This looks like a shake.'[1]

A second example of the influence exerted on members can be traced at Leicester, where Shukburgh Ashby was returned at a by-election on 14 February. His first vote on 27 February was with the coalition on a motion to adjourn. Four days later he wrote a public letter expressing astonishment that he had been represented as an opponent of the ministry, and dismissing his first vote as 'in a matter of no moment'. His recantation was almost abject. 'Last night I gave my vote in the minority. I never meant to oppose, nor ever shall oppose Mr. Pitt.' It was to no

---

[1] The 'last address' was Fox's motion of 1 March asking the king to dismiss his ministers. *Sarah Farley's Bristol Journal*, 17 & 31 January; 14, 21, 28 February; 6 & 27 March; 3 April; *Felix Farley's Bristol Journal*, 7 & 14 February; *H.M.C. Rutland MSS.*, iii, 77.

avail. The government was not mollified, and when Ashby lost his seat at the general election, Robinson expressed great satisfaction.[1]

Even on the leaders of the party the campaign had its effect, driving them gradually on to the defensive. It was true, admitted North, that there had been an address from Banbury, but none of his constituents had signed: Fox, smarting from a meeting in Westminster Hall where he had been assailed with cries of 'No Grand Mogul! No India Tyrant! No Usurper! No Turncoat!' and the like, was reduced to protesting that 'the people were deceived, they were causing their own ruin . . . those who understood the ground of the dispute . . . were with him'. In a brilliant stroke, Lord Camden summarised Fox's predicament: 'he is in the condition of a magician who is able to disturb the whole world by his enchantments so long as he remains in his circle, but becomes impotent the instant he leaves it.'[2]

Two issues dominated the second half of February—a revival of the project for a union of parties, and the question of postponing supplies.

The members of the St Albans Tavern group refused to accept the breakdown of the first negotiation as final. On 9 February they declared that they would seize any chance to promote a reconciliation, and on 11 February Charles Marsham introduced a motion in the House of Commons deploring the exclusion of either party from an administration. Fox was unexpectedly disarming. There was, he trusted, no personal objection on either side, and he complimented Pitt on his abilities and on 'what he had always understood to be his political principles'. The criticisms of his own Indian proposals might be met, and it was known

[1] *Leicester and Nottingham Journal*, 6 March; Laprade, 121. A public meeting at Lichfield, which had already addressed, instructed its members on 6 March not to impede the progress of the Mutiny bill or to withhold supplies. This was directed at George Anson: the other member, Thomas Gilbert, was a ministerialist. *Drewry's Derby Mercury*, 4/11 March.

[2] Debrett, xiii, 227, 207, 190; Camden to Thomas Walpole, 5 February, Lullings MSS.

that North's claims would not stand in the way of a settlement. But the constitutional rights of the House of Commons could not be set aside, and Pitt must first resign. Pitt's reply was in the same dulcet strain. No man, he was sure, could wish for union more sincerely than he did. He agreed that an administration not possessing the confidence of the House of Commons could not last, and he and his colleagues were ready to resign 'the moment there should be a prospect of an administration being formed by whom the country might be effectually served'. But despite his great respect for North's private character and talents, he could not bring himself to serve in a cabinet with him. North did not allow his new role of elder statesman to inhibit him when he rose to reply. 'Whenever it shall appear to be the sense of the public that I am the obstacle', he told the House, 'there is no love of power, no love of emolument, no object of ambition, that shall induce me to remain one moment the bar to so great a public benefit as a stable administration.' But were not the concessions all on one side?

The right honourable gentleman chooses to declare that he cannot act with me. But does he bend to the repeatedly declared opinion of the majority of this House that they can have no confidence in him? . . . the right honourable gentleman avoids the concessions which he owes to the House of Commons, but states it as a matter of principle to exclude me . . . Let the right honourable gentleman do what he ought to do to this House, and it is of little comparative importance indeed what becomes of me.

Marsham and Powys at once congratulated North on his altruism, and added their voices to the demand for Pitt's resignation.[1]

The first month of parliamentary warfare had had a sobering effect on both sides. Pitt was forced to recognise that he was little nearer to gaining a majority in the House, Fox that he was little nearer to reinstatement in office. The intervention of the House of Lords, though unimportant in other respects, served to remind the supporters of the coalition that even if they effected Pitt's

[1] Debrett, xiii, 93–104.

dismissal, their own measures of government could be frustrated. The king, as usual, put the least favourable construction on Fox's moderation: 'I am not surprised the language of Mr. Fox on union should have been less offensive this day; the temper of London and Westminster must make such an appearance necessary; but whilst resignation is coupled with it, no expectation can be grounded on it, nor any propriety in asking any further questions . . . on that head.'[1] But the ministers were aware how damaging any appearance of intransigeance might be, and when Marsham visited Pitt with fresh proposals, they agreed to re-open negotiations.

The king was horrified at the possibility, however slight, that he might be forced to re-employ Fox. On 15 February, he wrote to Pitt:

I confess I have not yet seen the smallest appearance of sincerity in the leaders of Opposition, to come into the only mode by which I could tolerate them in my service, their giving up the idea of having the administration in their hands, and coming in as a respectable part of one on a broad basis; and therefore I, with a jealous eye, look on any words dropped by them, either in Parliament or to the gentlemen of the St. Albans Tavern, as meant only to gain those gentlemen, or, if carrying further views, to draw Mr. Pitt, by a negotiation, into some difficulty.

Should the Ministers, after discussing this, still think it advisable that an attempt should be made . . . I will, though reluctantly, go personally so far as to authorize a message to be carried in my name to the Duke of Portland, expressing a desire that he and Mr. Pitt may meet to confer on the means of forming an administration on a wide basis . . .[2]

Marsham's hope was that a personal message from the king would meet Portland's constitutional objections, as being tantamount to a resignation by the ministers, and later that day Sydney carried an invitation to discuss with Pitt the formation of a ministry 'on a fair and equal footing'. Portland's reply was unaccommodating: Pitt must first resign, and the king, as an indication of confidence,

---

[1] The king to Pitt, 11 February, J. H. Rose, *Pitt and Napoleon*, 204.
[2] Stanhope, i, appendix, vi–viii.

must grant him an audience.[1] The king, jubilant at what he regarded as clear evidence of Portland's overweening pretensions, urged that the negotiations be broken off at once: 'the Ministers could not be five minutes in deliberating on the impropriety of the sentiments of such a proceeding.'[2]

But by this time the negotiators were inured to disappointments. The following day Pitt found them as 'indefatigable . . . but as ineffectual as ever'.[3] They made their final effort a week later, Marsham persuading Pitt to try to obtain the king's consent to grant Portland an audience. Portland's first reaction was that nothing short of an explicit resignation would satisfy the honour of the House of Commons. Fox was willing to waive that point, but was adamant that it should not be a joint ministry—the memory of the Shelburne–Rockingham administration was too painful:

Marsham and everybody must see that it lies completely open to the old objection of Pitt's being as it were an agent for the King, and I mention this the rather because in every conversation in which I have been present, Powys seemed to feel the whole weight of this difficulty as much as myself . . . You and not Pitt must be the King's agent as far as he is supposed to have one.[4]

In the event, however, the leaders of the coalition agreed to abandon the first point and compromise on the second. Sir Gilbert Elliot passed on to Harris an account he had received direct from Portland:

The Duke consented to see the King on the subject saying that he should in the outset of his audience treat His Majesty's application for his assistance in forming

---

[1] Aspinall, i, 35. Portland's letter is not completely explicit. Professor Aspinall suggested that he was seeking assurances of support from the royal household. I am inclined to think that the 'same proofs' he referred to were for an audience. The letter should be compared with Fortescue, vi, no. 4209.

[2] Aspinall, i, 36.

[3] Pitt to Rutland, 17 February, Stanhope, i, 184. The same day Lord Sydney wrote to Rutland that 'the foolish committee at the St. Albans are trying with Mr. Pitt to make out something of the steps that have been lately taken; but Mr. Pitt seems firm'. *H.M.C. Rutland MSS.*, iii, 75.

[4] Portland to Fox, 5.30 p.m. 24 February, Russell, ii, 238–40; Fox to Portland, 10 p.m. 24 February, Add. MS. 47561, f. 74.

a new administration as a virtual dissolution of the present one, without insisting either on the actual previous dismission of the ministers or even a declaration to that effect in the House of Commons. He consented also that the new administration should be considered as an accession neither to his former one nor to Mr. Pitt's, and that in his conference with Mr. Pitt he should act only as one individual treating with another, and not as the King's agent . . .[1]

Elliot, for one, felt that the leaders of the coalition had gone too far in making concessions, and that the dignity of the House of Commons would be 'sacrificed to the temporising spirit of the mediators'.

The conciliatory nature of Portland's answers seems to have placed Pitt in some difficulty. To the king he admitted that a refusal to treat might 'afford an advantage to Opposition'. The king gave the most grudging permission for 'this last trial' to be made, making no secret of his hope that it would fail: 'a subject requiring from his sovereign exact words . . . is very revolting.' He insisted on one condition: 'Mr. Powys shall explain specifically to that Duke that his being called upon is to give him no right to anything above an equal share to others in the new administration, not to be the head of it, whatever employment he may hold.' This condition, if communicated, would certainly kill the negotiation, since it raised once more the spectre of the 'independent peer' that had proved a stumbling block in March 1783. Consequently, when Portland asked for an explanation of what was meant by the term 'equal', Pitt refused to give it, writing evasively to Powys: 'Mr. Pitt has all along felt that explanation on all the particulars, both of measures and arrangements, . . . would be best obtained by personal and confidential intercourse. On this idea Mr. Pitt has not attempted to define in what manner the principle of *equality* should be applied.' The same day, the negotiation was broken off, leaving the country gentlemen of the St Albans Tavern to declare feebly that 'it would be no dishonorable step in either of the gentlemen to give way'. The king, however,

---

[1] 25 February, Minto MSS., Box M 43.

was delighted, 'as it could never have ended advantageously for this country'.[1]

It is clear that the negotiations did not really break down, as the members of the St Albans Tavern averred, over 'a doubt respecting a single word'.[2] Behind the verbal fencing lay the realities of power. Though the duke of Portland's conduct of the negotiations has been severely criticised, it is not easy to see why he should be singled out for censure.[3] Neither side was sincere, if by that is meant that they went into the negotiation willingly. But Portland's attitude was certainly far from inflexible, and some of his colleagues were dismayed at the concessions he was prepared to make. He is scarcely to be blamed for refusing to enter into an agreement the terms of which were to be revealed later: there was nothing that had happened since North's resignation in 1782 to convince him that he should put his trust in the king's sense of fair play. Pitt's counter-suggestion that the key-word should be first accepted, then defined, was at best illogical, at worst dishonest.

Nor can the charge that Portland's tactics were at fault be sustained. The test was the effect produced upon the country gentlemen. Elliot reported that Powys and Marsham were 'much disgusted' at Pitt's attitude, and this evidence is confirmed by the acerbity of their exchanges in the House of Commons. Indeed,

---

[1] Aspinall, i, 39; J. H. Rose, *Pitt and Napoleon*, 205; Stanhope, i, 187; *Annual Register*, 1784/5, 272. A coalition version of this exchange is given by Elliot in Malmesbury, ii, 5–6. 'The Duke answered that he could not subscribe to these words without some explanation of them for that he did not understand them . . . If Mr. Pitt meant that they should draw lots who should be at the head of the new administration, and then name to the different offices alternately, he would not agree to such a proposal . . . Pitt said he saw nothing in the Duke's reasons which induced him to change his opinion . . . Powys desired that he would only explain more clearly and precisely the sense in which his words were to be adopted, adding, that as for himself he really did not understand them . . . Pitt at last consented to give a fuller explanation, and is to give it in writing tomorrow morning.' Pitt's explanation was the letter quoted above.

[2] *Annual Register*, 1784/5, 272.

[3] Stanhope wrote that he 'made every possible difficulty'; E. C. Black, *The Association* (1963), 108–9 wrote that he demonstrated 'once and for all that the Whig politicians were not men of principle but predatory animals in a parliamentary Roman circus'. I must confess to not understanding what the second remark means.

one of the ministers tacitly admitted that the St Albans Tavern negotiation had told against them. In the debate of 20 February, Pepper Arden wondered by what means the country gentlemen had been 'drawn from their side to vote against them', and declared that they had been 'seduced' by their anxiety for union.[1]

The crucial test of the opposition's determination came when the ministers began to bring forward the routine business of supply. There was still no answer from the king to the address voted on 2 February when Pitt moved on the 10th to consider the Ordnance estimates. Fox insisted that supplies should not be approved until a reply had been received, though as a gesture of moderation the detailed consideration of the estimates was begun the following day.[2] No further progress was made during that week, and Monday 16 February was taken up by the quarrel with the House of Lords. When the estimates again came up for discussion on Wednesday 18 February, Pitt opened the proceedings with the provocative declaration that the king had not thought proper to dismiss his ministers and they had not resigned. Fox replied by moving that consideration of the estimates be postponed until Friday 20th to allow time for deliberation. The House of Commons had been given an answer such as had never been heard from a prince of the Brunswick line: its consequence was for ever destroyed unless some method of securing its honour could be discovered. The motion for adjournment was strongly supported by Powys and opposed by Pitt: it was idle to pretend that the supplies were merely postponed, they were 'to all intents and purposes stopped'. In a full house, Fox's motion was carried by a mere 12 votes, a majority significantly smaller than that which, two days previously, had been prepared to pursue the quarrel with the House of Lords.[3]

---

[1] Debrett, xiii, 212.

[2] Debrett, xiii, 88–90; *Gentleman's magazine*, 1784, i, 145; *Commons' journals*, 39, 911–2.

[3] Debrett, xiii, 138–58. The voting was 208–196, and the majority was the smallest the coalition had had, except on Pitt's India bill.

On Friday 20th the coalition rallied its forces once more, on a resolution, moved by Powys, begging the king to 'give effect' to the wishes of the House. If they took no note of the royal answer and proceeded to vote supplies, it would be construed as acquiescence: 'in what situation, then, can you ever be which can justify your demurring when this did not?' He accused Pitt of impeding the business of the nation by clinging to office. Lord Nugent's characteristically unsophisticated solution of the political crisis wracking the country was that the two leaders should meet at his house, 'get gloriously drunk', and lose their stiff reserve. Pitt's reply to the debate revealed the growing confidence afforded him by the evidence of public support. It was no small thing, he warned the House, to stop the supplies: was there anything in his character to justify the imputation that he was not to be trusted with the issue of public money? Resignation was out of the question: 'the situation of the times requires of me, and I will add, the country calls aloud to me, that I should defend this castle; and I am determined, therefore, I will yet defend it.' Powys's resolution was carried by a majority of 20, and a motion to present it as an address to the king by a majority of 21. Immediately afterwards the Ordnance estimates were approved.[1]

The presentation of the address took place on Wednesday 25 February. To those supporters of the coalition who clung to the belief that the king would at last yield, the royal answer was a sharp disappointment. He did not see that the dismissal of the ministers would promote the service of the public:

I observe, at the same time, that there is no charge or complaint, suggested against my present ministers, nor is any one or more of them specifically objected to; and numbers of my subjects have expressed to me, in the warmest manner, their satisfaction in the late changes I have made in my councils.

[1] Debrett, xiii, 162–214. The first division was 197–177; the second is given in *Commons' journals*, 39, 943 as 177–159, but Debrett and the *Gentleman's magazine*, 1784, i, 220 give it as 177–156. By approving these estimates, the coalition was conceding very little: there were others to come, as well as the Mutiny bill, and it allowed them to refute Pitt's assertion that postponement was the same as stopping supplies.

Under these circumstances, I trust my faithful Commons will not wish that the essential offices of executive government should be vacated until I see a prospect that such a plan of union as I have called for, and they have pointed out, may be carried into effect.[1]

The blandness of this answer in no way weakened its impact: it was, observed Elliot, 'a reply to the House of Commons not paralleled this hundred years'. But his hope that it would stimulate his colleagues to fresh endeavours proved ill-founded: rather, the king's steadfastness began to persuade waverers that the struggle was useless. At a meeting of the coalition at Fox's house on the 26th Elliot was perturbed to detect 'a sort of boggle about the extreme, but the only decisive measure, of refusing supplies'. Meanwhile it was agreed to postpone the naval estimates until the royal answer had been considered on Monday, 1 March, and to defer consideration of the Mutiny bill for a week.[2]

As Elliot anticipated, the ministers did not resist the suggestion that the royal answer be debated on 1 March, but objected strongly to any interruption of public business by an adjournment. The opposition got their wish by a majority of only 7 votes, dividing 175 against 168. They explained their poor showing by the fact that several of their supporters, unprepared for an early division, had been shut out. But although this seems to have been the truth,[3] it was an ominous mishap, suggesting that some, at least, of the opposition were no longer prepared to regiment themselves in what began to appear a lost cause. Fox was reported to have warned his supporters that if they did not attend rigorously, 'with the most decided majority, they might be beaten by superior vigilance'.[4] Elliot, one of the militants, wrote despondently to Harris that some 'patched accommodation' seemed the

---

[1] Debrett, xiii, 220–1.   [2] Elliot to Harris, 25 & 26 February, Minto MSS.
[3] *Sarah Farley's Bristol Journal*, 6 March, drawing on the London newspapers, gave the names of thirteen absentees, most of whom had been dining with the Prince of Wales. The explanation is confirmed by Elliot's letter to Harris (Malmesbury, ii, 4) where the defaulters are described as 'looking like the foolish virgins somewhere in the Bible'. There was no reason for Elliot to wish to deceive Harris.
[4] *General Evening Post*, 26/28 February.

probable outcome: ' I see the number of those who think as I do about it is too small, and that there is too much water gruel in the times to render any more manly conclusion . . . practicable.'[1]

On 1 March Fox moved the most forthright address to the king that had yet been attempted. Reiterating the right of the House to advise the king on the use of the prerogative, it expressed 'concern and disappointment' that no further steps had been taken to promote a strong and stable government and begged the king, in direct terms, to dismiss the ministers. Fox took the opportunity to review the whole constitutional issue. Had not George II, in the course of the Seven Years War, set aside his personal dislike of William Pitt, senior, in order to promote harmony and efficiency? Did not Sir Robert Walpole and Lord North both resign as soon as it was clear that they had lost the confidence of the House of Commons? 'What sort of government', asked Fox, 'could take place on a principle which did not imply the confidence of the House?' Powys was even more outspoken: if the address produced another negative, they should lay the mace at the foot of the throne, for they would no longer be a House of Parliament. Pitt declared his intention of avoiding in reply 'beaten themes and hackneyed arguments.' It was not right to assert that the monarch was under any necessity of dismissing ministers because the House expressed disapprobation of them, however, 'awkward and unpleasant' that might render their situation: to argue otherwise was to transfer the prerogative rights from the sovereign to the House of Commons and to destroy the balance of the constitution:

It was this mixed government which the prudence of our ancestors devised, and which it will be our wisdom inviolably to support. They experienced all the vicissitudes and distractions of a republic. They felt all the vassalage and des-potism of a simple monarchy. They abandoned both, and by blending each together, extracted a system which has been the envy and admiration of the world . . . This system it is the intention of the present address to defeat and destroy . . .

[1] Malmesbury, ii, 6.

In the lobby the coalition carried the address by 201 votes to 189, by far the lowest majority it had had on a question of this nature.[1]

The king, indignant at a further address, 'and the latter part of it in so dictatorial a style', advised a short answer. No charge or complaint, the House was reminded, had been offered against any of the ministers: if they were as obnoxious as the majority believed, it was absurd to press for their inclusion in an extended administration. The king knew of no further step he could take to meet the wishes of the House.[2]

It was now apparent that the coalition would experience the greatest difficulty in carrying any motion for the stopping of supplies; its majorities merely for postponing had been slender enough. The last shot in their armoury was the possibility of passing the Mutiny bill for a month only. But even this might not be decisive. The House of Lords might well amend it to extend for the full term, and begin another constitutional wrangle. Alternatively the ministry could carry on and present the supporters of the coalition with another agonising reappraisal at the end of the month's grace. There were rumours of a proposal to expel Pitt from the House of Commons,[3] but it is unlikely that the coalition's leaders gave it serious consideration. Even if a majority of the House supported them, the memory of the Wilkes case was fresh enough to deter them: in the existing mood of the country Pitt, if expelled, would have the choice of dozens of constituencies, avid to re-elect him. To impeach him meant bringing him before the House of Lords where he possessed a substantial majority. In short, the coalition had exhausted all constitutional expedients. 'I am sorry to see our majority dwindling', remarked Elliot on 4 March: 'it will not bear much curtailing, and I am still more sorry to think it pretty much decided

---

[1] Debrett, xiii, 230–52. Powys's speech is reported in the *Gentleman's magazine*, 1784, i, 294–5.
[2] Debrett, xiii, 253.
[3] Rutland to Gower, 10 March, Granville MSS.; *Whitehall Evening Post*, 9/11 March.

that we shall not carry the refusal of the supplies. There is some doubt even of our carrying a short Mutiny Bill.'[1]

On the 5th Fox moved to postpone consideration of the Mutiny bill until the royal answer had been debated on the 8th. Powys, once again, spoke in support, with great bitterness, wishing 'for time to regulate the funeral procession of this House of Commons . . . ministers were determined to continue their mad career and set prerogative above the privileges of the people'. Pitt contented himself with pointing out that time was short if the Mutiny Act was to be renewed. The adjournment was carried by 9 votes, 171 against 162.[2]

It was widely recognised that the debate of 8 March would probably be decisive. By 11 a.m. the strangers' gallery of the House was full, though the main business did not come on until 4 in the afternoon. At that hour Sir James Lowther, usually regarded as the most disagreeable man in eighteenth-century public life, complained that there was no room for one of his friends, and insisted that the gallery be cleared. Since the newspaper reporters were turned out with the rest, only fragmentary accounts of the debate have survived. Fox realised that more addresses to the king would be fruitless, and the proceedings took the form of a remonstrance, to which no answer was customary, justifying the actions of the majority, and intended as an appeal to public opinion. It warned the king that if, in the present critical situation, the House voted supplies, its forbearance should not be mis-understood. On the main point of issue, it argued:

We neither have disputed, nor mean in any instance to dispute, much less to deny, His Majesty's undoubted prerogative of appointing to the executive offices of state . . . but at the same time we must, with all humility, again submit to His Majesty's royal wisdom that no administration, however legally appointed, can serve His Majesty and the public with effect, which does not enjoy the confidence of this House; that in His Majesty's present administration we cannot confide; the circumstances under which it was constituted, and the

---

[1] Elliot to Harris, Minto MSS.   [2] Debrett, xiii, 255–67.

grounds upon which it continues, have created just suspicions in the breasts of his faithful Commons that principles are adopted . . . unfriendly to the privileges of this House, and to the freedom of our excellent constitution . . .

There is no report of any speech by Pitt,[1] and the main ministerial defence came from Henry Dundas. 'We are ever talking to one another within these walls about our dignity but do the people catch this strain from us? . . . Does the circulation of their blood run one iota faster on the subject . . .?' After a two hour speech on India by Burke, whose sense of occasion was seldom evident, the remonstrance was carried by a single vote, 191 against 190.[2]

The king, for one, had no doubt that the end was in sight. The letter acquainting him with the result of the debate was, he told Pitt, 'the most satisfactory I have received for many months': between them they had 'saved the constitution, the most perfect of human formations'.[3] His jubilation was justified. A meeting of the coalition the following morning agreed that a short Mutiny bill could not be carried: according to Cornwallis, several of the military men were not prepared to support it.[4] Accordingly, no opposition was offered when, that afternoon, Sir George Yonge moved that the bill should be in force for the normal term of one year. The struggle was over. 'The enemy seem indeed to be on their backs', Pitt informed Rutland: 'I write now . . . tired to death, even with victory, for I think our present state is entitled to that name.'[5]

---

[1] Philip Yorke told his uncle that Pitt intervened only on a point concerning the negotiations. Add. MS. 35382, f. 10.

[2] *Gentleman's magazine*, 1784, i, 296–9; Debrett, xiii, 268–77.   [3] Stanhope, i, appendix, x.

[4] Malmesbury, ii, 6–7; *Correspondence of Charles, first Marquis Cornwallis*, i, 170. Cornwallis's suggestion seems plausible. Sir Hugh Palliser, a Vice-Admiral, had been a close supporter of Sandwich and North, but was reported to have refused on 5 March to postpone the Mutiny bill. *Bath Chronicle*, 11 March. He wrote to Sandwich on 7 March begging him 'not to consider my having voted for the Mutiny Bill . . . to be *intended* unfriendly to you . . .' *The House of Commons, 1754–90*, iii, 247–8.

[5] Stanhope, i, 198. Sir James Bland Burges subsequently claimed that the collapse of the coalition's resistance was due to a suggestion he made Pitt that the Mutiny bill could originate in the House of Lords. According to the story, Pitt notified Fox, who surrendered on the spot. Although Lord Rosebery seemed to find some meaning in the

How had it been accomplished? Why was Pitt able gradually to pare away the coalition's majority? The deeper causes of the coalition's downfall will be discussed in a later chapter, but some explanation of the purely parliamentary situation can be attempted here, despite the fragmentary nature of the evidence.[1]

It was the boast of the coalitionists that they lost very few supporters once the struggle had begun, and this seems to have been the case: most of the conversions took place during the recess.[2] Once a member had taken sides, he was reluctant to expose himself to sarcasm and ridicule by deserting: 'you seem to be a little suspicious of me', wrote Lord Sheffield to Eden, 'but it is exactly the moment, and almost the only moment, when according to my nature it is impossible to be off . . . if only to avoid the appearance of *quitting* at such a time, I should seem to go on.' By the end of February, Elliot could observe that 'the number of those who are capable of conversion by the merits of any question is not considerable'.[3]

Three factors seem to have contributed to the coalition's decline in relative strength. First, government influence ensured that members attending for the first time tended to support the ministers. Elliot commented on the division of 8 March that 'Devonshire Parker', who had not previously taken part, 'voted against us, much to the surprise of those who knew him'. Some

---

expedient suggested, it appears to me quite unintelligible. Their Lordships' previous approval would certainly not prevent the House of Commons from rejecting the bill or amending it if they wished. Nor can I really believe that Bland Burges had triumphed where the finest legal minds had been baffled for weeks, though this is the impression he endeavoured to convey. Lord Rosebery, *Pitt* (1891), 56; *Letters and correspondence of Sir James Bland Burges*, ed. J. Hutton (1885), 71–4.

[1] There are no division lists extant for the period January to March 1784, and the suggestions offered are conjectural.

[2] Lord Palmerston wrote in March that the equality in the parties was 'owing to the attendance of new votes, rather than to the desertion of old ones', and Elliot, describing the division of 8 March declared that 'nobody went over, not one'. B. Connell, *Portrait of a Whig peer*, 152; Malmesbury, ii, 6.

[3] Auckland, i, 71/2. Sheffield wrote on 7 January but the argument operated with even greater force once the struggle had been resumed. Elliot to Harris, 25 February, Minto MSS.

light was thrown on the mystery two months later when the member in question was raised to the peerage as Baron Boringdon.[1] In similar fashion, it was asserted that General Luttrell, a supporter of the coalition, had been instructed to take up his duties in Ireland in order to remove him from the parliamentary scene.[2] These manoeuvres were possible only for government. Secondly, although pressure of public opinion seems rarely to have forced a member to change sides, it could persuade him to absent himself. Sir Charles Warwick Bampfylde, the member for Exeter, was under heavy attack in his constituency, which was one of the first to address in favour of Pitt: on 1 March he, like the members for Bristol, was reported to have abstained.[3] The voting pattern certainly suggests that abstention rather than conversion was the coalition's chief hazard: whereas the final vote on the government side was only 3 less than the vote of 12 January, the opposition vote had fallen by 41.[4] Finally, the ministry made a net gain of some six votes through by-elections during the period, and this was of some importance in so nicely balanced a situation.[5]

From 9 March onwards the fifteenth Parliament of Great Britain led a posthumous existence, with nothing but desultory

[1] Malmesbury, ii, 6. John Parker was member for Bodmin 1761–2 and for Devon 1762–84.

[2] *Morning Herald*, 4 February. Luttrell is best known as Wilkes's opponent at the Middlesex election of 13 April 1769.

[3] *H.M.C. Rutland MSS.*, iii, 77. The first address from Exeter, printed in the *London Gazette*, 31 January/3 February, was signed by the Mayor and 307 'principal inhabitants': a second was signed by 471 of the leading merchants of the city. Bampfylde's somewhat ineffective riposte was a third address, signed by only eighty-one persons, expressing a wish for a united administration. The *Exeter Flying Post*, 11 March carried a letter from 'Vindex' defending his conduct in supporting Fox.

[4] According to the newspaper list of 19 March, reprinted as an appendix to Stockdale's *Debates 1784–90*, the coalition should still have had a majority of 13. It lists 260 members against Pitt, 247 in his favour, and 51 absent.

[5] Irrespective of re-elections on taking office, there were ten by-elections between 29 December and 11 March. At St Albans and Aldborough, ministerialists replaced coalitionists; at West Looe, London, Leicester and Old Sarum (11 March) ministerialists replaced members who were habitual absentees or whose allegiance was doubtful; there was no change in the position in Yorkshire and Cornwall, or for the second seat at Old Sarum (6 January). The only coalition gain was at Truro.

skirmishing. Appropriately enough the business of the House on the 10th was to consider the treatment of 'criminals under sentence of death, and respited during His Majesty's pleasure'. This, *mutatis mutandis*, was no bad description of the coalition's predicament. Only a little band of Northites stayed in the field, Sir Grey Cooper, Eden and North himself arguing that there could be no dissolution before an appropriation act had been passed or the affairs of the East India Company regulated: the minister did not trouble to reply. On the 11th Robinson wrote that he had 'impressed on Mr. Pitt's mind that things draw much nearer', and his days were filled with electoral consultations. On the 22nd, the king wrote to Henry Drummond, the banker, to borrow £24,000 at five per cent: 'Mr. Drummond may be surprised to receive this from me', he opened engagingly, but it is doubtful whether the surprise was as overwhelming as all that. Two days later, in the House of Lords, the king explained that 'extraordinary circumstances' had led him to dissolve Parliament and seek the sense of his people. The theft of the Great Seal from the Lord Chancellor's house the same day, though the cause of much speculation and mirth, was not enough to save the supporters of the coalition from the fate that had so long hung over them.[1]

---

[1] Robinson to Jenkinson, Add. MS. 38567, f. 186; Aspinall, i, 42–3; *Gentleman's magazine*, 1784, i, 230.

CHAPTER II

THE GENERAL ELECTION

Although the excitement had gone out of the parliamentary struggle long before the dissolution, the campaign of addressing and the dissemination of numerous pamphlets, squibs, caricatures and ballads kept interest high among the general public. Readers of the *Caledonian Mercury* were assured in a letter from London that the talk in the capital was whether civil war would ensue. Party animosity in York was reported to run so high that gentlemen of different sides would not speak to each other in the streets. Edmund Burke's son fought a duel at the York assizes with a fellow lawyer who described Fitzwilliam's attack upon Pitt as the action of a blackguard, and a duel of a less serious nature took place at the opera where the duchess of Rutland shouted 'Damn Fox' and was replied to by Lady Maria Waldegrave with a shout of 'Damn Pitt'—a not very taxing level of political debate. 'Politics,' Horace Walpole informed Mann, 'are all in all. I question whether any woman intrigues with a man of a different party. Little girls say, "Pray, Miss, of which side are you?" I heard of one that said, "Mama and I cannot get Papa over to our side." '[1]

That the ministry would obtain a substantial majority was not open to question. North's followers, in particular, were in a vulnerable position, some of them, like George North himself, representing Treasury or Admiralty boroughs. In January, before public opinion had had time to express itself, newspapers were speculating that 100 coalitionists might lose their seats, and forecasting a majority of 60 in Pitt's favour.[2] Nothing had hap-

---

[1] *Caledonian Mercury*, 10 March; *General Evening Post*, 7/10 March; *The correspondence of Edmund Burke*, v, 130–3; Letters of the duchess of Devonshire, *Anglo-Saxon Review*, September 1899; Walpole to Mann, 26 March.

[2] *Sarah Farley's Bristol Journal*, 24 January; *Morning Post*, 27 January.

pened since to suggest that the coalition was likely to do better, and on the day of the dissolution the *Morning Herald* reported that Robinson anticipated a majority of 70.

Unfortunately the only list of Robinson's forecasts surviving is the one compiled in December 1783 before Pitt took office. There can be no doubt that Robinson changed his predictions considerably in the subsequent three months.[1] His original estimates had been extremely sanguine. He believed in December that after the general election, as a result both of conversions and defeats, the 'certain' opposition would be reduced to 123, against 253 ministerialists: a further 116 would be *Hopeful* and 66 *Doubtful*. On the assumption that the *Hopefuls* voted with government and the *Doubtfuls* against, the ministry would command 369 votes against 189, a majority of 180. But many of the expected conversions failed to materialise, and Robinson must have revised his estimates to take account of this. It is, however, possible to form a conjecture of Robinson's expectation in March since most of the calculations on which his anticipated electoral gains were based remained constant. In December he was hoping to make some 60 electoral gains at the dissolution. Applying this figure to the parliamentary situation in March, when the coalition still had on paper some 260 supporters against 247, he could expect a final total of 307 for government against 200 in opposition.[2]

The great majority of his electoral gains he hoped to make in the close boroughs, either by purchase from the great patrons or by the exploitation of government influence.[3] The support of the

[1] The December list is that printed in Laprade, 66–105. George Rose assisted Robinson in drawing up the revised list, and refers to it in his letter of 7 April, Laprade 123. There was only one copy. If it survives, one would expect it be in the Rose MSS., but I have not been able to trace it there.

[2] This is a very approximate calculation, first because of the difficulty of taking into account the fifty-one members who had been absent during the parliamentary struggle, and secondly because the intervening three months had made certain changes even in the purely electoral considerations.

[3] About forty-five of his expected gains were in the close borough section: most of the others were in Scotland.

duke of Northumberland, Lord Eliot and Lord Mount Edgcumbe was worth a net gain of 14 seats in Cornwall and Devon alone[1]; there was the possibility of about 20 gains in seats where the government had direct influence[2]; and there were other gains likely where the smaller patrons, such as Rutland and George Selwyn, had been caught with coalition members.[3] In addition, there were seats in boroughs like Wendover, where money might turn the scale in favour of ministerial candidates.

Money was however in short supply. Large sums had been spent on the previous general election, only three and a half years before, and it had been followed by some extremely expensive by-elections. When North left office in March 1782 the king was horrified to discover that there were further debts, which were not settled until after the 1784 election. This, and the depressed state of public credit, made it difficult for the king to obtain the necessary advances in March 1784, and the total spent on the election was considerably smaller than for the two previous general elections—£31,848, against nearly £50,000 in 1774 and £62,000 in 1780. This was not as severe a handicap as might appear. Since, from an electoral point of view, the government wasted most of its money, it is doubtful whether the outcome would have been significantly different had more funds been available.[4]

---

[1] Launceston 1; Bere Alston 2; Newport 2; Liskeard 1; Grampound 2; St Germans 1; Lostwithiel 1; Bossiney 1; Fowey 1; Plympton 2. The detailed position in these boroughs can be traced in *The House of Commons 1754–90*, i.

[2] Plymouth 1; Hedon 1; Harwich 1; Hastings 2; Rye 2; Seaford 2; Sandwich 1; Winchelsea 1; (these are classified by Robinson as open boroughs, though in some cases it seems questionable): Saltash 1; Queenborough 2; Malmesbury 2; Newport (Hants.) 1; Yarmouth 2. It is a very nice distinction to decide whether the 4 seats at Weymouth and Melcombe Regis and the 2 at Dartmouth were under government control or in the hands of local managers.

[3] Rutland nominated to one seat at Bramber, and at the general election replaced Henry Fitzroy Stanhope, a Foxite, by Daniel Pulteney; Selwyn's second seat at Ludgershall was occupied by Lord Melbourne, a Gentleman of the Bedchamber to the Prince of Wales.

[4] Fortescue, v, nos. 3669 & 3674; vi, nos. 3714 & 3715, 3753; Laprade, 57–62; Aspinall, i, nos. 51, 56, 59, 121, 129, 139, 140, 141, 143; Secret Service Accounts, Windsor Archives; *The House of Commons 1754–90*, i, 77, 84.

By 'wasted' I mean that the result was not influenced by the money spent—e.g. at

The ministry's adversaries approached the general election in a mood of stoic resignation: 'it is our business not to despair of the commonwealth', was the best that Elliot, beset with troubles, could manage. On 26 March, two days after the dissolution had been announced, and before a single vote had been cast, Burke was lamenting the 'great slaughter' of his friends and the 'many vexatious disappointments' they had already suffered.[1] Nevertheless, the party struggled to find places for the dispossessed and for aspiring newcomers, though the task was enormous and the resources slender. Much of the work was undertaken by Portland himself, by no means the figurehead he is sometimes represented as being; other attempts at coordination, particularly in Scotland, were made by William Adam, later to emerge as the opposition's chief electoral manager. A list drawn up by Adam of 'persons desiring seats', includes many of the retiring members—Richard Beckford, Stephen Lushington, Lord Melbourne, Lord Maitland, Sir Ralph Payne, Sir Grey Cooper, Samuel Salt, John Ord, Jacob Wilkinson and Percy Wyndham—and in a letter of 30 March, still before polling began, he added Sir Gilbert Elliot, Wilbraham Tollemache, 'and many others', to the number.[2] When one of the coalition's new supporters complained to Adam that his claims to a seat were being overlooked, he was told sharply that the first rule was to 'take care that those who had

---

Westminster where £9,200 did not suffice to keep out Fox. Had no money at all been spent, no more than ten extra seats would have fallen to the coalition. The matter is discussed in *The House of Commons 1754–90*, i, 95.

[1] Malmesbury, ii, 7; *The correspondence of Edmund Burke*, v, 134–5.

[2] D. E. Ginter, *Whig organization and the general election of 1790* (1967), 9–19. Lushington, Cooper and Ord sat for government boroughs at Hedon, Saltash and Hastings; Melbourne had been turned out of Ludgershall by George Selwyn, Wyndham out of Chichester by Richmond, Payne out of Plympton Erle by Mount Edgcumbe, and Tollemache and Salt out of Liskeard by Lord Eliot; Sir Gilbert Elliot had just abandoned the struggle for Roxburghshire; Jacob Wilkinson presumably did not relish fighting Honiton again, since it was an expensive borough and the interest of Sir George Yonge might be supported by government money; Beckford gave up Bridport, not wanting to stand a contest, and was found a snug seat after the general election by Lord Surrey.

lost their seats in the last parliament should . . . be preferred in the next to any other person'.[1]

The general election lasted five weeks, the last return coming in from London on 7 May.[2] It followed the usual pattern, voting for the English and Welsh boroughs taking place during the first week, succeeded during the next fortnight by the county elections, with the results from Scotland coming in last of all. Observers therefore had to piece together the probable outcome of the election from the returns as they were printed day by day in the newspapers.

During the first two days, thirty-nine boroughs made their returns, and the coalition held its ground tenaciously. Twenty of the boroughs returned the old members, while in another nine the change of personnel did not affect voting strength. The remaining ten boroughs provided Pitt with 8 gains in seats, and the coalition with 5 gains, a net gain to the ministry of only 3 seats.[3] The coalition's supporters must have been gratified to keep 3 of the 4 seats at Weymouth and Melcombe Regis, normally under government control, but to offset that were two notable casualties. Hertford, which went to the hustings on the first day, was a fairly independent borough, free from the grosser forms of corruption: its electorate of 500 contained a powerful Dissenting element, and it was one of the places where public opinion might have a chance to express itself. Moreover, it was contested by the three candidates who stood in 1780, when Thomas Dimsdale and William Baker had narrowly defeated John Calvert. Since then,

---

[1] Ginter, op. cit., 10.

[2] With the exception of the celebrated Westminster election which was protracted until 17 May.

[3] Pitt's gains were two at Seaford, two at Queenborough, and one at Hertford, Hull, Hedon & Bramber; the coalition's gains were two at Huntingdon (Lord Sandwich's borough), and one at Maldon, Stockbridge and Heytesbury. Some of these gains were more apparent than real. The Seaford result was quashed on petition, and the ministry eventually lost both seats, while at Stockbridge John Luttrell, a supporter of the coalition, was in negotiation with Pitt within five days of his return, thus neutralising the gain for the second seat. *The House of Commons 1754–90*, i, 454–7; iii, 67–8.

Dimsdale and Calvert, the latter returned in November 1780 for Tamworth, had supported Pitt, while Baker had taken a prominent part on the coalition side, moving the strong resolution of 17 December against reporting the king's opinion. The poll could provide a reasonably fair test of election prospects as a whole. Baker came third, polling 223 against 292 for Dimsdale and 365 for Calvert, and had no doubt that he was a political victim, remarking in his farewell address on the 'popular fury of the Times', and warning the voters to be on their guard against any repetition of 'a late most extraordinary transaction'.[1] The second day's casualty was at Hull, an open borough with some 1,200 voters, where David Hartley, the American negotiator, was beaten by Wilberforce and Samuel Thornton: his speeches in the House were however so didactic and tedious that some of his coalition colleagues may have received the news without undue grief.

By the end of the fourth day half the English boroughs had made their returns, and the pattern was emerging more clearly. A further 13 net gains for Pitt had wiped out the coalition's majority.[2] Three of their leaders went down without a shot fired. Thomas Erskine, the future Lord Chancellor, ended his brief House of Commons career when the corporation of Portsmouth, seized by 'the madness of the day', refused to re-elect him[3]; the corporation of Bury St Edmunds rejected the duke of Grafton's nomination of General Conway and insisted on a change of

---

[1] *Annual Register*, 1784/5, 276–7. The veiled reference is to the king's intervention.

[2] I estimate Pitt's gains as follows: Honiton 1, Harwich 1, Poole 1, Rochester 2, Boston 1, Newark 1, Southwark 1, Chichester 1, Horsham 1, Steyning 2, Sandwich 1, Portsmouth 1, Maidstone 1, Bury 1, Sudbury 2, Worcester 1, Beverley 1, Pontefract 1; in addition, the Speaker's return for Rye in place of Thomas Onslow, if not a ministerial gain, was an opposition loss: Fox's gains were: Colchester 1, Boroughbridge 1, Winchelsea 1, King's Lynn 1, Newport 1, Malmesbury 2, Richmond 1, Ilchester 1. I count it as a gain when the sitting member who was replaced had been a permanent absentee, like Sir Richard Worsley or Thomas Walpole. The political behaviour of the two new members for Woodstock is too obscure to make an assessment possible.

[3] *The House of Commons 1754–90*, i, 299. He was also defeated at Truro, standing on the Basset interest.

candidate[1]; at Southwark, Sir Richard Hotham declined before the poll opened, providing the borough with its first uncontested general election for more than fifty years.[2] The most remarkable feature of the results at this stage was the success achieved by the ministry in the very large boroughs: in the nine that had made returns, the government had gained six seats against one doubtful gain by the opposition[3]; at Oxford there had been no change, and at Nottingham the coalition member, Daniel Parker Coke, held his seat by judiciously refusing to discuss political questions, 'as they very often caused confusion'.[4] 'Plenty of bad news from all quarters', wrote Fox on 3 April.[5]

After a week's polling, nearly all the English boroughs had made their returns: they were 'beyond the hopes of the most sanguine friends', commented the king,[6] and the *London Chronicle* confirmed on 7 April that the ministers were 'likely to have a more considerable majority than was at first expected'. The position of the rival leaders pointed the contrast. Pitt, having turned aside excellent offers for London and Bath, was returned top of the poll for the University of Cambridge, beating the two sitting members with conspicuous ease. Fox was running third in his own constituency of Westminster, more than 100 votes behind Sir Cecil Wray, a political mediocrity: he had 'gone too far at present to give up', wrote Portland on the 8th, and 'though there is no chance . . . of success, he should not appear to desert his friends'.[7] Lord John Cavendish, the *chevalier sans peur et sans*

---

[1] The king to Pitt, 28 March, J. H. Rose, *Pitt and Napoleon*, 206. That this was an objection to Conway's political activity may be inferred from the fact that the corporation elected Grafton's substitute candidate without opposition.

[2] *London Chronicle*, 30 March/1 April.

[3] By 'very large' I mean a borough with more than 1,000 voters. Pitt's gains were at Southwark, Worcester, Beverley, Hull, Maidstone, Newark. At Colchester, Christopher Potter ousted Sir Robert Smyth. While Smyth was certainly a supporter of Pitt, Potter's allegiance was doubtful, and it was not certain that he could hold the seat on petition.

[4] *The House of Commons 1754–90*, ii, 233.

[5] Russell, ii, 267. [6] J. H. Rose, *Pitt and Napoleon*, 207.

[7] Portland to Lady Rockingham, Portland MSS. Pw F 9193. The poll for Westminster stood at the end of 6 April as Lord Hood 3262, Sir Cecil Wray 2985, Charles Fox 2868.

reproche of the Rockinghams, was defeated in their own citadel of York, which he had represented since 1768. Successes for the coalition to set against these disasters were hard to find. They could claim a defensive victory at London where Atkinson failed by 7 votes to oust Sawbridge from fourth place, with the result that government and opposition shared the seats. William Windham's victory at Norwich was hailed by Portland as 'the only very satisfactory event that has happened since this cursed dissolution', but it was a very near thing, and only technically a coalition gain.[1] Some of the other coalition successes were undoubtedly counterfeit in character. At Bedford, William Colhoun declared his complete sympathy for the corporation's dislike of the coalition, was returned unopposed, and at once joined Fox.[2] At Scarborough, George Osbaldeston, a friend of Lord Fitzwilliam, was so hard pressed that he was obliged 'publicly to explain away' his reported opposition to the ministry: 'he dared not declare himself in our favour, but at heart he is with us', wrote a friend to Fitzwilliam.[3] To such evasions were the coalitionists reduced.

The county elections, which began on 6 April, brought the opposition nothing but tribulation. At the county meeting at Dorchester, Humphrey Sturt admitted that he would have supported Fox's India bill had he been present: the subsequent show of hands was so strongly against him that he abandoned the seat he had occupied for thirty years without a struggle to a young man of twenty-nine.[4] In Norfolk, Thomas William Coke, of whom Robinson had written that 'his connections carry him dead', suffered a similar fate. An onlooker described the county meeting at Norwich:

---

[1] Portland to Windham, 7 April, Add. MS. 37845, f. 3. The voting was Sir Harbord Harbord 2305, Windham 1297, Henry Hobart 1233. The sitting member whom Windham replaced had taken no part in the proceedings of the fifteenth Parliament.
[2] *The House of Commons 1754–90*, i, 207–8.
[3] *Ibid*, iii, 234–5; Preston to Fitzwilliam, 5 April, Wentworth Woodhouse MSS.
[4] *Sherborne Mercury*, 12 April.

Coke was not suffered to speak; Windham made two attempts, but such vehement marks of dislike were expressed by general hissing and hooting that neither of them was heard. Coke's bringing forward one of Fox's desperate resolutions has ruined him with all thinking men . . . he was rejected with the utmost abhorrence, and left the hall with great confusion of face . . .[1]

In Yorkshire, the two coalitionist candidates, faced with overwhelming evidence of hostility from all parts of the county, declined the night before the poll.

Coalition supporters who resolved to try the hustings fared no better. Winchcombe Henry Hartley took on two supporters of Pitt in Berkshire and declined on the first day, having polled 301 against 677 and 678: his second sortie into Gloucestershire was even more dispiriting, producing 20 votes against 357 and 443 for his opponents. A day's polling was enough to convince Sir Charles Bunbury in Suffolk that his cause was hopeless. A visiting French nobleman found the situation faintly subversive:

He has been a member of Parliament for the country for thirty years; [in fact since 1761] he was supported by all the gentlemen of the county and consequently by the more enlightened part of it. I myself saw him rejected by farmers and freeholders who have only the bare qualifications of an elector because he was a supporter of the coalition . . .[2]

By the time Buckinghamshire went to the poll on 21 April it was *sauve qui peut*, and opposition candidates struggled to rid themselves of the curse of the coalition. '*I can venture to pledge myself*', declared Joseph Bullock on behalf of Lord Verney, '*that he is not connected with Lord North or Mr. Fox but is totally independent of them.*' His correspondent, the redoubtable Lord Abingdon, was not appeased: 'why did he support them then, and in such measures too?', and in due course Verney went down to defeat.[3] In

---

[1] J. Freeman to Lord Sydney, 11 April, Brotherton MSS.

[2] François de la Rochefoucauld, whose comments are printed in *A Frenchman in England*, ed. J. Marchand (1933). His understanding of the English constitution was far from perfect. It was an odd time to be observing that 'it is always the king who is bound to yield and royalty in England is, in fact, a wandering phantom which finds itself seated on a throne in a democratic state'.

[3] This exchange is in the Thame MSS. at C.R.O., Oxford.

only one county, Bedfordshire, did a coalitionist survive when faced with a poll, and that by 1 vote. In all, Pitt made 12 net gains from the forty English counties.[1]

By the middle of April the magnitude of the disaster was apparent to the coalitionists. 'We are cut up root and branch', confessed Eden to Sheffield: 'the country is utterly mad for prerogative.'[2] The fact that in Scotland the opposition almost succeeded in holding its own and that Dundas's forecasts had been wildly optimistic afforded scant consolation.[3] The best that the coalition could do was to fling all its resources into the desperate struggle at Westminster, where, after a poll of forty days, Fox succeeded in gaining second place: only the ineptitude of the government's handling of the scrutiny enabled the opposition to pass it off as a famous victory.[4]

In total, Pitt made some 70 net gains—rather more than Robinson and Rose had anticipated. They were fortunate in that their lack of success in Scotland was balanced by the gains in the English counties, so that the final result was not far from their

---

[1] His gains were Berkshire 2, Suffolk 1, Surrey 1, Yorkshire 1, Staffordshire 1, Somerset 1, Dorset 1, Norfolk 1, Buckinghamshire 2, Hertfordshire 1 and Middlesex 1. The coalition's only gain was in Derbyshire, where Nathaniel Curzon, an early convert to the ministry, was forced to decline and his seat taken by Edward Miller Mundy.

[2] 10 April, Add. MS. 45728, f. 15.

[3] There were no net gains in the Scottish burghs, where ministerialists captured Glasgow and Dumfries, but lost Aberdeen and Elgin. In the counties there was one net gain, ministerialists taking Roxburgh, Sutherland, Berwickshire and Lanarkshire, but losing Buteshire, Clackmannanshire and Ross-shire. Clackmannanshire alternated in representation with Kinross, which had been represented by a government supporter: Buteshire alternated with Caithness, whose member, John Sinclair, had been an early convert to the ministry. In December, Robinson had hoped for 12 electoral gains in Scotland, as follows: Clackmannanshire, Dumbartonshire, Dumfries burghs, Glasgow burghs, Haddington burghs, Inverness-shire, Linlithgow burghs, Linlithgowshire, Perth burghs, Roxburghshire, Tain burghs and Wigton burghs. The coalition was protected from its own unpopularity by the oligarchical nature of the Scottish representation, which allowed little expression of public opinion: the total electorate of the thirty-three Scottish counties was about 2,500, half that of the city of Bristol.

[4] The Westminster campaign can be studied in the compilation of speeches, ballads and broadsheets published at the time entitled *The history of the Westminster election*. W. T. Laprade, 'William Pitt and Westminster Elections', *American Historical Review*, xviii, 253–74, argued that Westminster was a Foxite victory and demonstrated that the coalition was not unpopular. I do not think he proved his case.

forecast. William Adam estimated the new Parliament as ministerialist 306, opposition 200, and 38 doubtful.[1] In the first division of the new House, on the Westminster scrutiny, Pitt had the pleasure to find himself in a comfortable majority, with 233 votes against 136.

Severe though the coalition's defeat was, it is important not to exaggerate it. Most of the estimates of the opposition's losses are inflated. Lecky wrote that no fewer than 160 members, 'nearly all of them belonging to the opposition, were driven from parliament', and later historians have echoed his opinion without bothering about the reservation.[2] Lecky's computation of the number of members not re-elected was very near the mark: according to *The House of Commons 1754–90*, it was 163.[3] But by no means all of these had been coalitionists. Forty-six of those not re-elected had been supporters of administration; another 21 had been absent from the critical debates and cannot be classified: the number of coalitionists who disappeared was 96.[4] Nor were all of these political victims. John Yorke had been anxious to retire before the 1780 election and had agreed to continue only to oblige the family interest; Thomas Staunton was in his late seventies and extremely unwell; George Forester could certainly have been returned for Wenlock had he wished, and James Wemyss chose to stand down in favour of his son in Sutherland.

The coalition's casualties were at once dubbed 'Fox's Martyrs', and a pamphlet of that name describing their sufferings had an

[1] Blair–Adam MSS.

[2] J. H. Rose, *William Pitt and national revival*, 170; D. L. Keir, *The constitutional history of modern Britain* (1938), 380; J. S. Watson, *The reign of George III* (1960), 272.

[3] *The House of Commons 1754–90*, i, 98. This was by no means an unusual number: in fact, it was rather smaller than in the three previous general elections.

[4] The list of affiliation given as an appendix to Stockdale's *Debates* showed 260 members as coalitionists, 247 as Pittites, and 51 absentees. On a *pro rata* proportion of losses, the coalition would have expected to lose 74 old members. Twenty-two does not, of course, represent their net political loss, since in few cases were coalitionists who retired, for whatever reasons, replaced by fellow coalitionists. The 163 new members I estimate as follows: Government 109; probable government 6; total government 115: Opposition 29; probable opposition 5; total opposition 34: doubtful 14.

immense success. The inclusion in the list of such notable Foxites as Bunbury, Baker, Cavendish, Coke and the Hartleys appears to bear out the description. Recently it has been suggested that most of the victims were followers of Lord North.[1] In fact, the losses came from both wings of the coalition with surprising impartiality. 'An Authentic List of the whole House of Commons', published in March 1784, identified 130 members as Foxites and 112 as Northites. Of the 96 members of the coalition who did not reappear in Parliament, 47 were followers of Fox and 43 of North.[2]

These figures need some explanation. It had been generally assumed that North's followers would suffer most, since his long tenure of power had enabled him to find government boroughs for many of his political associates. But the public traditionally over-estimated the extent of the government's direct borough influence, and therefore exaggerated the proportion of North's following that was *en prise* to the new administration.[3] At the most generous definition, the government's borough interest might encompass 35 seats in some eighteen boroughs.[4] But some of North's former friends, like Charles Jenkinson and John Robinson, representing Saltash and Harwich respectively, had already changed sides. In the eighteen boroughs were left 24 coalitionists, of whom 17 were Northites.[5] Had every one of

---

[1] *The House of Commons 1754–90*, i, 89.

[2] F. O'Gorman, *The Whig party and the French Revolution* (1967), prints as appendix I a useful assessment of party strength between 1780 and 1784. Since our estimates of Foxite and Northite losses in 1784 do not exactly coincide, I have printed the evidence for my calculation as appendix I.

[3] *Sarah Farley's Bristol Journal*, 24 January 1784, wrote of the Admiralty commanding 28 seats, the Treasury more than 50, as well as all the Cinque Port seats, with one exception. This exaggerates the government's command by about four times.

[4] Dover 1, Harwich 2, Hastings 2, Hedon 2, Malmesbury 2, Newport (Hants.) 2, Plymouth 2, Portsmouth 2, Queenborough 2, Rochester 2, Rye 2, Sandwich 2, Saltash 2, Scarborough 1, Seaford 2, Yarmouth (Hants.) 2, Weymouth and Melcombe Regis 4, Winchelsea 1. There is scarcely one borough in this list of which some reservation or qualification should not be made.

[5] The Northites were John Henniker, George North, Lord Palmerston, John Ord, John St John, Sir Frederick Rogers, George Darby, Charles Frederick, Sir Walter Rawlinson, George Finch Hatton, Thomas Onslow, William Dickinson, Sir Grey Cooper, Sir

them lost his seat the effect would have been far from catastrophic. But in practice the coalitionists proved surprisingly hard to dislodge. Six of them were able to transfer to other seats and reappear; another 6 stood their ground and survived.[1] At the end of the clearing operation, there were still 16 coalitionists sitting for the eighteen boroughs, against 20 Pittites.[2] Considering that these were boroughs where the government was reputed to be at an advantage, the results were mediocre—indeed, rather worse than the national average.[3]

Fox's following, on the other hand, suffered more severely than they may have expected, mainly because, as candidates for the counties and large towns, they were more exposed to the chill blast of public opinion. North's losses in the counties at the general election of 1780 meant that only 4 of his 112 followers were knights of the shire, as against 29 of Fox's 130.[4] Only one of his supporters, Lord Lewisham, fell victim to county opinion, whereas 10 of Fox's failed to secure their return. A similar pattern can be traced in the large towns. In the thirty-two boroughs

---

Thomas Rumbold, Welbore Ellis, William Rumbold and John Purling. Fox's six were Thomas Erskine, Sir Henry Fetherstonhaugh, Robert Gregory, John Trevanion, Edward Morant and John Nesbitt. One other coalitionist, Stephen Lushington, had been brought in for Hedon just before the change of ministry in December 1783. Sir Richard Sutton, Sir Richard Worsley, Christopher D'Oyley and John Durand I class as doubtful.

[1] The six who moved were George North, Palmerston, Ord, Rawlinson, Onslow and Sir Thomas Rumbold. The six who held their seats were Fetherstonhaugh, Dickinson, Morant, Ellis, Purling and Nesbitt.

[2] I.e. 10 new coalitionists had joined the 6 survivors. The other two members were the Speaker, and Henry Flood, returned eventually for Seaford after a series of contests, whom I classify as doubtful. After the 1780 general election, the same boroughs had returned 33 government supporters and only 5 members of opposition.

[3] In some places the government manager seems to have been unreliable—e.g. at Weymouth and Malmesbury. In others, it is difficult to resist the conclusion that the operation of Crewe's Act, disenfranchising revenue officers, had made the government's position insecure. The matter is discussed by B. Kemp in an article in the *English Historical Review*, 1953, but I am not wholly convinced by her conclusion that 'the government did not lose seats in 1784 as a result of Crewe's Act'. John Robinson, in his estimates, thought the act might have some effect on Hastings, Rye, Seaford, Winchelsea, Harwich and Scarborough. In 1780, these six boroughs had returned 11 government supporters: in 1784 they returned 5 government supporters and the Speaker.

[4] For the 1780 general election, see I. R. Christie, *The end of North's ministry*, 157–63.

classified as 'large' by *The House of Commons 1754-90*, the representation at the dissolution was Fox 28, Pitt 24, and North 6, with 8 others.[1] Of the 16 coalition victims in this group, 11 came from Fox's wing and 5 from North's.

Allegations were, of course, widespread at the time that the government's success had been achieved by bribery on a lavish scale. 'Nothing but the want of cash lost the elections', insisted a coalition partisan in *The History of the Westminster Election*, and Burke complained that the 'great support' of the contest was 'money furnished by the oppression and devastation of India'.[2] On this, and the evidence available in Robinson's papers, W. T. Laprade founded an elaborate theory that the 1784 election saw the 'commercial magnates' beginning to use their wealth to buy political power, and that even Robinson himself was appalled at the introduction of 'crude wealth as a stark force for the purpose of overturning the established order in the constituencies'.[3] In particular he drew attention to the remark added by Robinson to certain electoral proposals that they were 'a wild wide calculate of the money wanted for seats, but which I always disapproved and thought very wrong.' But an analysis of the estimates in question suggests the possibility of another explanation of Robinson's comment, for they are ludicrously unrealistic. The total sum envisaged comes to £193,000, not including any money to be spent at Westminster, York, Bristol, Gloucester, 'and other places'—i.e. more than had been spent at the five previous general elections put together, and a strange contrast with the £32,000 actually available. In other words, Robinson may be expressing professional horror at the crudity of the

---

[1] The total includes 4 members for London. The 8 others were 4 absentees, 1 doubtful (H. Rawlinson for Liverpool) and 3 members who can only be described as 'coalition'.
[2] Burke to Sir William Lee, 27 March. Horace Walpole told Mann, 30 March: 'the court struck the blow at the ministers, but it was the gold of the Company that really conjured up the storm and has diffused it all over England'.
[3] Laprade, introduction, xviii.

estimates rather than any forebodings that 'the old order was doomed'.

The role of the East India Company in the campaign is hard to trace. In view of the part played by Indian affairs in the development of the political crisis, one would expect members of the Company to take the keenest interest and the problems of India to be warmly discussed. According to Wraxall, the committee of the proprietors had, in the course of December, sent circular letters to 'almost every town or corporate body throughout Great Britain' warning them to be on their guard.[1] Richard Atkinson, one of the Directors, had become in the course of the struggle against Fox's India bill, a close confidant of Robinson, Jenkinson and Dundas, and was much consulted over electoral arrangements. In January 1784 it was said that nothing was done at the India House 'but to think of how they shall defeat Mr. Fox's bill'.[2] The government was particularly anxious, in view of the financial stringency, to encourage wealthy supporters, Indians or not, to undertake at their own expense the task of driving the Rockinghams out of the open boroughs, where they were strongly entrenched. Paul Le Mesurier, who contested Southwark at a by-election in June 1784 explained afterwards that he had been 'drawn into public life much earlier than he ever thought he should be'—presumably because of the part he had taken in opposing Fox's bill.[3] Some candidates at the general election were certainly tempted to hint that the resources of the Company were behind them. An election manager at Boston reported of Dalhousie Watherstone, who though once a Bengal army officer was certainly not prominent in Company politics, that 'it is given out among the freemen that he is sent down by the India Company, who are to bear all the expense, which is talked of very largely . . . This makes the freemen mad.'[4]

[1] Wraxall, iii, 253.
[2] T. Graham to Henry Burt, 30 January, Lynedoch MSS. 3591, f. 170.
[3] *The House of Commons 1754–90*, iii, 33–4.
[4] *Ibid*, iii, 610–11.

But it is a long step to move from evidence of this kind to an assertion that there was an 'organised and systematic attempt' by the Company to intervene. If that had been the case, with events favouring them, one would expect to find a dramatic increase in the number of members of the East India interest returned to Parliament. There is no sign of this.[1]

The elections took place amid one of the most extensive publicity campaigns of the eighteenth century. Mrs M. D. George has shown that the number of caricatures produced in the first five months of 1784 reached record proportions.[2] Fitzwilliam was warned, in the course of February, that pamphlets against Fox's India bill were being industriously circulated throughout the country: a 'determined set of people', with a well-organised system was said to be at work on behalf of Pitt in Yorkshire.[3] London newspapers devoted great space to the parliamentary debates and, later, to electioneering matters, while the provincial papers reported local meetings in considerable detail, and often found space for polemical correspondence. Administration seems to have spent more than £1,000 on the press in the course of the year.[4] Some of the pamphlets and squibs undoubtedly made effective propaganda, particularly Stockdale's publication of

---

[1] It is true that the figures for members in the East Indian interest quoted in *The House of Commons 1754–90*, i, 152 show a rise from 31 in the fifteenth parliament to 45 in the sixteenth, but two reservations must be made. First, this is the continuation of a trend which had been developing from 1754 onwards: secondly, since the figures are the total for each parliament, and the sixteenth lasted nearly twice the length of the fifteenth, one would expect the numbers to be substantially higher.

A better comparison is between the number of members sitting at the dissolution and those returned at the general election. According to C. H. Philips, *The East India Company 1784–1834*, there were 58 members of the Indian interest at the dissolution and 60 returned at the general election. This again should be seen as part of the general trend, since the numbers rise to 72 in 1790, to 75 by 1796, and to 95 in 1802.

My own calculation is: *at the dissolution* 36 members (James had died but Lushington had come in): returned at the general election 34, raised to 36 by the end of the year through by-elections. Of the 34 members, 24 supported Pitt and 10 the coalition.

[2] *Catalogue of political and personal satires* (1938), vi, xvi.

[3] Rev. H. Zouch to Fitzwilliam, 9 February; Peter Wentworth to Fitzwilliam, 11 & 16 February, Wentworth Woodhouse MSS.

[4] A. Aspinall, *Politics and the press, c. 1780–1850* (1949), 68.

The Beauties of Fox, North and Burke, which recalled the pre-coalition abuse that had passed between them.[1] In the field of caricature, administration had a marked superiority, both in numbers and quality. Pitt offered very little to the caricaturist, though he occasionally made an appearance as 'Master Billy' or 'The Infant Hercules': Fox and North, on the other hand, offered splendid targets, and innumerable variations were produced on the union of this ever-diverse pair; they appeared as coal-heavers, bandits, chimney-sweeps, Fox and the Badger, Herod and Pilate, Carlo-Khan and the fair Northelia, while Fox alone was pilloried as Guy Fawkes, Satan, Phaeton, Cataline, Gorgon, and repeatedly as Cromwell.

It would, however, be misleading to suggest that the coalition was buried beneath a pile of hostile propaganda. The sums needed for newspaper subsidies were comparatively small, and well within the capacity of the coalition to raise.[2] They were well aware of the importance of publicity. Fitzwilliam was told by one of his Yorkshire supporters: 'I wish we had a good paragraph out into the York and Leeds papers . . . to state the dispute betwixt the King and Parliament properly, for it is amazing to think how ignorant people are on the subject; they have no idea but that Mr. Fox wants to get the better of the King and be the Lord Protector.'[3] In Sheridan the coalition possessed a man with very good contacts with publishers and printers, and, before its dismissal, it had itself been accused of maintaining 'a tribe of hireling newspaper scribblers'.[4] One historian of the press has even suggested that, with the exception of the *Morning Post,* control of which had been purchased by George Rose in the early months of 1784, all the

---

[1] Stockdale was paid £228 18s. 6d. by the ministers in 1784 for 'various pamphlets and publications'. *Ibid.,* 166.

[2] £200 a year was an average subsidy to the editor of a London newspaper. Compared with the cost of contesting Westminster, usually paid for by subscription, this was insignificant.

[3] Carr to Fitzwilliam, 11 March, Wentworth Woodhouse MSS.

[4] The accusation came from Sir Richard Hill during the debate on the third reading of Fox's India Bill. Debrett, xii, 385.

London newspapers supported the coalition.[1] But this is to over-simplify the position. Few, if any, editors were so devotedly partisan that they would refuse to insert paragraphs from the other side, and in the majority of papers one finds coalition puffs followed immediately by government puffs. John Almon, of the *General Advertiser*, seems to have been in receipt of subsidies from both sides, while the *Morning Herald*, for years the most staunch coalition journal, figures in the list of newspapers receiving money from the government.[2] In the absence of a detailed and authoritative study of the press during this period, one can only venture the opinion that in terms of space the coalition was not outclassed, though the government's publicity may have had the edge in vigour and effect.

The interpretation of the general election of 1784 has for many years been a matter of dispute between historians. The publication in 1922 by W. T. Laprade of the electoral papers of John Robinson encouraged the belief that public opinion counted for little or nothing in the final result.[3] Although this assumption was at once challenged, notably by J. H. Rose, it gained wide acceptance.[4] In 1937, however, Mrs M. D. George redressed the balance by drawing attention to the indisputable evidence that public opinion was massively in favour of Pitt.[5] The two most recent summaries of the problem, by N. C. Phillips and in *The House of*

---

[1] L. Werkmeister, *The London Daily Press, 1772–92* (1963), 78.

[2] *Ibid.*, 131–3; Secret Service Accounts, Windsor Archives.

[3] Laprade's views can also be studied in his article 'Public Opinion and the General Election of 1784', *English Historical Review*, 1916. 'It is doubtful, in view of the nature of the political machinery then in use, whether in 1784 the popular wish, if there had been such a consensus of opinion, could have influenced the result of a parliamentary election... Nothing remotely resembling what we understand by the term "public opinion" played a decisive part in the Election'.

[4] Rose's article, entitled 'The rout of a coalition' is in *The nineteenth century and after*, March 1924. For a somewhat uncritical acceptance of Laprade's thesis, see C. E. Fryer, 'Historical Revision', *History*, 1924.

[5] 'Fox's Martyrs; the General Election of 1784', *Transactions of the Royal Historical Society*, 1939.

Commons 1754–90, agree that the result was due to the normal attractive influence of government, augmented by public opinion, which helped to turn defeat into a rout.[1]

That the 1784 election was more 'political' than its predecessors will hardly be denied. Of the 1768 election it has been written that it 'had little to do with politics and almost nothing with party'.[2] One could not begin to make sense of the 1784 election if one ignored politics and party. The very fact that there was a general election in 1784, when the fifteenth parliament had another three years to run, testifies to the importance of political considerations: one might say that this was the first political, as opposed to statutory, dissolution since 1714.[3] It is true that the number of contests in 1784 was in no way remarkable,[4] but this is not in itself evidence of lack of public concern. Indeed, in several instances, the absence of a contest was the most dramatic demonstration possible of the coalition's unpopularity—in Dorset, Yorkshire or Norfolk, for example, where the canvass alone was sufficient to convince the coalitionist candidates that their cause was hopeless. That the political issues of the day were very widely discussed is apparent from the number of pamphlets, cartoons and broadsheets, as well as from references in national and provincial newspapers and in private correspondence. Coalition supporters shared to a considerable degree the bewilderment of the French observer of Bunbury's *débâcle*. 'My mind misgives me,' wrote Lord Spencer to his mother, 'when I see the accounts daily pouring in from every quarter of the defeat of our

---

[1] N. C. Phillips, '*Yorkshire and English National Politics, 1783–4*' wrote that the 'current hypothesis . . . permits public opinion a role, though not a deciding one, in the election'. John Brooke, commenting on the argument whether the result owed more to manipulation or public opinion, concluded: 'it was, of course, both these things at the same time'. *The House of Commons 1754–90*, i, 89.

[2] J. Brooke, *The Chatham administration* (1956), 338.

[3] There had of course been premature dissolutions before—in 1747, 1774 and 1780—but in each case the parliament had run most of its term. This was the first dissolution since 1714 that could be considered as punitive.

[4] *The House of Commons 1754–90*, i, 96. The total for 1784 was eighty-three, as against seventy-six in 1780 and ninety-five in 1774. These estimates are of course approximate.

partisans in all places where they offer themselves; and it is very plain that politicks are at the bottom of all the contests.'[1]

Even in places where there appears to have been little political activity, one can sometimes detect evidence by probing beneath the surface. The member for Stirling burghs, James Campbell, an early convert to administration, was returned without serious opposition at the general election. Yet the *Caledonian Mercury*, 7 April, reported a declaration by the corporation of Inverkeithing, one of the constituent burghs, that it would support 'no candidate whose principles were understood to be adverse to the present administration'. The situation in Pembroke boroughs and Pembrokeshire seems at first glance to be even more devoid of interest: in the boroughs Hugh Owen was returned unopposed, as he had been in 1774 and 1780, while in the county his cousin, Sir Hugh Owen, was also returned unopposed. *The House of Commons 1754–90* does not devote a single line to either election. But the freeholders of Pembrokeshire were well aware of the political crisis, and in a unanimous address to the two members begged them to 'persevere in maintaining the dignity of the House of Commons . . . not suffering us to be enslaved by the backstairs influence of the Minister and his train of new made lords'.[2] Some of these can no doubt be dismissed as pious resolutions, designed to support the member's political attitude, but it is certain that more political excitement was generated than can be traced by a bare examination of election returns.

But to suggest that there was widespread public interest and overwhelming support for the ministry is not to argue that it was a decisive factor: it does not follow that public opinion could make itself felt through the hardened arteries of the unreformed representative system. Mrs George was right in observing that 'within the limits of the system a mandate could scarcely have been more emphatic', but those limits were still severe. In borough after borough the techniques of electoral management stood

[1] 2 April, Spencer MSS.   [2] *Sarah Farley's Bristol Journal*, 17 April.

firm. Lord North was threatened with a contest in his own family borough of Banbury, but although the interloper was cheered by the inhabitants, the corporation gave his lordship his eleventh consecutive unopposed return. The number of constituencies in which public opinion could be decisive was still a small proportion of the whole, and had the popular tide flowed as strongly for the coalition as it did for Pitt, there can be little doubt that the administration would still have obtained a majority.

In some respects the address campaign was a more remarkable demonstration of public opinion than the general election. It may well have had more effect in that it took place at a time when the issue was still in the balance, whereas the election came after it had been decided. With unrepresented towns like Alnwick, Bideford, Blandford, Halifax, Maidenhead, Leeds, Rotherham, Wakefield and Wolverhampton taking part, it broke through the boundaries of the unreformed system. The implications of this wider public participation were portentous. From a Tory point of view, William Eden was right to question the wisdom of Pitt and the king summoning such forces to their aid.[1] For the time being, they were allies: would it always be so?

The rout of the coalition was so devastating and the hostility of the people so manifest that the victims themselves tended to subscribe to the view that the result was due to popular frenzy. 'The people did not like our work,' wrote Burke, 'and they joined the court to pull it down.'[2] A few sensational examples, such as the defeats of Coke and Lord John Cavendish, gave plausibility to this explanation, but it was, nevertheless, mistaken. The basic cause of the defeat was the influence of government, and its

---

[1] 'His Majesty seems to be placing his crown upon the back of a runaway horse. It was offensive enough when Fox used to talk of the majesty of the people, but I never expected to see the Court of St. James enter into that co-partnership.' Add. MS. 45728, f. 30. The author of the pamphlet, *We have been all in the wrong*, 1785, made a similar point when he wrote: 'such an appeal may serve the turn of the day to a Minister; but under pretence of serving the King, it brings ruin on the Throne'.

[2] Burke to William Baker, 22 June 1784. See also his speech of 1788: 'the mob of 1784 destroyed the House of Commons, destroyed their best friends.' Debrett, xxiii, 342.

magnitude was the result of the peculiar political situation of the day. For the first time since the Hanoverian succession, the government changed hands immediately before a general election, leaving its former possessors to withstand the full brunt of its influence. Had the election of 1741 come just after the fall of Walpole, the distress of his followers might have been as great as that of the coalition's. Had there been a general election in 1762 when Newcastle, after years in power, led his troops into opposition, the same might have happened.[1] But in each case the general election was postponed several years, giving an opportunity for the trimmers and waverers to adjust themselves to the changed circumstances. If the fifteenth parliament had run its full term, until 1787, the coalition would, *ceteris paribus*, have suffered the same fate, but it would have been by gradual stages; by deaths, desertions and by-election losses, followed by a much less dramatic clearing-out of the survivors when the general election came. What seemed to some in 1784 *Vox Dei* and to others *Vox Populi* was merely the routine working of the electoral system under most unusual circumstances.

[1] The nearest equivalents would be the general elections of 1710 and 1715.

CHAPTER 12

CONCLUSION

The meeting of the sixteenth parliament on 18 May 1784 found Charles Fox back in his old position—the political wilderness. North and Burke never held office again: Fox was excluded for all but the last six months of his life. The party was dazed by defeat. Some talked of secession: others, like Burke, demanded vigorous counter-attack. The debate on the Westminster scrutiny brought Fox into action, but by August he was complaining that the exertions of the previous eight months had left him 'completely tired out . . . body and mind', and in October Burke declared that he could not find the faintest traces of any plan of campaign: 'everything is left to accidents.'[1]

Nevertheless, the coalition did not, as many expected, fall to pieces in adversity. On the contrary, it cohered so well that it ceased, in effect, to be a coalition at all, and became the opposition party under Fox's leadership. North's position suffered a steady eclipse.[2] Hampered by ill-health and growing blindness, at fifty-two he had no political future, and his following was not replenished. His personal reputation remained high, and he slid easily into the role of elder statesman, intervening frequently in debate and listened to with respect. But his following suffered a slow attrition. Several of them died in 1785, a small cluster

---

[1] Add. MS. 47561, f. 81; *The correspondence of Edmund Burke*, v, 177.

[2] *The House of Commons 1754–90*, iii, 212, exaggerates when it suggests that the election of 1784 'almost wiped out his party'. Sixty-nine of his followers were returned, and of these 40 were still voting in opposition at the time of the Regency crisis of 1788–9. To what extent they still regarded North as their leader, it is impossible to say: with parliamentary reform a dead issue after 1785 there were few questions to distinguish the two wings of the coalition. Two calculations in 1788, the first crediting him with only seventeen supporters and the second with five seem serious under-estimates. *MSS. P. V. Smith, H.M.C. 12th Report*, ix, 373; Buckingham, ii, 13.

resigned their seats in 1787, and others went over to administration. John Luttrell and Lord Delaval abandoned the losing side in great haste, the first making contact with Pitt within five days of his re-election, the second taking the very earliest opportunity to recant and express his conviction that Pitt had been borne into power 'on the shoulders of the people'.[1] A more substantial loss, since it deprived the opposition of one of its best debaters, particularly on economic questions, was that of William Eden, who accepted in December 1785 an appointment as negotiator for a commercial treaty with France. Savagely attacked as an apostate, he received from one friend some consolation:

As to Charles Fox . . . I am perfectly convinced that nothing but the death of the King or a war can bring him forward, and therefore I consider him destined to pass the greatest part of his life in opposition. I have heard the king speak of him with that indignation that I really believe he would rather sacrifice everything than allow him to come forward. He therefore ought not to expect that people who are by no means proscribed should continue their adherence beyond certain limits . . .[2]

This was no unfair description of Fox's plight. Debating victories, as on the government's Irish proposals or the plan for fortifying Portsmouth and Plymouth, could bring him no nearer to restoration: Pitt, he declared ruefully, was a minister who 'thrives by defeat and flourishes by disappointment'.[3] For a few months, in the winter of 1788–9, the king's illness held out hopes of a return to power, but they were delusive. The following year, with the outbreak of the French Revolution, the whole context of politics was transformed, and the process inaugurated that led to the break-up of the opposition and the gradual regrouping of parties on ideological lines.

Several of the factors contributing to the defeat of the coalition have already been discussed. It is scarcely possible, from the

---

[1] *The House of Commons 1754–90*, iii, 68; *Parl. Hist.* xxiv. 835.
[2] Sir Andrew Hamond to Eden, 10 December, Auckland, i, 362.   [3] Debrett, xix, 224.

fragmentary evidence available, for the historian to gauge precisely the relative importance of revulsion from the coalition itself, Fox's India bill and the Receipt Tax in creating a hostile public opinion.

But in the intricate network of causes, four seem to me to be worth emphasising. The first, and the foundation on which everything depended, was the unwavering hostility of the king. The crisis revealed how great were the prerogatives surviving to the monarch, provided that they were used with determination and in favourable circumstances: the seventy years since the Hanoverian succession had not seriously eroded the monarch's powers, and he was still, in a very real sense, the centre of government. North's opinion, in February 1783, that the 'appearance of power' was all that the king could expect was wide of the mark: a sounder, though more flippant comment, came from Lord Townshend, who declared afterwards that he had 'always foreseen the coalition ministry could not last, for he was at court when Mr. Fox kissed hands, and he observed George III turn back his ears and eyes just like the horse at Astley's, when the tailor he had determined to throw was getting on him'. More than twenty years later the king was still protesting that, 'even at the hazard of a civil war', he would not employ Fox.[1] In a direct and personal clash between an eighteenth-century monarch and one of his subjects, however able, the monarch was bound to win, unless the exigencies of war made that subject's services indispensable.

The second factor in bringing about the downfall of the coalition was the success of Pitt's lie to the House of Commons. It is hardly possible to exaggerate the extent to which the anti-coalition campaign was based upon the new minister's reputation for purity and integrity. His virtuous restraint in not appropriating

---

[1] Russell, ii, 28; *The diaries and correspondence of George Rose*, ii, 156–7. There is a discussion of the origins of the king's dislike of Fox in Mr Brooke's biography in *The House of Commons 1754–90*, vol. ii.

for himself the valuable sinecure of the Clerkship of the Pells when it fell vacant in January 1784 was extolled in dozens of speeches and newspaper paragraphs. The immaculateness of his character was held up in contrast to the grubby reputations of Fox and North. 'The salvation of the country', insisted Lord Mulgrave in February 1784 'required virtue as well as talents, and in this respect . . . there could not be a question.' Pitt's chief advantage over Fox, thought Wraxall, was his 'moral character, high integrity, and indisputable rectitude of intention'. One of Fitzwilliam's followers reported to him that the Yorkshire electors considered Pitt their champion, and 'they can see in him no error'. Could this reputation have survived had Fox been able to demonstrate that Pitt was not merely privy to the royal intervention, but an instigator of it? Wilberforce himself conceded that if the bedchamber peers had been influenced, he would consider it an unconstitutional and most scandalous use of the royal name. But what, he asked, had these allegations to do with the present ministers? Never did crying 'Wolf' redound more dramatically on its authors than on the Rockinghams: for years 'secret influence' had been their cry, and when it happened, they were listened to with bored indifference.[1]

Pitt's reputation would have been less decisive had it not contrasted so pointedly with the public image of his main rival. Indeed, it is not easy to explain why a man, so attractive in his private circle, should have been so distrusted by the public at large. It would be too simple to see Fox as the victim of unrelenting propaganda. Paragraph after paragraph, it is true, dwelt on his debts, his gambling, his love affairs, and reminded readers that his father had once been called 'the public defaulter of unaccounted millions'. The accusation of 'Cromwell' was particularly effective. It was reported to be the 'received notion among the inferiors' in Yorkshire that Fox was 'attempting to dethrone

[1] Debrett, xiii, 64; Wraxall, iii, 232; Sinclair to Fitzwilliam, 3 March 1784, Wentworth Woodhouse MSS.

the King and make himself an Oliver Cromwell'. In Lancashire the name of Fox was said to be 'most universally execrated', and in Gloucestershire 'the Good Women and the Mob' exclaimed against him and the India bill 'with an honest vehemence that will not permit them to discriminate between the Minister and the Man'. But he was hounded in this way because he was peculiarly vulnerable, and because the public was prepared to believe the worst of him. A belated recognition of the damage that his character had done his party seems to lie behind his remark in the summer of 1784: 'it is impossible not to see that the majority is much more *against* us than *for* the Ministry, and their behaviour on the India bill, which had begun to excite much discontent till I opposed it, is a very sufficient lesson in my mind.'[1]

Some of this dislike may have been a residue from the American war, when the Rockinghams had at times flirted with treason; some was undoubtedly a general disillusion with politicians associated in any way with the loss of an Empire and mortifying defeats at the hands of the national enemy. But the main ingredient in the dislike of Fox seems to have been moral disapprobation. The wit, cynicism and urbanity of much of the fashionable world should not blind us to the fact that large sections of the community were sober, god-fearing and respectable, took their tone from the king, and were genuinely disgusted at the spectacle of Fox's furniture being put into the streets, or the leader of the opposition hurrying from the House of Commons to conduct a Faro bank. 'Can you, as honest, rational men,' appealed a broadsheet to the Parents of Westminster, 'give your support to the high priest of drunkenness, gaming, and every species of debauchery that can *contaminate the principles you would early wish to inculcate in your offspring* . . .?'[2] It was the paradox of Fox's life that, incomparably

---

[1] The 'India Bill' referred to was, of course, Pitt's bill, introduced into the House of Commons on 6 July 1784. Parker to Fitzwilliam, 26 April, Wentworth Woodhouse MSS.; T. Blackburne to H. Addington, 19 April, Sidmouth MSS.; R. Cumberland to G. Cumberland, 7 April, Add. MS. 36494, f. 298; Fox to Portland, 1 August, Add. MS. 47561, f. 81.   [2] *History of the Westminster election*, 99.

the sharpest weapon in his party's armoury, he was also its most grievous liability.

The last factor relates to the overall strategic situation. The coalition's leaders in general, and Fox in particular, have been criticised for running to extremes during the crisis. I think it is nearer the truth to say that, in the last resort, they were too moderate, and flinched from the logic of the situation. They continued to put their trust in the normal working of the constitution, in majorities and addresses and appeals to the king, long after it was apparent that the constitution was not functioning normally. There is something almost comical in the coalition's lack of comprehension. 'I am unable to conjecture what the ministers mean,' Eden had written on 4 January: 'I cannot see that they have any practical resource of any kind.' That they might defy adverse votes in the House of Commons was never in his mind. General Conway, writing the same day, was equally baffled: 'a system against the bent of the House of Commons, and supported only by the Crown, I take . . . to be impracticable.' But Lord Camden, explaining the events to Thomas Walpole in Paris, saw the situation as the breakdown of executive government and 'little less than a declaration of open war between the King and his servants'. The only possible retort was an appeal to arms by the king's adversaries. It was never contemplated. The moderate, aristocratic nature of the Rockinghams and their allies meant that, for all their adulation of the Glorious Revolution of 1688, the thought of emulating it in practice did not occur to them. The king called their bluff.[1]

---

[1] Eden to Sheffield, 4 January, Add. MS. 45728, f. 12; Grafton, 388; Camden to Walpole, 7 January, Lullings MSS.

Later on the mood of the people was enough to discourage any such appeal. But the marked reluctance on the part of the coalition's supporters to withhold supplies or to pass a short mutiny bill confirms their caution.

The coalition's predicament seems to me not dissimilar to that of the Liberals in Prussia during the 1860s, when they, with a majority in the Assembly, were confronted by a minister appointed by the crown, and determined to govern with or without their consent. The Liberals also flinched. Since Bismarck's part in this crisis is not always admired, I am a little surprised at the enthusiasm commonly shown for Pitt's conduct.

In 1784 it was not unreasonable to hazard a guess that the success of the king's intervention would usher in a period in which royal power would be most vigorously asserted. Horace Walpole thought that the wound given by Pitt to the House of Commons might prove 'very fatal to the constitution', while in his last parliamentary speech General Conway declared bitterly that he had 'hitherto been fool enough to consider the House of Commons as of consequence to the country and weight in the constitution . . . but the right honourable gentleman had proved it to be a cypher'. Nor were these apprehensions confined to the opposition. Even Pitt seems to have had misgivings and feared at times a stab in the back by the king. Over parliamentary reform in 1785 he warned the king that the 'one issue of the business to which he could look as fatal' would be 'the possibility of the measure being rejected by the weight of those who are supposed to be connected with government'. In the event, all these fears were groundless. The House of Commons was neither destroyed, nor its power seriously weakened; while the fifty years from 1784 to 1834 witnessed a substantial decline in the influence of the crown.[1]

Why did the defeat of the House of Commons not produce dire consequences? First it must be conceded that, though in the course of the struggle the king was prepared to use questionable means, there was never any intention of subverting the constitution. The 'settled plan to destroy, not the form, but the essence and the efficacy of the House of Commons' existed only in Burke's imagination.[2] Indeed, once the crisis was over, the king reverted to a very correct view of constitutional propriety, and was hurt that anyone should think him capable of wishing to influence the votes of members of Parliament: 'on a question of such magnitude', he replied to Pitt about reform, 'I should think

---

[1] Walpole to Mann, 30 March 1784; *Parl. Hist.* xxiv, 773 (a different version of Conway's speech is given in Debrett, xiii, 306); Pitt to the king, 19 March 1785, quoted D. G. Barnes, *op. cit.*, 125–6.

[2] Debrett, xv, 153. The charge was made during his 'coroner's inquest' speech of 14 June 1784.

very ill of any man . . . who would suffer his civility to anyone to make him vote contrary to his own opinion.'[1]

The general factors behind the decline in the influence of the crown in the later eighteenth and early nineteenth centuries have been well established: they include the diminution of patronage, tighter parliamentary control of expenditure, and the growth of an organised public opinion.[2] To these we may add arguments from the nature of the royal victory itself. It was a very close run thing. The stubbornness of the coalition's resistance meant that even the most bigoted royalist would think twice before embarking upon a repetition of the struggle, and there was some truth in Eden's suggestion that the coalition had snatched victory from defeat: to Elliot he wrote, on 26 March: 'you see that our Parliament is dissolved in displeasure for the first time since the revolution. There is one use in this—it (serves?) a good constitutional principle—it is better to pack a new Parliament than to try to govern in defiance of the old one.'[3] Although the king had won, in a direct confrontation with a majority of the House of Commons, circumstances had been greatly in his favour: he had the support of public opinion, of a sizeable minority in the Commons, of a large majority in the Lords, and of a minister of quite unusual popularity, while his adversaries were deprived of their most effective counter-argument by the fact that the royal intervention could not be proved. It would be rash to suppose that such a combination of favourable factors was likely to be repeated.

But perhaps the main reason why the king's victory proved deceptive is that, in pursuing his anti-party crusade, his supporters had been forced to adopt the techniques of party itself—letters of

[1] D. G. Barnes, *ibid.*, 127.
[2] A. S. Foord, 'The waning of the influence of the crown', *English Historical Review*, 1947; A. Aspinall, 'The cabinet council 1783–1835', *Proceedings of the British Academy*, 1952; D. Large, 'The decline of "the party of the Crown" and the rise of parties in the House of Lords, 1783–1837', *English Historical Review*, 1963; B. Kemp, *King and Commons 1660–1832* (1957), ch. iv, section iii; R. Pares, *King George III and the politicians*, ch. vi.
[3] Minto MSS., M. 1260.

attendance, pairing arrangements, coordinated tactics, organised propaganda, and electoral planning. The dream of non-party government was further away in 1784 than it had been in 1782. That staunchest of non-party politicians, General Conway, admitted at the end of his career in 1784 that 'in the late contest, he had gone much further than he had ever gone in party before', and he was not the only one.[1] The traditional role of the independents had been shown to be scarcely tenable, and their numbers had declined substantially. Daniel Pulteney in December 1783 referred to the 'thirty or forty' independent members, and three months later most of these had committed themselves.[2] The attempts in 1788 and 1797 to revive independency under the banner of a third party, aloof from Pitt or Fox, are remarkable chiefly for the poor support they received. 'In these desperate times', wrote an observer in 1796, 'a man must choose his party and stick to it. Voting and acting according to Conscience will not do.'[3]

The growth of party organisation was most marked in the ranks of the coalition, particularly after it had become the opposition. The mere fact that it survived as an effective political force in the face of what appeared to be a hopeless position suggests a good deal of cohesion and resilience. The harshness of its fate may itself have stimulated reform and reorganisation. Of the 1780 general election it has been pointed out that the opposition could show 'nothing comparable with the range of Treasury election organization and activity'.[4] But the evidence from the Blair Adam MSS. establishes that in 1784 the opposition made a determined effort to match the government's campaign, promoting candidatures and providing seats.[5] This organisation was not allowed to lapse and by 1790 William Adam was acting as the shadow patronage secretary. Between 1788 and 1790, according to Professor Ginter, Adam and Portland are known to have been

[1] Debrett, xiii, 306.   [2] *H.M.C. Rutland MSS.*, iii, 73.
[3] *The girlhood of Maria Josepha Holroyd*, ed. J. H. Adeane (1896), 388–9.
[4] I. R. Christie, *The end of North's ministry 1780–82*, 107.
[5] D. E. Ginter, *Whig organization in the general election of 1790.*

concerned in the affairs of at least eighty-three constituencies, and efforts were being made to offset the government's financial advantage by setting up a party election fund.[1]

In other areas the development of party organisation may be detected. Professor Ginter has suggested that the period saw the beginnings of a paid party secretariat, operating from Carlton House. The formation of the Westminster Whig Club in May 1784 recognised the need for more formal arrangements than Brookes's could provide and led to the establishment of a series of clubs throughout the provinces to disseminate propaganda and rally the faithful. The Esto Perpetua Club, founded by some of the leading coalitionists to launch literary attacks on their opponents, commenced life with the production of the *Rolliad*. If it did little to improve the coalition's political fortunes, the effect upon *morale* was good. Another step in the direction of party solidarity was the adoption by the coalition, including Lord North, of the famous blue and buff colours.[2]

These changes, it is clear, stemmed from the coalition's unhappy plight. Unable to see any way in which they were likely to regain the confidence of the crown, the opposition was forced to overhaul its techniques for enlisting the support of the public. 'It must be from movements out of doors and not in Parliament', wrote Fox in 1801, 'that opposition can ever gain any strength. I mean of course *as* opposition. What the king's death or illness might produce is another question.'[3] After the acute disappointment of the Regent's change of heart in 1810, the same logic forced them to embrace the cause of parliamentary reform, lest their stay in the wilderness should last, not thirty or forty years, but for ever. 'Put not your trust in Princes' implied putting it in the people.

One of the most significant demonstrations of the importance of party in the period 1782–4 is in its effect upon family

[1] *Ibid.*, Introduction, xxxvii–xxxviii; see also A. S. Foord, *His Majesty's Opposition 1714–1830* (1964), section viii. F. O'Gorman, *The Whig party and the French Revolution*, devotes a section of his first chapter to the consolidation of party organisation after 1784.
[2] Wraxall, iii, 349–50. [3] Russell, iii, 190–1.

relationships, regarded by some historians as the basis of eighteenth-century parliamentary groupings.[1] Family after family was hopelessly split. Thomas Grenville voted for a motion that implied censure on his brother Lord Temple; Philip Yorke and his uncle John voted on opposite sides at the end of the debate of 12 January 1784; Lord Sandwich was horrified to discover that, though he was 'engaged to support the coalition to the utmost', his son, Lord Hinchingbrooke, abhorred it as an attempt to keep the king in 'perpetual subjection'; Lord Bute was a devoted supporter of the king, while Lord Mountstuart, his son, was 'decided for Mr. Fox, and taking a warm part'; George Damer, 'a most violent party man', voted for Fox's India bill in the House of Commons, while his father, Lord Milton, voted against it in the House of Lords; Lord Midleton voted 'in all the violent questions' against his uncle, Lord Sydney, for whose borough he sat: 'so much for obligation and friendship', commented Cornwallis.[2]

One must resist the temptation to make sweeping inferences from a study of two years, particularly when they are, in so many respects, of an unusual nature. Yet so little work has been done on the political life of the later eighteenth century, that it may be helpful to suggest how this study relates to the discussion about the development of party.

The modern study of this question may be traced from the Romanes Lectures given by G. M. Trevelyan in 1926.[3] As one might expect from an historian born and bred in the Whig tradition, Trevelyan argued that 'the two perennial groups

---

[1] E.g., D. Marshall, *Eighteenth century England* (1962), 60: 'In the eighteenth century, men acted together because they were related, or because they had been friends at school, or were connected by marriage alliance'; R. Walcott, *English politics in the early eighteenth century* (1956), 45, writes that in the early period 'the fundamental units of party organisation' were 'friends and relations'.

[2] Buckingham, i, 309–10; Add. MS. 35381, f. 215; Sandwich to Fox, 27 November 1783, Sandwich MSS.; Thomas Coutts to Charles Stuart, 23 December 1783, *A prime minister and his son*, ed. Hon. Mrs E. Stuart Wortley (1925); *Correspondence of Charles, first marquis Cornwallis*, i, 166, 168.

[3] 'The two-party system in English political history.'

labelled Whig and Tory' ... constituted 'the most lasting element in our public life from the days of Clarendon and Shaftesbury to the days of Salisbury and Gladstone', and he called for a new investigation into party history. At the time he spoke L. B. Namier was already hard at work on such a project, and his conclusions, published in 1929, appeared to leave little of the Trevelyan thesis intact. In his own period of study, the era of Newcastle and Bute, party could be ignored: 'the political life of the period could be fully described without ever using a party denomination.'[1] Other scholars took up the new thesis, until it seemed that party might be eradicated from the historiography of the eighteenth century in the way George III had hoped to eradicate it from the practice. K. G. Feiling declared it to be a fundamental truth that 'organized continuous party existed neither in the seventeenth nor in the eighteenth century'.[2] Professor Walcott, in his work on Anne's reign, rejected the Whig-Tory dichotomy, and insisted that the more one studied the period 'the more it seems to have in common with the structure of politics in the Age of Newcastle as explained to us by Namier'.[3] Professor D. G. Barnes accepted that Namier's conclusions were broadly true for the period 1783–1806. Namier himself, when he came in turn to deliver the Romanes lecture, was led by this evidence of support to extend his argument outside the boundaries he had at first carefully prescribed: even before 1714, he told his audience, there was no clear party division, and in the early nineteenth century 'no trace ... at all of party in the modern sense'.[4]

The new orthodoxy was soon challenged. It was not suggested that a party system existed in the eighteenth century, or that political parties were fully developed, but successive historians came forward to testify that their own periods of study could not be properly understood without reference to party loyalties.

---

[1] *The structure of politics at the accession of George III*, Preface to the first edition.
[2] K. G. Feiling, *The second Tory party, 1714–1832*, 2.
[3] *English politics in the early eighteenth century*, 160.
[4] 'Monarchy and the Party System', printed in *Personalities and powers* (1955), 32, 34.

Professor J. R. Jones, in his work on the politics of Charles II's reign, specifically denied that Namier's conclusions applied there, and insisted that the whole nation was concerned with political issues; Professor Kenyon, in his biography of Lord Sunderland, declared that the terms 'Whig' and 'Tory' were 'indispensable' to a correct interpretation of the 1690s, and Mr G. S. Holmes, in his admirable work on Anne's reign, wrote: 'whatever the complexities of the body politic in the early years of the eighteenth century, its life-blood was the existence and conflict of two major parties.'[1] The problem has also been examined in relation to the other end of the century. Professor Ginter has argued that party played a dominant part from the 1780s onwards, and Mr A. M. Mitchell wrote that a 'namierite' interpretation of politics in the 1810s and 1820s 'distorts' the true situation.[2]

This study of the period 1782–4 adds a little more evidence pointing in the same direction. It could not have been written except in party terms: indeed, its main theme is the relationship between party and its claims and the prerogatives of the monarch. One may perhaps suggest that the period of study with which Namier was familiar, far from manifesting characteristics which could be traced more widely, begins to look increasingly like an aberration from the normal pattern. It may be that historians have underestimated the extent to which the heritage of Jacobitism distorted the natural development of party in the middle years of the eighteenth century. Since the Tory party was placed under the ban for a whole generation after the catastrophe of 1715, it is scarcely surprising that party alignments began to disintegrate, and politics to take the form of struggles between Whig factions. Even so, it is necessary to remember that a substantial Tory party survived throughout the reign of George II.

---

[1] J. R. Jones, *The first Whigs: the politics of the exclusion crisis, 1678–1683* (1961), 2–4; J. P. Kenyon, *Robert Spencer, earl of Sunderland* (1958), 248 note; G. S. Holmes, *British politics in the age of Anne* (1967), 6.

[2] D. E. Ginter, *op. cit.*, liv–lvii; A. M. Mitchell, *The Whigs in opposition, 1815–1830* (1967), 4.

To trace the evolution of party is a complex and sometimes baffling task: its behaviour resembles that of the Cheshire Cat, appearing and disappearing in the most disconcerting fashion. Yet two factors seem to me to have made the search even more difficult than it might be. Sir Lewis Namier, in his Romanes lecture, called for a study of 'party-names'. This, I suspect, is the least hopeful way of tackling the problem. To demonstrate that the names 'Whig' and 'Tory' are not meaningful at a particular period is not the same as showing that the politics of that period was not based on party: Namier was right to observe that the description of Pitt as a 'Tory' is quite unhelpful, but it does not follow from that that Pitt was not supported and opposed on a party basis. Names are often the least significant part of political life: in Denmark the party which calls itself 'Venstre' (Left) is on the extreme right of the political spectrum. One may suggest that a more profitable line of investigation would be into party organisation and voting discipline.

Secondly, the differences between eighteenth-century parties and 'modern' parties have sometimes been made to appear even greater than they are by an undue emphasis on the incoherence of the one and the coherence of the other. Mr Brooke, in his work on the Chatham administration, devoted considerable discussion to the structure of the Rockingham party, but I am not sure that his evidence always bears out his contention that they were an incoherent and disorganised group.[1] He describes party as follows: 'The history of party in the eighteenth century tells how little groups, clustered first round a great nobleman or prominent

---

[1] J. Brooke, *The Chatham administration* (1956), chs. vi & vii. From his analysis of the Nullum Tempus division of February 1768, he argues that the Rockinghams made 'a poor figure' (243–7). But was it so poor? 44 per cent of the total House of Commons took part in the division. According to Newcastle's list of the Rockinghams, 60 per cent of their supporters voted, 59 for the motion and 2 against. I should have thought that this suggests a good deal of party discipline. Of the fifty M.P.s described by Mr Brooke as 'Rockinghams' in 1768, fourteen were still in the House of Commons in the spring of 1784. Of these, twelve were supporting Fox, one was absent and one was supporting Pitt. This argues at least some measure of party continuity.

politician, blossom into maturity and then die; evanescent
creatures, they live for a day, but their place is quickly taken by
others.' Metaphors are always dangerous, particularly when they
are as graceful as this one, and later we are specifically told that
Rockingham's party 'was not dissolved by his death'.[1] In other
words, the Rockinghams were moving away from a strictly
personal connection.

That twentieth-century parties have developed an organisa-
tional and polemical apparatus quite beyond that of eighteenth-
century ones is too obvious to need demonstration; but this does
not necessarily place them in a category by themselves. In other
respects, many of the 'imperfections' of eighteenth-century
parties can be found in 'modern' ones. If it is true that the 'two-
party system' did not operate in the eighteenth century, it is
worth remembering that it has rarely operated in classical
simplicity in either the nineteenth or twentieth century. It
would be a mistake to assume that 'modern' parties never split, or
form coalitions, or change their policies abruptly, or contain
diverse elements, or are accused of being ideologically indistin-
guishable from their adversaries. Nor will mere size allow us to
distinguish 'modern' parties from their predecessors. The Liberals
are a small faction compared with the Rockinghams, and their
voting discipline has sometimes been sadly lacking, yet few would
deny that they constitute a political party.

To the argument that the period 1782–4 witnessed a consolidation of parties, it may be objected that the very formation of the
coalition showed that party was still in a highly fluid state. Yet the
realignment of parties is by no means the same as the abandonment
of parties. Indeed, Sir Ivor Jennings may be right in suggesting
that the indignation with which the coalition was greeted
demonstrates that party was already widely accepted: nobody
could protest if independents exercised their right to regroup.[2] In

---

[1] J. Brooke, *The Chatham administration* (1956), 219, 293.
[2] *Party politics*, vol. ii, *The growth of parties* (1961), 47–8.

the same way, the furious attacks on Fox and North for dereliction of principle could hardly have been made without subscribing to the view that political groups ought to have distinctive and enduring ideologies. Lastly, one may wonder why George III devoted so much of his energies to the extirpation of party if it did not exist.

APPENDIX

COALITION LOSSES AT THE 1784 GENERAL ELECTION

In the Bond MSS. and Abergavenny MSS. are copies of *An authentic list of the whole House of Commons*, which appears to have been published in a newspaper in March 1784, and is a detailed and well-informed attempt to assess the affiliation of all members immediately before the 1784 election. It divides the membership into ten groups:

The supporters of Lord North's administration voting with Mr Pitt.	130
The members of the old Opposition with Mr Pitt.	82
The friends of Lord North voting with Lord North	112
Old Opposition voting with Mr Fox	130
New members voting with Mr Pitt	28
New members voting with the coalition	12
Doubtfuls	3
Old Doubtfuls voting with Mr Pitt	11
Old Doubtfuls voting with coalition	3
Not voted	47
	558

The ninety-six supporters of the Coalition who were not re-elected in 1784 are classified in the *Authentic list* as follows:

I THE FRIENDS OF LORD NORTH VOTING WITH LORD NORTH

Anthony Bacon; Francis Basset; Andrew Robinson Bowes; Reginald Pole Carew; Henry Seymour Conway (Downton); Sir Grey Cooper; John Craufurd; George Darby; George Daubeny; Francis Eyre; Martyn Fonnereau; Sir Charles Frederick; George Graham; Joseph Gulston; Francis Hale; William Hanger; George Finch Hatton; Sir John Henniker; Sir Robert Herries; Lord Lewisham; Henry Lawes Luttrell; James Mansfield; Sir James Marriott; David Michel; George Onslow; Sir Ralph Payne; Sir Frederick Rogers; George Ross; William Rumbold; Henry St John; John St John; Hugh Scott; Lord Sheffield; Lord Shuldham; Humphrey Sibthorp; Hans Sloane; Anthony Storer; William Strahan; Andrew Stuart; Charles Townshend; Robert Vyner; James Wemyss; John Yorke (43)

2 OLD OPPOSITION VOTING WITH MR FOX

Evelyn Anderson; William Baker; Wilson Braddyll; Sir Charles Bunbury; George Byng; Lord John Cavendish; Sir Robert Clayton; Thomas William Coke; Henry Seymour Conway (Bury St Edmunds); Henry Dawkins; Sir Gilbert Elliot; Thomas Erskine; George Fitzwilliam; George Forester; Robert Gregory; Thomas Grenville; Booth Grey; Thomas Halsey; David Hartley; Winchcombe Henry Hartley; Philip Honywood; Sir Richard Hotham; George Hunt; Lord Lucan; Thomas Lucas; John Luther; Sir Horatio Mann; Hugh Pigot; Sir John Ramsden; Charles Ross; Thomas Bates Rous; George St John; Sir Thomas Skipwith; John Mansell Smith; Richard Smith; Henry Fitzroy Stanhope; Thomas Staunton; Humphrey Sturt; Beilby Thompson; Wilbraham Tollemache; John Townshend; John Trevanion; Lord Verney; Richard Walpole; William Weddell; Jacob Wilkinson; Percy Charles Wyndham (47)

3 NEW MEMBERS VOTING WITH THE COALITION

James Craufurd; Somerset Davies; Francis Ferrand Foljambe; Stephen Lushington (4)

4 DOUBTFULS

John Elwes

5 OLD DOUBTFULS VOTING WITH COALITION

Henry Rawlinson

BIBLIOGRAPHY

PRIMARY SOURCES

I MANUSCRIPTS

British Museum

Add. MSS. 27914 & 27918: Leeds papers
Add. MSS. 22930: Flood papers
Add. MSS. 29155 & 29161: Hastings papers
Add. MSS. 33087–130: Pelham papers
Add. MSS. 34412–71: Auckland papers
Add. MSS. 34883–5: Gibbon papers
Add. MSS. 35349–36278: Hardwicke papers
Add. MSS. 36494: Cumberland papers
Add. MSS. 37833–5: Robinson papers
Add. MSS. 37842–935: Windham papers
Add. MSS. 38190–489 & 38564–81: Liverpool papers
Add. MSS. 38716: Northington letter-book
Add. MSS. 40177–80 & 40733: Temple letter-books
Add. MSS. 42772–846: Rose papers
Add. MSS. 47449–597: Fox papers
Add. MSS. 51467–8: Holland House papers
Egerton MSS. 2136: Dashwood papers
Egerton MSS. 2232: Thurlow transcripts

Public Record Office
Chatham papers
Foreign Office papers
Granville papers
Manchester papers

Bodleian Library
Bland Burges papers
Clarendon papers
North papers

National Library of Scotland
Lynedoch papers

Melville papers
Minto papers
Robertson–Macdonald papers
Scottish peerage papers

Scottish Record Office
Dalhousie papers
Dundas of Arniston papers
Melville papers

University of Leeds
Brotherton papers

University of Nottingham
Portland papers

Sheffield Public Library
Wentworth Woodhouse papers

Manuscripts in County Record Offices
Buckinghamshire: Lee papers
Devon: Sidmouth papers
Essex: Smyth papers
Hertford: Baker papers
Huntingdonshire: Manchester papers
Kent: Waldeshare papers
Northamptonshire: Fitzwilliam papers
Oxfordshire: Thame papers
Somerset: Dickinson papers
West Suffolk: Grafton papers

Manuscripts in private collections
Abergavenny papers
Camden papers
Jolliffe papers
Kenyon papers
Lansdowne papers
Lullings papers
Sandwich papers
Spencer papers

2 PUBLICATIONS OF THE HISTORICAL MANUSCRIPTS COMMISSION

Abergavenny. *Tenth Report, appendix*, part vi: *MSS. of the Marquis of Abergavenny*, 1887.

Bathurst. *Report on MSS. of Earl Bathurst*, 1923.

Carlisle. *Fifteenth Report, appendix*, part vi: *MSS. of the Earl of Carlisle*, 1897.

Charlemont. *Twelfth Report, appendix*, part x: *MSS. of the Earl of Charlemont*, vol. i & ii, 1891, 1894.

Dartmouth. *Eleventh Report, appendix*, part v; *Fourteenth Report, appendix*, part x; *Fifteenth Report, appendix*, part i: *MSS. of the Earl of Dartmouth*, 1887, 1895, 1896.

Donoughmore. *Twelfth Report, appendix*, part ix: *MSS. of the Earl of Donoughmore*, 1891.

Emly. *Fourteenth Report, appendix*, part ix: *MSS. of Lord Emly*, 1895.

Fortescue. *Thirteenth Report, appendix*, part iii: *MSS. of J. B. Fortescue, Esq.*, vol. i, 1892.

Kenyon. *Fourteenth Report, appendix*, part iv: *MSS. of Lord Kenyon*, 1894.

Knox. *Report on MSS. in various collections*, vol. vi: *MSS. of H. V. Knox, Esq.*, 1909.

Lothian. *Report on the MSS. of the Marquess of Lothian*, 1905.

Lonsdale. *Thirteenth Report, appendix*, part vii: *MSS. of the Earl of Lonsdale*, 1893.

Manchester. *Eighth Report, appendix*, part ii: *MSS. of the Duke of Manchester*, 1881.

Morrison. *Ninth Report, appendix*, part ii: *MSS. of Alfred Morrison, Esq.*, 1883.

Rutland. *Fourteenth Report, appendix*, part i: *MSS. of the Duke of Rutland*, vol. iii, 1894.

Smith. *Twelfth Report, appendix*, part ix: *MSS. of P. V. Smith, Esq.*, 1891.

Stopford-Sackville. *Report on MSS. of Mrs. Stopford-Sackville*, vol. i, 1904.

Sutherland. *Fifth Report, appendix*, part i: *MSS. of the Duke of Sutherland*, 1876.

3 NEWSPAPERS

(a) *London*

> *General Evening Post*
> *London Chronicle*
> *London Gazette*
> *London Packet*
> *Morning Herald*
> *Morning Post*

Parker's General Advertiser
Public Advertiser
St James' Chronicle
Whitehall Evening Post

(b) Provincial

Aris's Birmingham Gazette
Bath Chronicle
Bonner and Middleton's Bristol Journal
Caledonian Mercury
Drewry's Derby Mercury
Exeter Flying Post
Felix Farley's Bristol Journal
Glocester Journal
Jackson's Oxford Journal
Jopson's Coventry Mercury
Leicester and Nottingham Journal
Lincoln, Rutland and Stamford Mercury
Nottingham Journal
Reading Mercury and Oxford Gazette
Sarah Farley's Bristol Journal
Sherborne Mercury and Western Flying Post
Worcester Journal
York Courant

4 PAMPHLET LITERATURE

The beauties and deformities of Fox, North and Burke, 1784.
A candid investigation of the present prevailing topic, by George Rous, 1784.
The coalition, or an essay on the present state of parties, 1783.
A defence of the earl of Shelburne, by D. O'Bryen, 1782.
A defence of the Rockingham party in their late coalition with Lord North, by William Godwin, 1783.
A dialogue on the actual state of Parliament, 1783.
An examination into the principles of the earl of Shelburne, 1783.
Fox's Martyrs, or a new book of the sufferings of the faithful, 1784.
History of the political life of Charles James Fox, 1783.
A letter to the earl of Shelburne on his speech July 10 1782, by Thomas Paine, 1782.
A letter to the earl of Shelburne on the peace, by Portius, 1783.
A letter to Lord North and Mr Fox, by Francis Dobbs, 1784.
A letter from a member of the House of Commons to his constituents, on the great constitutional questions lately agitated in Parliament, 1784.

Letters to a member of the present Parliament upon the extraordinary and unprece-dented transactions in the last House of Commons, 1784.

The ministerialist, 1783.

Monitory hints to the minister in a letter to the earl of Shelburne, 1783.

Observations on 'a defence of the Rockingham party', 1784.

Observations on the East India bill proposals by Charles James Fox and William Pitt, 1784.

Observations on the ministerial anarchy, 1783.

A reply to the defence of the earl of Shelburne, 1782.

A short but serious reply to the defence of the earl of Shelburne, 1782.

Serious considerations on the political conduct of Lord North, by Nathaniel Buckington, 1783.

Thoughts on the peace in a letter from the country, 1783.

Thoughts on the peace, by Thomas Paine, 1783.

A vindication of the earl of Shelburne, 1782.

We have been all in the wrong, or thoughts upon the dissolution of the late, and conduct of the present Parliament, 1785.

A word at parting to the earl of Shelburne, 1782.

A. S. Foord, *His Majesty's Opposition, 1714–1830*, 395–8, gives the titles of other pamphlets.

5 JOURNALS AND MAGAZINES

Annual Register.
Cobbett's Parliamentary History.
Court and City Register, or Gentleman's complete annual Kalendar.
Debrett's Parliamentary Register, 1780–90.
Gentleman's Magazine.
History of the Westminster Election, 1784.
Journals of the House of Commons.
Journals of the House of Lords.
Monthly Review, or Literary Journal.
Political Magazine, and Parliamentary, Naval, Military and Literary Journal.
State Trials, A complete collection, ed. T. B. Howell.
Stockdale's Debates and Proceedings of the House of Commons 1784–90.

6 BOOKS

Adeane, J. H., ed. *The girlhood of Maria Josepha Holroyd*, 1896.
Albemarle, Earl of, *Memoirs of the marquis of Rockingham*, 2 vols., 1852.
Anson, W. R., ed. *The autobiography and political correspondence of Augustus Henry, third duke of Grafton*, 1898.

Argyll, duke of, ed. *Intimate society letters of the eighteenth century*, 2 vols., 1910.

Aspinall, A., ed. *The later correspondence of George III*, 4 vols., 1962–8.

—. *The correspondence of George, Prince of Wales, 1770–1812*, 5 vols., 1963–8.

Bickley, F. ed. *The diaries of Sylvester Douglas, Lord Glenbervie*, 2 vols., 1928.

Browning, O., ed. *The political memoranda of Francis, fifth duke of Leeds*, 1884.

Buckingham and Chandos, duke of, *Memoirs of the court and cabinets of George III*, 4 vols., 1853.

Connell, B. *Portrait of a Whig peer, compiled from the papers of the second Viscount Palmerston*, 1957.

Copeland, T. W., ed. *The correspondence of Edmund Burke*, 1958–68.

Dobrée, B., ed. *The letters of King George III*, 1935.

Fitzgerald, B., ed. *The correspondence of Emily, duchess of Leinster*, 3 vols., Dublin, 1949–57.

Fitzmaurice, Lord. *Life of William, earl of Shelburne*, 2 vols., 1912.

Fonblanque, E. B. de. *Political and military episodes in the latter half of the eighteenth century*, 1876.

Fortescue, Sir John, ed. *The correspondence of King George III*, 6 vols., 1927–8.

Gleig, G. R. *Memoirs of the life of Warren Hastings*, 3 vols., 1841.

Hewins, W. A. S., ed. *The Whitefoord papers*, 1898.

Hogge, G., ed. *The journal and correspondence of William Eden, Lord Auckland*, 4 vols., 1860–2.

Hutton, J., ed. *Selections from the letters and correspondence of Sir James Bland Burges*, 1885.

Ilchester, countess of, and Lord Stavordale. *The life and letters of Lady Sarah Lennox*, 1902.

Laprade, W. T., ed. *The parliamentary papers of John Robinson, 1774–1784*, 1922.

Llanover, Lady, ed. *The autobiography and correspondence of Mary Granville, Mrs Delany*, 6 vols., 1861.

Malmesbury, earl of, ed. *The diaries and correspondence of James Harris, first earl of Malmesbury*, 4 vols., 1845.

Marchand, J., ed. *A Frenchman in England, 1784*, 1933.

Minto, countess of, ed. *The life and letters of Sir Gilbert Elliot*, 3 vols., 1874.

—. *A memoir of the Rt. Hon. Hugh Elliot*, 1868.

Nicholls, J. *Recollections and reflections personal and political as connected with public affairs, during the reign of George III*, 2 vols., 1820–2.

Norton, J. E., ed. *Letters of Edward Gibbon*, 3 vols., 1956.

Ross, C., ed. *Correspondence of Charles, first Marquis Cornwallis*, 3 vols., 1859.

Russell, Lord John, ed. *Memorials and correspondence of Charles James Fox*, 4 vols., 1853.

Sedgwick, R., ed. *Letters from George III to Lord Bute 1756–66*, 1939.

Sinclair, Sir John. *The correspondence*, 2 vols., 1831.

Smith, W. J., ed. *The Grenville Papers*, 4 vols., 1852.

Stanhope, Earl. *Life of the Rt. Hon. William Pitt*, 4 vols., 1861.

—. *Miscellanies*, 1863.

Stirling, A. M. W. *Coke of Norfolk and his friends*, 2 vols., 1908.

Stuart Wortley, E., ed. *A Prime Minister and his son*, 1925.

Tayler, A. & H., eds. *Lord Fife and his factor*, 1925.

Walpole, Horace, *Letters of Horace Walpole, fourth earl of Orford*, ed. P. Toynbee, 16 vols., 1903–5; Supplement, 3 vols., 1918–25.

—. *Correspondence*, ed. W. S. Lewis, 1937–68.

—. *Memoirs of the reign of King George the Third*, ed. Sir D. le Marchant, 4 vols., 1845.

—. *Journal of the reign of King George the Third, 1771–1783*, ed. Dr Doran, 2 vols., 1859.

Warner, R. *Literary recollections*, 2 vols., 1830.

Wheatley, H. B., ed. *The historical and the posthumous memoirs of Sir Nathaniel William Wraxall*, 5 vols., 1884.

Wilberforce, R. I. W. & S. W. *Life of William Wilberforce*, 1838.

Windham, William. *The Windham Papers, with an introduction by Lord Rosebery*, 2 vols., 1913.

Wyvill, C., ed. *Political Papers*, 6 vols., 1794–1802.

Yorke, P. C. *The Life and correspondence of Philip Yorke, earl of Hardwicke*, 3 vols., 1913.

SECONDARY SOURCES

I ARTICLES

A. Aspinall. 'The cabinet council, 1783–1835', *Proceedings of the British Academy*, xxxviii, 1952.

I. R. Christie. 'The political allegiance of John Robinson, 1770–1784', *Bulletin of Institute of Historical Research*, xxix, 1956.

—. 'Economical reform and the "Influence of the Crown", 1780', *Cambridge Historical Journal*, xii, 1956.

—. 'George III and the Debt on Lord North's Election Account, 1780–84', *English Historical Review*, lxxviii, 1963.

A. S. Foord. 'The waning of "The Influence of the Crown" ', *English Historical Review*, lxii, 1947.

C. E. Fryer. 'Historical Revision: the General Election of 1784', *History*, ix, 1924.

W. R. Fryer. 'King George III, his political character and conduct, 1760–84; a new Whig interpretation', *Renaissance and Modern Studies*, vi, 1962.

M. D. George. 'Fox's Martyrs: the General Election of 1784', *Transactions of the Royal Historical Society*, 4th series, xxi, 1939.

D. M. Joslin. 'London bankers in wartime, 1739–84', *Studies in the Industrial Revolution*, ed. L. S. Pressnell, 1960.

B. Kemp. 'Crewe's Act, 1782', *English Historical Review*, lxviii, 1953.

W. T. Laprade. 'William Pitt and Westminster Elections', *American Historical Review*, xviii, 1912–13

—. 'Public opinion and the General Election of 1784', *English Historical Review*, xxxi, 1916.

D. Large. 'The decline of "the party of the Crown" and the rise of parties in the House of Lords, 1783–1837', *English Historical Review*, lxxviii, 1963.

L. B. Namier. 'Monarchy and the party system', *Personalities and Powers*, 1955.

—. 'King George III, a study of personality', *Personalities and powers*, 1955.

C. S. Philips. 'The East India Company Interest and the English Government, 1783–4', *Transactions of the Royal Historical Society*, xx, 1937.

E. A. Reitan. 'The civil list in eighteenth-century British politics: parliamentary supremacy versus the Independence of the Crown', *Historical Journal*, ix, 1966.

J. H. Rose. 'The rout of a coalition', *The nineteenth century and after*, March 1924.

E. A. Smith. 'Earl Temple's resignation, 22 December 1783', *Historical Journal*, vi, 1963.

G. M. Trevelyan. 'The two-party system in English political history', Romanes lecture, 1926.

2 BOOKS

Aspinall, A. *Politics and the press, c. 1780–1850*, 1949.

Barnes, D. G. *George III and William Pitt, 1783–1806*, 1939.

Black, E. C. *The association: British extraparliamentary political organization, 1769–1793*, 1963.

Binney, J. E. D. *British public finance and administration, 1774–1792*, 1958.

Brooke, J. *The Chatham administration, 1766–68*, 1956.

Butterfield, H. *George III, Lord North and the people, 1779–80*, 1949.

—. *George III and the historians*, 1957.

Christie, I. R. *The end of North's ministry, 1780–82*, 1958.

Christie, I. R. *Wilkes, Wyvill and reform: The parliamentary reform movement in British politics, 1760–85*, 1962.

Conn, S. *Gibraltar in British diplomacy in the eighteenth century*, 1942.

Copeland, T. W. *Edmund Burke*, 1950.

Craig, M. J. *The volunteer earl*, 1948.

Derry, J. W. *William Pitt*, 1962.

—. *The Regency crisis and the Whigs, 1788–9*, 1963.

Doren, C. C. van. *Benjamin Franklin*, 1939.

Emden, C. S. *The people and the constitution*, 2nd. ed., 1956.

Feiling, K. *The second Tory party, 1714–1832*, 1938.

Fergusson, A. *Henry Erskine*, 1882.

Foord, A. S. *His Majesty's Opposition, 1714–1830*, 1964.

Furber, H. *Henry Dundas, first Viscount Melville, 1742–1811*, 1931.

George, M. D. *English political caricature to 1792*, 1959.

—. *Catalogue of political and personal satires*, 1938.

Ginter, D. E. *Whig organization and the general election of 1790*, 1967.

Gore Browne, R. *Chancellor Thurlow: the life and times of an eighteenth-century lawyer*, 1953.

Harlow, V. T. *The founding of the second British Empire, 1763–93*, 1952.

Hobhouse, C. B. *Fox*, 1934.

Holmes, G. *British politics in the age of Anne*, 1967.

Jennings, Sir Ivor. *Party politics*, 3 vols., 1960–2.

Johnston, E. M. *Great Britain and Ireland, 1760–1800: a study in political administration*, 1963.

Jones, J. R. *The first Whigs: the politics of the exclusion crisis, 1678–1683*, 1961.

Judd, G. P. *Members of Parliament 1734–1832*, 1955.

Keir, D. L. *The constitutional history of modern Britain*, 1938.

Kemp, B. *King and Commons, 1660–1832*, 1957.

—. *Sir Francis Dashwood, an eighteenth-century Independent*, 1967.

Lascelles, E. *The life of Charles James Fox*, 1936.

Lecky, W. E. H. *A history of England in the eighteenth century*, 8 vols. 1878–90.

Lillywhite, B. *London coffee houses*, 1963.

Lucas, R. *Lord North, second earl of Guildford*, 2 vols., 1913.

McDowell, R. B. *Irish public opinion, 1750–1800*, 1944.

Madariaga, I. de. *Britain, Russia and the armed neutrality of 1780: Sir James Harris's mission to St Petersburg during the American Revolution*, 1962.

Marshall, D. *Eighteenth-century England*, 1962.

Marshall, P. J. *The impeachment of Warren Hastings*, 1965.

Matheson, C. *The life of Henry Dundas, first Viscount Melville*, 1933.

Mitchell, A. M. *The Whigs in opposition, 1815–1830*, 1967.

Morris, R. B. *The peacemakers*, 1965.

Namier, Sir Lewis. *The structure of politics at the accession of George III*, 2nd edition, 1957.

—. *England in the age of the American Revolution*, 1930.

—. & Brooke, J., eds. *The House of Commons, 1754–90*, 3 vols., 1964.

Natan, A., ed. *Silver renaissance*, 1961.

Norris, J. *Shelburne and reform*, 1963.

O'Gorman, F. *The Whig party and the French Revolution*, 1967.

Olson, A. *The radical duke, career and correspondence of Charles Lennox, third duke of Richmond*, 1961.

Pares, R. *King George III and the politicians*, 1953.

Pemberton, N. W. B. *Lord North*, 1938.

Pemberton, W. S. C. *The earl bishop: the life of Frederick Hervey, bishop of Derry, earl of Bristol*, 2 vols., 1925.

Perry, T. W. *Public opinion, propaganda and politics in eighteenth-century England*, 1962.

Philips, C. H. *The East India Company, 1784–1834*, 1940.

Phillips, N. C. *Yorkshire and English national politics, 1783–4*, 1961.

Porritt, E. and A. G. *The unreformed House of Commons*, 2 vols., 1903.

Redlich, J. *The procedure of the House of Commons; a study of its history and present form*, 3 vols., 1908.

Rose, J. H. *William Pitt and national revival*, 1911.

—. *Pitt and Napoleon, essays and letters*, 1912.

Rosebery, Lord. *Pitt*, 1891.

Sichel, W. *Sheridan*, 2 vols., 1909.

Sutherland, L. S. *The East India Company in eighteenth-century politics*, 1952.

Turberville, A. S. *The House of Lords in the eighteenth century*, 1927.

—. *The House of Lords in the age of reform, 1784–1837*, 1958.

Valentine, A. *Lord North*, 2 vols., 1967.

Walcott, R. *English politics in the early eighteenth century*, 1956.

Watson, J. S. *The reign of George III, 1760–1815*, 1960.

Werkmeister, L. *The London daily press, 1772–92*, 1963.

Williams, B. *Carteret and Newcastle*, 1943.

INDEX

N.B. Constituencies are given for the members of the fifteenth parliament, 1780–4, only.

Peers are entered under their titles, thus:

Beaufort, Henry Somerset, 5th duke of (1744–1803)

Aberdeen, addresses, 187n, 215n

Abingdon, Willoughby Bertie, 4th earl of (1740–99), 135, 214

Acland, John (1756–1831), MP Bridgwater, 115n

Adam, William (1751–1839), MP Wigtown burghs, 27, 31, 44n, 48n, 49, 102, 209, 216, 236–7

Addington, John Hiley, 154n

Address campaign supporting Pitt, 185–90, 226

Aldborough, by-election, 204n

Almon, John, 223

Alnwick, address, 226

Althorp, George John Spencer, Lord (1758–1834), MP Northampton and Surrey, later 2nd Earl Spencer, 25n, 84, 148, 186, 224–5

Alvensleven, Count, Hanoverian ambassador; acts as intermediary, 130–2

Ambler, Charles (1721–94), MP Boroughbridge, 161

America: independence, 6, 14–15, 17–18, 23, 32–3, 40–3; peace proposals, 13–18, 32–7, 51–8; and Fox's resignation, 22–4; treatment of loyalists, 16, 33–4, 39, 41, 45–6, 50, 53

American Intercourse Bill, 89n

Anderson, Francis Evelyn (1752–1821) MP Beverley, 245

Anne, Queen, dislike of party, ix

Anson, George (1731–89), MP Lichfield, 190n

Anstruther, John (1753–1811), MP Anstruther Easter burghs, 157

Apsley, Henry Bathurst, Lord (1762–1834), MP Cirencester, 118

Arden, Richard Pepper (1744–1804), MP Newtown, I.o.W., 146, 154, 166, 196

Ashburnham, John Ashburnham, 2nd earl of (1724–1812), 7

Ashburton, John Dunning, 1st Baron (1731–83), MP Calne, xi, 3n, 11, 56, 66, 72, 83, 101, 103, 129

Ashby, Shukburgh, (1724–92), MP Leicester, 189–90

Astley, Sir Edward, 4th Bt (1729–1802), MP Norfolk, 178

Atkinson, Richard, 76, 77–8, 127, 131, 132–3, 164, 167, 170n, 213, 220

Aubrey, John (1739–1826), MP Wallingford, 25

Audley, George Thicknesse, 9th Baron (1758–1818), 100

Aust, George, 137n

Aylesbury, 186

Bacon, Anthony (1717–86), MP Aylesbury, 244

Baker, William (1743–1824), MP Hertford, 23, 146; attacks use of

Burges, Sir James Bland, claims credit for coalition's defeat, 202n

Burgoyne, John (1723–92), MP Preston, 10, 120

Burke, Edmund (1729–97), MP Malton, defends party, x; and Indian affairs, 11, 107–12, 121, 202; counsels against resignation, 21–2; attacks Shelburne 23–4; resigns 25; as Paymaster 93–4; xii, 10, 31, 40n, 43–4, 75, 83, 135, 186, 209, 219, 226, 228, 234

Burke, Richard, 22n, 83, 206

Burrell, Sir Merrick, 1st Bt (1699–1787), MP Great Bedwyn, 157

Burton, Francis (1744–1832), MP Heytesbury, 160

Bury St Edmunds, 211

Bussy-Castelnau, Charles Joseph Patissier, Comte de, 43

Bute, John Stuart, 3rd earl of (1713–92), ix, xn, 145, 182n, 238

Buteshire, 215n

Byng, George (1735–89), MP Middlesex, 185n, 245

Cabinet: Lord Rockingham's, 3n, 5–6; Lord Shelburne's, 21–3, 25–6, 36–7; the Duke of Portland's, 73–6, 82–4; William Pitt's, 145, 153–5; constitutional position, 19, 21n, 51

Caithness, 215n

Calvert, John, senior (1726–1804), MP Tamworth, 158n, 210–1

Calvert, John, junior (1758–1844), MP Malmesbury, 158n

Cambridge University, election, 212

Camden, Charles Pratt, 1st earl (1714–94), opinion on Fox-Shelburne split, 26; 3n, 9–10, 25, 37, 44, 56, 67, 104, 138, 145, 154, 190, 233

Campbell, James (1737–1805), MP Stirling burghs, 225

Carew, Reginald Pole (1753–1835), MP Penryn, 159n, 244

Carlisle, Frederick Howard, 5th earl of (1748–1825), 23, 27, 45, 51–2, 73, 139

Carmarthen, Francis Godolphin Osborne, 5th marquess of (1751–99), 14n, 24, 30, 56, 78, 148; becomes Secretary of State, 153–4; 161, 166–7, 173–4, 177

Caswall, Timothy (1733–1802), MP Brackley, 157n

Catholic Emancipation, royal intervention in 1801, 143

Cavendish, Lord John (1732–96), MP York, resigns, 21–2, 25; attacks peace, 53–4, 57–8; negotiates loan, 86–7; budget, 87–8; defeated at York, 212–3, 217, 245; 3n, 18, 68n, 73, 76, 95, 108, 148, 177, 226

Chamberlain, Joseph, 63

Chandos, James Brydges, 3rd duke of (1731–89), 118, 136

Charlemont, James Caulfeild, 1st earl of (1728–99), 11–12, 91

Charles I, king, 125n, 143

Charteris, Francis (1749–1808), MP Haddington Burghs, 116, 162

Chichester, 209n, 211n

Churchill, Winston Spencer, 63

Clackmannanshire, 215n

Clarendon, Thomas Villiers, 1st earl of (1709–86), 100, 124; secret negotiations with Pitt, 129–32; memo on a dissolution, 150

Clayton, Sir Robert, 3rd Bt (1740–99), MP Bletchingley and Surrey, 245

Clerkship of the Pells, 231

Owen, Sir Hugh, 5th Bt (1731–86), MP Pembrokeshire, 225
Oxford, 212
Oxfordshire, address, 187

Paget, Henry Bayly, 10th Baron (1744–1812), 82, 100
Paisley, address, 188n
Palk, Robert (1717–98), MP Ashburton, 121n
Palliser, Sir Hugh, 1st Bt (1723–96), MP Huntingdon, 202n
Palmerston, Henry Temple, 2nd viscount (1739–1802), MP Hastings, assesses situation in Jan. 1784, 166; 203n, 217n, 218n
Pardoe, John (1756–96), MP Camelford, 121n
Parker, George Parker, Lord (1755–1842), MP Woodstock, 160
Parker, John (1735–88), MP Devon, 203–4
Parliamentary reform; Rockingham's cabinet split, 6; Pitt's motion defeated, 10, 91–3; Shelburne's attitude, 31; Pitt's cabinet divided, 155; 20, 27, 49–50; 127–8; 187; 234–5; 237
Party; attitude towards, ix–xi, 175, 224; estimates of party numbers, 25n, 30–1, 54–6, 72, 132–3, 161–2, 216, 228–9; party organisation, 235–8; eighteenth-century parties discussed, 238–43; party names, 241; see also Union of parties
Payne, Sir Ralph (1739–1807), MP Plympton Erle, 209, 244
Peace negotiations, 13–18, 32–7, 45; debates on, 40–3, 51–8; 89–90; 86
Peachey, John (1749–1816), MP New Shoreham, 157
Peel, Sir Robert, 63

Pelham, Thomas (1756–1826), 44n, 57, 103n
Pembroke, Henry Herbert, 10th earl of (1734–94), 7n
Pembroke boroughs, 225
Pembrokeshire, 225
Penzance, address, 188
Perceval, Charles George (1756–1840), MP Launceston, 158n
Percy, Lord Algernon (1750–1830), MP Northumberland, 149n, 158
Perth burghs, 215n
Peyton, Sir Henry, 1st Bt (1736–89), MP Cambridgeshire, 116
Pigot, Arthur, 107n
Pigot, George Pigot, 1st Baron (1719–77), 106
Pigot, Hugh (1722–92), MP Bridgnorth, 25n, 245
Pitt, George (1751–1828), MP Dorset, 157
Pitt, Thomas (1737–93) MP Old Sarum, advice to the king, 71–2, 79–80; 43, 53, 89, 92, 155
Pitt, William, senior, later 1st earl of Chatham (1708–78), 63, 74n, 85, 182n, 199
Pitt, William, junior (1759–1806), MP Appleby; relations with Shelburne, 8, 9, 18, 60; proposes parliamentary reform, 10, 91–3; accepts office, 22, 25; defends peace, 41, 57–8; hostility to North, 44, 47, 60–1, 67; meets Fox, 48; attacks coalition, 54, 78; refuses lead, 65–7, 75, 76–8; resigns as Chancellor, 80; Fox's opinion of, 102–3; plans with Temple, 104–5, 113; attacks Fox's India Bill, 115–20; advises royal intervention, 128–32; dismisses accusations as hearsay, 140; First Lord of the

Treasury, 145; constructs ministry, 145, 153–5; and Temple's resignation, 147–51; lies to the House, 165, 230–1; produces India Bill, 164, 167–9, 170–1; considers dissolution, 171–4; in negotiations for union, 176–9, 190–6; public approval of, 184–90, 230–1; protests at postponement of supplies, 196–8, 201; refuses to resign, 178–9, 196, 197, 199–200; gains victory, 202; elected for Cambridge University, 212; xn, xii, 24, 39, 40, 44n, 46, 56, 68n, 69, 72, 82, 87, 88, 94, 95, 99, 102, 114, 122, 127, 133, 134, 135, 143, 144, 148, 151, 156, 159n, 160, 161, 167, 182, 183, 229, 233n, 234, 241

Plymouth, address, 185; 208n, 217n, 229

Plympton Erle, 208n, 209n

Pochin, William (1731–98), MP Leicestershire, 116

Pontefract, 88n, 211n

Poole, 211n

Portland, William Henry Cavendish Bentinck, 3rd duke of (1738–1809); Irish policy, 12–13, 91; candidate to succeed Rockingham, 20; forms ministry, 72–6; dispute over Prince's establishment, 95–100; asks for peerages, 100–1; dismissed, 144; union of parties, 176–9, 190–6; xn, 25, 41 ,68n, 69, 70, 85, 86, 103, 126, 127n, 129, 133, 136, 137, 138, 142, 148, 156, 159, 186, 209, 212, 213, 236–7

Portsmouth, 7n, 211, 217n, 229

Potter, Christopher, 212n

Powell, John, 93–4

Powys, Thomas (1743–1800), MP Northamptonshire; criticizes Pitt, 172, 175, 178, 179, 180; and union of parties, 191–6; withholds supplies 196–8; deplores Pitt's refusal to resign, 199, 201; 55, 58, 118, 121

Prerogatives of the crown; choice of ministers, ix–xi, 21, 69–71, 169, 181–2, 185, 199–200, 201–2; peerages, 70, 82–3, 100–2, 155–6, 158–60; right of dissolution, 124, 141, 145–7, 152–3, 164–6, 169, 171–4; right of veto, 124; right to intervene, xiii, 136–7, 141–3, 164–6, 230–1; how exercised, 50, 116–17; 163

Press, influence of; 117–18, 221–3, 231–2

Preston, 88n

Pulteney, Daniel, 115n, 150, 208n, 236

Purling, John (1722–1800), MP Weymouth and Melcombe Regis, 121n, 218n

Queenborough, 208n, 210n, 217n

Ramsden, Sir John, 4th Bt (1755–1839), MP Grampound, 158n, 245

Rawlinson, Henry (1743–86), MP Liverpool, 219n, 245

Rawlinson, Sir Walter (1734–1805), MP Queenborough, 217n, 218n

Rayneval, Joseph-Matthias Gérard de, French envoy, 34, 37

Reading, 186

Receipt Tax, 88–9, 230

Redruth, 185n

Richmond, 211n

Richmond, Charles Lennox, 3rd duke of (1735–1806); against resignation, 21–3; criticises Oswald, 33; leaves Shelburne's cabinet, 45–6; 3n, 6, 10, 18, 20, 24, 37,